China and the Middle East

There are currently few sources of reference from a Middle Eastern standpoint on the role that the People's Republic of China is currently playing in the Middle East and North Africa region. In this book, Dr Muhamad Olimat aims to analyse different perspectives in order to deepen the understanding of scholars and strategic planners alike, in order to offer a complete economic and political overview of the situation. China and Middle Eastern relations date back from the Silk Road and stretch to the current 'Arab Spring'. China's relations with the Middle East are highlighted in terms of energy, trade, arms sales, culture and political ties with key countries in the region: Saudi Arabia, Iran, Israel, Algeria and the United Arab Emirates. China's bilateral relations with each of these countries are based on a particularly critical aspect that determines its interest in the region. The core of China's relations with Israel, for instance, is weapons sales and advanced technology, while relations with Saudi Arabia are based on oil. Iran and China are tied with deep historical, civilizational, cultural and political bonds, although oil is also the primary focus of China's current interest in Iran. China's national interests in and relations and strategic partnerships with the Middle East are only increasing; this book aims to analyze and interpret these relations in this time of major change in the Middle East.

The book includes discussion of and comment on:

- China's deep involvement in the Middle East since the Silk Road
- The new Silk Road of trade, oil, arms sales, political and cultural relations
- China's oil investments in the Middle East
- China's reaction to the Arab Spring

Muhamad S. Olimat, is an Assistant Professor of international relations at Khalifa University of Science, Technology and Research (KUSTAR) in Abu Dhabi, United Arab Emirates. Prior to joining KUSTAR, Dr Olimat taught and conducted research at the University of South Florida in St Petersburg, Missouri State University and several other US higher educational institutions. His area of expertise is Middle East politics, and his research focuses on China and the Middle East, socio-political and economic development in the Middle East, and US foreign policy towards the region. He has published several articles and book chapters on China and the Middle East, the Arab Spring, transition to democracy, women and politics in the Middle East, and the role of Islam in the politics of the Middle East.

China and the Middle East

From Silk Road to Arab Spring

Muhamad S. Olimat

Routledge
Taylor & Francis Group
LONDON AND NEW YORK

First edition published 2013
by Routledge
2 Park Square, Milton Park, Abingdon, Oxfordshire OX14 4RN

Simultaneously published in the USA and Canada
by Routledge
711 Third Avenue, New York, NY 10017

First issued in paperback 2014

Routledge is an imprint of the Taylor and Francis Group, an informa business

British Library Cataloguing in Publication Data
A catalogue record for this book is available from the British Library

Library of Congress Cataloging in Publication Data
Olimat, Muhamad.
China and the Middle East : from Silk Road to Arab Spring / Muhamad Olimat. – First edition.
pages cm
Includes bibliographical references and index.
1. China–Foreign economic relations–Middle East. 2. Middle East–Foreign economic relations–China. 3. Silk Road. 4. Arab Spring, 2010- I. Title.
HF1604.Z4M628 2012
382.0951'056–dc23
2012028085

ISBN 978-1-85743-631-0 (hbk)
ISBN 978-1-85743-796-6 (pbk)
ISBN 978-0-203-07312-4 (ebk)

Typeset in Times New Roman
by Taylor & Francis Books

Europa Commissioning Editor: Cathy Hartley

In loving memory of my parents, Salem and Eda
To my children, Jennah and Kasum

Contents

Illustrations

Figures

Tables

Acknowledgements

I would like to acknowledge the support and encouragement of my family, especially my brothers Ahmed and Hmoud. Special thanks to my good friend and editor Emilia Garofalo. Your encouragement, editing skills and support made all the difference in the completion of the book. I would also like to thank my colleagues and friends at the Institute for Civil and International Security at Khalifa University, especially Micheline Ishay for her encouragement and support, as well as David Goldfischer and Mohamad Zieneddin. Thanks to colleagues at KUSTAR's library especially Patricia and Dorothy.

Many thanks also to Greg Moore, Ken Rutherford, Frank Biafora, Thomas Smith, Hugh LaFollette, Beat Kernen and Margie Buechner for their support and encouragement. I am grateful to Di Wang, Sangeeta Sinha, Hamid Ali and Ryad Yemany for their assistance in data collection. Finally, thanks also to Cathy Hartley at Routledge for her enthusiasm for the project and her support throughout the process of submitting the proposal and on to publication.

Abbreviations

ADNOC	Abu Dhabi National Oil Company
AEW	Airborne EARLY WARNING
AU	African Union
AWACS	Airborne early warning and control system
CCP	Chinese Communist Party
CIA	Central Intelligence Agency
CNOOC	China National Offshore Oil Corporation
CNPC	China National Petroleum Corporation
CSCE	China State Construction Engineering Corpn Ltd.
DR	Dongfeng or East Wind Missiles CSS-2
EIA	Energy Information Administration, USA
FDI	Foreign direct investment
FLN	National Liberation Front
FOCAC	Forum on China–Africa Cooperation
FTZ	Free trade zone
GA	General Assembly
GCC	Gulf Cooperation Council
GNPOC	Greater Nile Petroleum Operating Company
IAEA	International Atomic Energy Agency
IAI	Israel Aerospace Industries
ICBC	Industrial and Commercial Bank of China
ICI	Israel–China Institute
IEA	International Energy Agency
IMF	International Monetary Fund
Intifada	Uprising
KPC	Kuwait Petroleum Corporation
MENA	Middle East and North Africa
MTCR	Missile Technology Control Regime
NPT	Nuclear Non-proliferation treaty
OFFP	Oil-for-food Programme
OIC	Organization of Islamic Cooperation
PFLP	Popular Front for the Liberation of Palestine
PFOAG	Popular Front for the Liberation of Occupied Arabian Gulf

PLO	Palestinian Liberation Organization
PNA	Palestinian National Authority
PRC	People's Republic of China
R&D	Research and Development
ROC	Republic of China (Taiwan)
SABIC	Saudi Basic Industries Corpn
SAVAK	Sāzemān-e Ettelā'āt va Amniyat-e Keshvar, or Organization of Intelligence and National Security (Iran)
SC	Security Council
SCF	Strategic Cooperation Forum
Sinopec	China Petrochemical Corporation
SIPRI	Stockholm International Peace Research Institute
The P 5+1	Permanent members of the UN Security Council and Germany
UAE	United Arab Emirates
UAV	Unmanned aerial vehicle
US(A)	United States (of America)

Introduction

The aim of this book is to provide a distinctive perspective on China's Middle Eastern relations. My interest in the topic of Chinese Studies, and subsequently in Sino–Middle Eastern relations, was prompted by my association with Chinese Studies at Missouri State University where I taught for two years, 2005–07, and where I became a member of the Association of Chinese Political Studies (ACPS). My friends and colleagues at the association, particularly Greg Moore and Dennis Hickey, encouraged me to research Sino–Middle Eastern relations, given the growing interest in the topic. Since then, I have been studying, collecting material and interacting with Chinese and other scholars on Chinese Studies. The idea of expanding my research into a manuscript came from previous collaboration on two book chapters and an article, one with Dennis Hickey and Baogang Guo's book *Dancing with the Dragon*, published by Lexington in 2010, another chapter with Shaun Breslin in his book *Handbook of China's International Relations* published by Routledge in 2010, in addition to an article published in the *Journal of Chinese Political Science* in 2009 entitled the Political Economy of Sino–Middle Eastern Relations.

During my research, I noticed a shortage of manuscripts, which certainly does not reflect China's heavy involvement in the Middle East and North Africa. The goal of this book is to fill that void, and to contribute to the ongoing debate on Sino–Middle Eastern relations in the hope of motivating future research in the field. To grasp the depth of China's relations within the region, in the overview chapter I went back to the Silk Road period to highlight major events that characterized the connection between the two regions up to the current Arab Spring. I was struck by the centuries-long relationship that tied China to the Middle East. The Silk Road opened up timeless routes of trade and cultural interaction; some of its remnants are still present in modern-day China, Central Asia, Iran, Iraq, Syria and Turkey.

Islam revolutionized the links between China and the Middle East. Although early Islam was characterized by conquest, China was spared the Islamic incursion twice. Islamic–Chinese relations were predominantly characterized by peaceful and civil co-existence, with one exception: the Talas River Battle in 751, in what is currently Kyrgyzstan. The Muslim army emerged triumphant but chose not to pursue an all-out conquest of China, preferring trade relations and peace. The Abbasids, an enlightened civilization led by open-minded caliphs, emphasized modern administration, science, craftsmanship, agriculture, irrigation systems, water canals and highways, and developed an efficient postal service in a huge empire. They were greatly interested in China's knowledge of astronomy and agriculture, and fascinated by its culture in particular. Therefore trade, cultural contacts and the exchange of knowledge were sources of major interaction between the two sides.

The Tang dynasty was also an enlightened, multicultural civilization that promoted similar values of trade relations and cultural and scientific interaction with the Islamic Empire and other neighbouring civilizations. During China's years of turbulence, Muslim armies came to its assistance to maintain its territorial integrity and unity. Muslim merchants and warriors from Persia, Arabia and Central Asia who resided in China came to be known as Hui, a reference to their Muslim religious affiliation. Although they lived side by side with the Han majority, Hui Muslims preserved their cultural distinctiveness, but have been subjected to some major episodes of violence ever since the ninth century. Sino–Middle Eastern contacts weakened between the sixteenth and mid-twentieth centuries as both the Islamic and the Chinese civilizations declined. However, since WWII, China's engagement with the Middle East has intensified to the extent that China has become an integral part of Middle Eastern international relations. Currently, China is heavily involved in Middle Eastern politics dealing with major issues such as the Arab Spring and its subsequent revolutions, the Iranian nuclear standoff and the Arab–Israeli conflict.

Book organization

This book is divided into nine chapters covering Sino–Middle Eastern relations from the Silk Road to the Arab Spring. The first four chapters discuss Sino-multilateral relations with the Middle East region, while the remaining five chapters deal with bilateral relations with key Middle Eastern countries, each of which is chosen for strategic elements in its bilateral relations with China.

In Chapter 1, I provide an overview of Sino–Middle Eastern relations highlighting the most significant events that have occurred between China and the Middle East from the emergence of the Silk Road to the current Arab Spring. In Chapter 2, I have developed a five-dimensional approach or five pillars: China's relations with the region are examined by looking at energy, arms sales, trade, political co-operation and cultural ties. In fact, in order for China to maintain its current growth rates and industrial momentum, the essence of its involvement in the Middle East has to deal with its quest for energy security defined in terms of securing access to Middle Eastern oil resources. China's bilateral trade relations with the region are also growing and forging strategic trade partnerships. China is heavily involved in political developments, especially within the paradigm of the Arab Spring in terms of its politics, repercussions, constraints and opportunities. China is an exporter of arms and a major importer of weapons from the Middle East. Its partnership with Israel is built on defence co-operation, importing high-tech weaponry and exporting light and medium types of arms to the region. Chinese–Middle Eastern cultural relations are characterized by cultural events such as festivals, New Year celebrations, educational opportunities and cuisine.

Chapter 3 offers a tridimensional approach to Sino–Middle Eastern relations viewed as an outcome of interaction between three actors in each scenario. China's efforts to maintain its interests have proved to be challenging, especially when dealing with contending regional powerhouses in the Middle East. The chapter describes scenarios and elements that balance, for example, China's relations with Iran and Saudi Arabia, two rivals in the region. Similarly, China has been successful in developing a strategic partnership with Israel while maintaining its traditional support of the Palestinian people. Chapter 4 presents an analysis of China's reaction to the Arab Spring and the current revolutions that shake the Middle East. China has been stunned as much as the United States, France or Britain by the events occurring in the region. China was acting on the assumption that Middle Eastern authoritarian regimes were 'change proof,' an assumption that proved to be inaccurate. Therefore, its reaction so far has been characterized by inconsistency and confusion at times, and problematic and retroactive statements at other times.

China's leadership closely followed the events that led to the demise of the Mubarak regime in Egypt in 2011. To some extent, the swift changes in Tunisia were reassuring to China and other countries concerned about stability in post-revolutionary situations in the Middle East. However, the Libyan, Syrian and Yemeni cases were characterized by widespread violence. China supported international efforts at the UN Security Council to pressure Gadhafi to halt the violence, but continued to ship arms to his regime until the final stages of the conflict in 2011. China supported the transition in Yemen, but has vehemently opposed any international military intervention in Syria to stop the genocide currently occurring in the country. In close co-ordination with Russia, China exercised a double and unprecedented veto on 4 February 2012 that prolonged the violence in Syria. For that, China and Russia earned the displeasure of Arab public opinion. For the first time, Chinese and Russian flags were burnt to substitute for the traditional burning of Israeli and American flags. The chapter also offers an in-depth analysis that provides scenarios to discern China's justification for its strong defence of the Syrian regime. In fact, Syria serves as a case study for China's views on the Arab Spring.

in 2012

Chapters 5 to 9 are devoted to case studies. Chapter 5 deals with Sino–Israeli relations; the main theme is China's renowned military partnership with Israel that stands at odds not only with China's traditional allies, the Arab world, but also with Israel's main supporter, the United States. Israel provides China with what other countries in the region lack: advanced weapons systems developed by Israeli corporations that have access to US military technology, and IT knowhow especially in the area of agro-technology. Israel was the first Middle Eastern country to recognize the People's Republic of China (PRC) in early January 1950 and the last Middle Eastern country to establish diplomatic relations with China in 1992.

Chapter 6 looks at Sino–Saudi relations. The core of their bilateral ties is energy co-operation. Saudi Arabia is the major source of oil currently sustaining China's industrial enterprise, and is also heavily involved in investing in China. For their part, Chinese corporations are developing some of the most ambitious expansion projects in the kingdom, such as highways and railways. Saudi–Chinese bilateral ties shifted from extreme animosity between 1949 and 1980 to cautious rapprochement between 1980 and 1990, to a strategic partnership in 2006 represented by the milestone visit made by the current Saudi monarch, King Abdullah, to China in 2006.

Chapter 7 investigates Sino–Iranian relations. In addition to oil as the core of their bilateral ties, this liaison is characterized by historical links that go back to the early days of the Silk Road. Persia influenced China and maintained familial, cultural and trade ties throughout history. The scope of bilateral relations, however, extends to other fields such military co-operation, natural gas exploration, goods and services and construction. China is also active in resolving the current Iranian nuclear programme crisis, a standoff between Iran and the international community that is sounding an alarm worldwide. Chapter 8 examines Sino–UAE relations. The core of their bilateral relations is trade. The UAE serves as a primary hub for Chinese corporations not only for the Gulf or Middle East regions, but also for Africa and the world. The UAE is the home of the Dragon Mart, the largest Chinese business complex outside mainland China; UAE's real estate corporations and port management firms are making headway in Chinese markets as well.

Chapter 9 analyses Chinese–Algerian relations. The core of their bilateral ties is political support and genuine friendship and admiration. China supported the Algerian National Liberation movement during its War of Independence from 1950 to 1964, and became the first non-Arab country to recognize Algeria's independence and to establish full diplomatic relations in 1958, four years before Algeria's official independence. In return, in 1971, Algeria co-sponsored the resolution to readmit China to the United Nations. Algeria lobbied before the international community and headed a global shift of support from the Republic of China (Taiwan) to the PRC. China is heavily involved in Algerian economic development. In fact, Chinese corporations are building highways, airports, housing, bridges, roads and even the Grand Mosque of Algeria.

China is determined to enhance its ties with the Middle East, but Western countries are alarmed by the magnitude of its involvement. China is simply following in American footsteps and the US's gradual involvement in the Middle East in the aftermath of the British departure from the region before and after WWII. Although the US is not expected to suddenly leave the Middle East, it is shifting some of its attention to South-East Asia and the Far East, aiming at reducing some of its security commitments in the Middle East. Yet, it is hard to imagine that the US would completely abandon its enduring commitments in the Middle East such as defending Israel's security, the security of its friends and allies in the Gulf region, and its reliance on Middle East energy resources.

Although there is currently some resentment towards China's policies over the Arab Spring, the people and governments of the Middle East are eager for China's greater involvement in the politics of the region. However, this may be a desire they will regret in the future. US involvement in the region was solicited in the Middle East as early as 1916, post WWI, but resented post WWII. China might find itself in the same situation. Its growing presence in the Middle East should attract scholars' attention to Chinese–Middle Eastern studies. This field will certainly develop along the lines of American–Middle Eastern relations post WWII. It is my hope that this book will contribute in part to its furtherance and to continued in-depth study.

1 Sino–Middle East relations

An overview

The aim of this chapter is to examine the depth of Chinese–Middle Eastern relations and to highlight some of the major events that have taken place in the history of the two regions over the past three millennia. There are several periods that can be identified: the Silk Road, the Islamic, the Colonial, the post-World War II and the post-Mao periods.

The Silk Road period

Around 300 BC, China had strong trade relations with the Middle East through a network of Asian merchants. The main trade route extended for 4,000 miles from the city of Xian in China to Constantinople in Turkey. It was known as the Silk Road and the core of the exchange was silk, a precious Chinese commodity that played a leading role in the promotion of trade between China and the rest of the world. Silk was in high demand especially among wealthy merchants and ruling elites from Central Asia to the Middle East to Europe. In addition to trading in other commodities such as spices, amber, porcelain and ivory, many countries took advantage of the Silk Road: India introduced unique spices to the world; Persia exported precious rugs in high demand; and Arabia traded its horses and camels, prized for their strength, patience, ability to travel long journeys and endure the harshness of the world's main thoroughfare.

Rather than looking at the Silk Road as just another economic route, China saw it as a corridor for speed and movement to boost its military capabilities. For instance, Central Asian nations, especially Kazakhstan, were the very first to domesticate horses. For its defence and expansion westward, China needed the lightweight, swift and strong Arabian horses that far exceeded other breeds in their speed and endurance. They were in great demand throughout history, and continue to be. These are the horses that carried Arabs as far east as China, and as far west as the heart of Europe. The peak of the Silk Road period occurred during Islamic rule, in which Muslims extended their domain from Western China to Southern and Western Europe. The Chinese Tang Dynasty, in particular, strengthened mutual trade relations with the Islamic empire.

Sino–Islamic relations

The advent of Islam on the Arabian scene marked a new phase in the relationship between China and the Middle East. Prophet Muhammad once said, 'Seek knowledge, even if it's in China' with reference to the importance of seeking knowledge despite the geographical distance, and in reference to China as a source of enlightenment and wisdom. Realizing China's strategic importance, his followers took drastic steps to establish solid diplomatic and economic relations with Chinese emperors and people. In the seventh century, the swift triumph of Islam brought the religion to the borders of China in record time, and at times into its heartland. In fact, a considerable number of Muslims were to be found in 'Chinese Turkistan about AD 630', that is during the lifetime of the Prophet (570–632).[1] Clearly, Islam reached China before it reached some parts of Arabia and North Africa precisely through Muslim merchants on the Silk Road. The Arab conquest of the Persian Empire speeded up the arrival of Islam in China in a more systematic way and, since then, the conquest of Central Asia has had a dramatic impact on Sino–Islamic relations.

When military clashes between Muslim armies and Persia began in the third decade of the seventh century, 'Persian King Yazdegerd sent a delegation to China seeking military assistance in his conflict with Muslims, but the reply was that Persia was so far away, and China could not give military assistance.'[2] The Persian envoy alarmed Chinese emperors about the rising power of Islam and piqued their curiosity. Tai-tsung (Gaozong), the powerful Tang Dynasty emperor, sent a diplomatic mission to Medina in the year 651 to meet with Caliph Othman. The goal of the 'mission was to present the cause of the Persians.'[3] Some sources state that Caliph Othman sent a return mission in the same year 651 led by Sa'ad ibn Abī Waqqās, a revered military general and a skilled diplomat, which 'was received with every distinction.'[4] The objective of the Waqqās mission was to convey the message of Islam to China and to the emperor personally, and to extend a hand of friendship. Although Emperor Gaozong did not convert to Islam, he showed unprecedented admiration towards the religion and towards Muslims. In fact, to commemorate the envoy and to express his friendship, he ordered the building of the first mosque in the capital city of Chang'an, which became the centre of Islamic presence in the empire. Chinese Muslim communities maintain that Commander Sa'ad resided and died in China, but the official annals of the Tang Dynasty and prominent Muslim historians such as Ibn Al Athir have no records of this narrative. At any rate, the Tang Dynasty was an enlightened civilization that celebrated diversity and multiculturalism; foreigners were warmly welcomed. Its capital and its other main city, Luoyang, became cultural and economic centres whose citizens consumed the famed products of Central Asia, Arabia and Persia. Arab and Muslim merchants traded with China, and some even resided in the country to form the first Muslim community in Xian. From that point on, Islam had a strong following in China that also spread to East Asia.

In the period between 651 and 714, Muslim armies led by Kutiba bin Muslim pushed to conquer the hinterland of Central Asia, building on the total conquest and absorption of the Persian Empire. Crown Prince Firuz, son of Yazdegerd, the last Persian king, fled to China where he was well received; he resided in Xian in 671. Kutiba's soldiers defeated Central Asian armies and marched into Kashgar, in Chinese East Turkistan, or what is currently Xinjiang. Since then, an alliance formed between Muslims, Uyghur and Tibetans. Although Muslims considered Central Asia an extension of the Islamic world, given that the people had accepted Islam and became part of the Islamic *Ummah*, China continued to consider the region to be under its sphere of influence and clashed with Muslims particularly at its borders at a later stage.

The epic encounter between China and the Umayyad Dynasty occurred in 714 AD, 96 *Hijrah* (Muslim calendar), when Kutiba bin Muslim marched towards Kashgar, or Shi in East Turkistan (Xinjiang), which was under Chinese rule at that time, and began the conquest of China. Gaozong asked Kutiba to halt his advance and sent him some of his advisers to negotiate for peace. Kutiba agreed to the negotiations and, in so doing, he was adhering to Islam's theory of war and peace: Muslim armies should give a warning, invite enemies to accept Islam, pay a tribute in exchange for peace and protection or go to war. Emperor Gaozong opted for the second option: a tribute and a peace treaty. Ibn Al Athir, the famous Muslim historian, narrates the story in his book, *Al Kamil* (The Complete History). Upon the emperor's request, Kutiba sent ten of his military commanders and advisers led by a skilled diplomat, Hubira Ben Mushamraj Al Kelaabie. On the first day, these ten members of the Muslim delegation wore soft, white attire. They also sprayed themselves with cologne and sat at the imperial court for several hours, but the emperor did not speak to them, so they excused themselves and left. The emperor asked his advisers what they saw. They replied that they saw men as soft as women. The next day, the Muslim delegation had a semi-rough appearance and wore semi-rough attire. They wore silk turbans and covered their faces except the eyes, then walked into the court, sat, again did not exchange conversation and then left. The emperor then asked his advisers what they saw, and they replied that they saw 'sort of men.' On the third day, the Muslim delegation marched towards the court on horseback, with full battle uniform, swords, shields and arrows. The emperor asked them to leave but to send him back Hubira, the head of the diplomatic mission. In the meantime, the emperor asked his advisers what they saw. They replied that they saw warriors such as they had never seen before. The emperor asked Hubira to explain to him the meaning of the attire. He complied by explaining that on the first day they wore soft cloth as if among family and friends. On the second day, they wore semi-rough clothing as when they feel safe among their leaders, and on the third day, they dressed as if they were facing the enemy. The emperor liked what he heard. He told the diplomat to inform Kutiba to leave or he and his army would be destroyed. Hubira replied that

Kutiba swore by Almighty God that he would step on China's soil, force it to pay a tribute and stamp on its kings. In Islam, an oath like this is firm and must be carried out. The wise emperor replied: 'As for stepping on China's soil, I will send him soil and he can walk on it: this will fulfil his oath. As for a tribute, we will pay it; and I'll send with you four princes for Kutiba to stamp on, and he did just that.'[5] Therefore, the wise emperor avoided imminent defeat at the hands of the Muslim army, which withdrew to its bases in Samarkand and Bukhara in Central Asia.

Between 714 and 751, Muslim armies continued their expansion and conquest in all directions, except in China. Even with internal developments and conflicts such as the assassination of Kutiba bin Muslim in a power struggle, Muslims honoured the agreement between Kutiba and Emperor Gaozong, and trade prospered on both sides. Taking advantage of dissent and fighting within the Muslim Empire, China attempted to pursue its interests in Central Asia, especially in the rich Ferghana Valley, a wealthy multi-ethnic land shared by Uzbekistan, Kyrgyzstan and Tajikistan. Ever since the Han Dynasty, China had sought control of this land. Developments on the political and military scenes on both sides brought them into collision in 751 near the Talas River, in what is currently Kyrgyzstan. Earlier, Arab armies had deposed King Ikhshid of the Ferghana Valley and installed King Alutar in his place. In turn, Ikhshid asked for China's help. This was a stroke of luck for the Chinese who not only were in a position to support him militarily, but wanted to correct what they thought had been a mistake in allowing Arabs to advance into Central Asia and occupy East Turkistan to intimidate China. Chinese sources estimated the Chinese contingent that met near the Talas River at 10,000 soldiers, but Ibn Al Athir estimated it at around 100,000 soldiers and did not mention a figure for the size of the Muslim military. Abu Muslim Al Khurasani, the ruler of Khurasan (Iran, Afghanistan, Central Asia), mobilized an army estimated by Chinese sources at 100,000 soldiers. The Muslim army was triumphant: it killed about 50,000 Chinese and allies and took 20,000 captive while the rest fled to China. This makes the fleeing army an estimated 30,000.[6]

After the battle, the Abbasids consolidated their dominance in Central Asia, and Islam spread among the Turkic people, and in East Turkistan, or Xinjiang. According to Arab sources, the Talas Battle put an end to Chinese expansion in Central Asia. In fact, had the Muslim armies been willing to invade China, the latter could have fallen under Abbasid dominance like other parts of Asia, Southern Europe and West Africa. However, the Muslim armies maintained control over Xinjiang, the border with the Chinese empire, and pursued a co-operative relationship with China. As Keay put it, 'the victorious Arab and Tibetan forces failed to follow up their triumph, and defeated Chinese had already written off Ferghana. World history was the only loser.'[7] Xinjiang became part of the Islamic dominion and 'the Chinese retreated … it was not until the Qianlong Emperor's conquest, one thousand years later, that the Chinese intervened successfully again in Turkistan, and they haven't left since.'[8]

The Abbasids and the Tangs

When the Abbasids took over the Umayyad Dynasty in 750, military tension between China and the Islamic Empire was reduced, with one exception: the aforementioned Talas Battle. It took place at a juncture of time in which the Abbasids were in the process of consolidating power; therefore, a limited confrontation with China was unavoidable as the latter pursued its territorial interests in Central Asia after the Kutiba–Tang agreement in 714. However, after Talas, relations between the Abbasids and Tangs improved significantly. The multicultural nature of both the Tang and the Abbasid empires facilitated open immigration of Arabs and Muslims to China, welcomed and encouraged by the Tang Emperors. The Muslim community enhanced China's international trade and strengthened its alliance with the Abbasids. When the Tangs needed Muslim help to suppress internal revolutions, the Abbasids never hesitated to intervene. Between 755 and 763, 'a Tartar named An Lusan, a general stationed at the border, rebelled against emperor Hsuang-tsung and proclaimed himself lord of China. The emperor handed over the throne to Su-tsung, who with the help of the Arabs defeated the Tartar. The 4,000 Arabs who had given him this assistance were given permission to settle within the border of the empire.'[9] The Chinese emperors found in Arabs and Persians an industrious community, endowed with a strong work ethic and knowledge of science, mathematics, astronomy and geography; they employed them in the imperial court and in key government positions, especially in management.

The Abbasids were trade and science oriented. They promoted trade relations with the entire world, translated world literature into Arabic, took a major interest in architecture and music and relaxed tensions with conquered nationalities through decentralization of their administration. Political and economic missions to China continued, and intensified during the Abbasid rule, from 750 to 1257, during which time trade relations were the centrepiece between the two sides. The Abbasids' ultimate goal was a foreign policy that promoted the establishment of an enduring civilization. The process of building such a civilization peaked during the reign of Haroun Al Rashid and his sons, Ameen and Mamoun, in the eighth and ninth centuries. They promoted trade and science, built monuments and palaces and translated written world heritage literature and previous civilizational contributions.

The Abbasids acknowledged Chinese contributions, especially in paper-making, astrology, irrigation and other fields. Chinese methods of manufacturing paper were introduced in the capital cities of Central Asia, spread to Baghdad, and from there to Spain, Europe and eventually to the entire known world. The Abbasids utilized paper very well. In fact, they embarked on the ambitious project of documenting world civilizations. To that end, they established the House of Wisdom in Baghdad. Major Chinese, Greek, Indian and other works were housed there and translated into Arabic. This process continued until the savagery of the Mongol invasion destroyed the bulk of the

House of Wisdom in 1257. The invasion was the first and most shattering attack on Islam. It is not an exaggeration to say that its devastating consequences had repercussions for many centuries and will continue for many centuries to come, as the Islamic civilization never fully recovered from it. The Chinese civilization suffered a similar fate in 1212: it took China over three centuries to partially recover from it.

Both the Tang and the Abbasid dynasties were multicultural and trade oriented; diversity was welcomed, celebrated and embraced. Tang rulers found Muslims to be a vibrant merchant class, and provided Arab Muslim merchants with all the support they needed. They also found Muslims to be disciplined and law-abiding people, as instructed by Islam's principles, and for this they admired them. The Muslim community concentrated on trade as its main goal, but at the same time reflected a positive image of Islam as a religion and of Muslims as a people. They and the Tang had identical goals; therefore, trade between China and the Islamic world flourished. As early Muslims in China observed the pillars of faith, they influenced their neighbours, but the spread of Islam was inadequate with the missionary nature of Islam itself or the strength of the Muslim community in China. Nevertheless, Muslims' approach to the propagation of Islam in China proved to be practical. For example, when other religions, especially Buddhism, were under state oppression, Muslims were left alone to practise their faith as they had not articulated a plan of conversion for the Chinese people or advocated Islam as a religion.

One of the tragic events that occurred to the prosperous Muslim communities in China during the Tang Dynasty happened in 878 AD. The Han majority protested against the successful Muslim community because they were jealous of the economic prosperity of Arab immigrants. The protests led to the massacre of over 100,000 Muslims. 'The tragedy led Arab immigrants to migrate to South East Asia and settle in that region. Therefore, the spread of Islam to Malaysia and South East Asia comes first from China (East), not from India and the Arabian region (West).'[10] Islam established a foothold to the extent that Indonesia became the largest Islamic country with a population that exceeds 200 million. The remaining Muslim community in China rebuilt itself and once again became more influential under Mongol rule in the thirteenth century. Karl Ludvig reports that emigration to China continued 'under the Yuan Dynasty, the ports and provinces of China were legally opened to Arabs and Persians, and an extensive migration resulted.'[11] Other major waves of violence against Muslims were also reported in the eighteenth and nineteenth centuries. Ludvig maintains that:

> following a rebellion among [Muslims] in 1785 a number of severe decrees were issued affecting all Mohammadans. Pilgrimages to Mecca were forbidden, and also the building of mosques. Their condition became practically that of serfs. They were under this repressive restraint till 1863. Then there were uprisings of the whole Mohammadan

> population in north and west China. Millions were killed in the terrible fighting. Peace came only when the adventurous Chieftain Yakoob Beg had gained supreme power and formed Mohammadans kingdom up in East Turkistan. Unfortunately he was removed by death as early as 1877. At his death all crumbled and after an incredible amount of bloodshed came under the rule of China once more.[12]

The Silk Road continued its primary role in world trade until sea routes gradually began to shift trade practices from the eighth century onward. The advantages of ocean routes were speed, reduced taxes, safety and security and bypassing the harsh weather conditions across Central Asia in particular. Arab dominance across the seas lasted until the thirteenth century when Europe began its rise and Middle Eastern power and influence waned. China pursued naval dominance for over 300 years, between the thirteenth and sixteenth centuries, but Chinese emperors concluded that it was in their best interests to concentrate on their internal affairs and defend the empire's borders from the escalating attacks of rising regional powers. In addition, China determined that there was not that much to learn from the existing world at the time, as the country was far more advanced than the rising European powers in terms of ship-building, naval strength, agriculture and paper-making. This policy of isolationism lasted until the 1840s when it was broken by British forces.

The rising West and the declining East

Both the Islamic empire and China went through episodes of civilizational rise and decline. 'During the chaotic century from 860 to 960 following the disintegration of the Tang dynasty, political and military powers devolved to the local level. … the effects of fragmentation were less benign in the north. Many of the regional warlords there were not Chinese but Turks from the garrison armies.'[13] Fragmentation continued, and China fell under the control of Mongols, Tibetans and Jurchens, Tanguts and Khitans. As mentioned earlier, the Mongol invasion was most devastating to both Chinese and Islamic civilizations. 'Mongol armies first swept across the north China plain in 1212–13, they left ninety-odd cities in rubble. When they sacked the Jurchen's northern capital at Beijing in 1215, it burned for more than a month.'[14] The Mongol wave of destruction continued westward, and its wrath reached Bukhara and Samarkand in Central Asia in 1219, with a destructive force of over 200,000 troops who levelled cities in their path. The devastation extended to Baghdad in 1257, the seat of the Abbasids and of Islam, and continued to Russia and Central Europe.

Beyond the brutality and violence exercised against conquered nations, the Mongols lacked the skills to manage the land and the people under their rule. They learned how to recruit and reward loyal subjects and armies. They recruited the Turkic armies to fight on their side, especially against Russia and Central Europe. Khubilai, the grandson of Genghis Khan, moved the Mongol capital from Karakorum in Mongolia to Beijing. In his battles against the Song Dynasty in Central and Southern China, he employed advisers from all nationalities including Chinese and Central Asians. 'The Mongols employed Chinese, Korean, Jurchen, Uighur, and Persian experts in naval siege warfare. Muslim engineers designed artillery that sent a barrage of rocks weighing up to a hundred pounds each.'[15] Their 'invasion marked the closure of the Song period, and led to the establishment of the Yuan Dynasty (1279–1368) and the incorporation of most of China into the Mongol Empire. It was to prove traumatic, with the Chinese finding themselves under alien rule and reduced to lowly status.'[16] Muslim artisans and labourers were moved by force from Central Asia in particular to Mongolia and China to work as slaves for Mongol warlords and for the state. This explains the increasing number of Muslims in China under Mongol rule. However, upper class Muslims and Central Asians of Uyghur, Turk and Persian backgrounds were privileged as they collaborated with the Mongol occupation – something the Chinese never forgave. Muslim co-operation was facilitated by the fact that the Mongols embraced Islam and became co-religionist. Some Muslim communities felt that they related to the Mongols more than the Han, given that the Han had massacred Muslims in ethnic tensions earlier. At this juncture, the pure image of Muslims in China began to change. Their association with the Mongol invaders proved to be devastating to Islam and Muslims in China. They came to be viewed as barbarians, traitors, savages and oppressive tax collectors. The Mongols had created a system whereby merchants, mostly Muslims from Central Asia, bid against each other on contracts from the Mongol rulers to collect taxes. This further stained the emerging negative image of Muslims as greedy traitors.

Under foreign rule, life was difficult for the Chinese, but as a civilization and as a people, they managed to survive and finally to liberate themselves from the Mongols. Chinese culture and civilization learned resistance to foreign rule, attempted to assimilate foreigners, sharpened and strengthened itself and nurtured a spirit of resistance to alien domination. The Ming Dynasty (1368–1644) came to restore China's dignity. The rise of the Ming Dynasty coincided with the continued decline of the Islamic civilization, and the rise of European conquest. Several competing tendencies vis-à-vis China's foreign policy can be identified in the early Ming Dynasty's rule. There was a momentum for reinstating the tributary system, extending China's traditional influence into Central Asia and pursuing naval exploration. It was also in this period that the concept of the Hui with reference to Muslims began to take shape. 'The term of Islam was the religion of the Hui (Huijiao), and to call oneself a Hui persona (Huimin) was to state a religious affiliation. Yet while Hui means "Muslim" for several centuries after Islam's entry into China, the concept also contained a racial component.'[17]

As for building a naval power, the Ming's third emperor, Chengzu, sent out a series of emissaries to visit potential tributary states. The grandest of these were the overseas voyages of 1405 to 1433 led by one of his most trusted servants, a Muslim admiral named Zheng He, who sailed to Arabia, Africa and East Asia.[18] China was unsurpassed by any existing power in terms of ship-building and maritime knowledge. Chinese naval dominance on the high seas was a testament to China's superior ship-building skills, navigational knowledge and scientific advancement. However, China decided to isolate itself from the world and focus on its internal affairs until the advent of the British encroachment in the 1840s. Had China pursued the naval exploration voyages, it could have been a global–imperial power with territorial possessions in the Americas, in Africa, in the Middle East and in Asia. China could have been richer than England, Spain, France, the Netherlands or Portugal. Instead, it was subjugated by rising Western naval powers for over a century, the century of humiliation.

Martin Jacques attributes the Ming policy of isolationism, China's failure to continue Zheng He's voyages or pursue its naval capabilities to several factors. He highlights the fact that, because of sensitivities about the northern borders, the Ming Dynasty moved the imperial capital from Nanjing to Beijing, which reduced interest in oceanic voyages. The cost of these voyages was a concern, while the priority was to protect China's territory and assimilate the newly annexed lands after the defeat of the Mongols. In addition, China believed in its civilizational superiority and felt it had nothing to learn from the outside world. All these factors encouraged China to shrink its naval ambitions.[19]

During the Manchu-controlled Qing Dynasty, China embarked on the most ambitious process of expansion westward, 'from 1644 to late 18th century, when the territory under Chinese rule more than doubled. This involved the conquest of lands to the north, notably those occupied by the Mongols, and to the north-west, the homeland of diverse Muslim populations of Turkistan. Many of the conquered people, particularly in Central Asia and Tibet, had little or nothing in common with the Han Chinese.'[20] Jacques affirms that 'these lands became colonial possessions of China, and China used a combination of military and cultural means to assimilate newly annexed lands, especially in Central and southern China and the steppe land.'[21] However, he notes that 'the Qing conquest of the north-west and the west was different, being achieved by the use of particular force and brutality. Most of the Zunghars for example, a Muslim people who occupied much of what we know now as Xinjiang, were exterminated.'[22] The violent incorporation of the bordering lands and the subjugation of the people came as a reaction to the Hans' humiliation by the Mongols. China also consolidated its control over the territory and the newly annexed lands, and shielded itself from potential 'barbarian' invasions. These measures never relieved China from the encroachment of the rising Western threat, which humiliated China as much if not worse than the savagery of the Mongol invasion.

In the post-Mongol era, trade with Central Asia and Turkic lands continued as China frantically embarked on a process of exploiting its imperial possessions in neighbouring lands. Internally, around the middle of the nineteenth century, as economic difficulties began to grow, the Qing Dynasty was shaken by a series of local revolts. 'In the southwest and northwest, Muslim and Miao rebellions flared up, revealing the potential for ethnic separatism to lead provinces on the periphery to break away from central control.'[23] Muslims in Yunnan, Gansu and Xinjiang rebelled against continued discrimination and near enslavement to the Hui by the Han. Their six-year rebellion was finally suppressed in 1879 by provisional generals.

Towards the mid-nineteenth century, Western, Russian and Japanese encroachment on Chinese and Central Asian territory – China's traditional sphere of influence – seemed to be unstoppable. Russia, in particular, had always had a keen interest in bordering Central Asia, whereas Britain, France and later the United States had trade interests in China and South and East Asia. The Japanese had territorial claims to make as well, and were able to press such claims and subjugate China with a brutal occupation comparable to the Mongol invasion. The Century of Humiliation, from 1848 to 1950, was replete with events that highlighted the bitter rivalry among leading world powers over concessions in China. 'China's impotence in the face of growing foreign intervention stimulated a movement for reform aimed at modernizing the country.'[24] The Chinese intelligentsia appealed for reform and change, but 'the imperial government for most part … neither understood nor accepted the necessity, let alone the urgency of modernization, remaining passive or actively opposed, unlike in post-1868 Japan, where the state was the key agent of modernization.'[25] Furthermore, the call for modernization and reform was 'associated with the West at a time when the latter was colonizing and humiliating the country: far from being seen as patriots, they [reformers] were regarded as tainted by the West, or worse, as traitors. As a result, the growing hostility amongst Chinese toward the West was to work against the process of reform.'[26] China's resistance together with such unsettling events as the Boxer Uprising of 1900 were not powerful enough to put an end to foreign occupation. This weakness only led to closer co-ordination between British, Japanese, American and French colonial powers, which further discredited China and forced it into treaties with degrading terms.

In the early years of the twentieth century, China witnessed some internal upheavals, wars of liberation against colonial powers, especially Japan, and a brutal civil war in which warlords, nationalists and communists were embroiled in brutal clashes between 1911 and 1949. The conflict between communists in mainland China who established the PRC and nationalists who moved their government of the Republic of China (ROC, Taiwan) to the island of Formosa never officially ended, although it became less antagonistic. China regained its strength, even though its spirit was wounded by the disgaraceful foreign presence and the brutality of the Japanese occupation. The scars of each period are embedded in the collective memory of today's China, and continue to influence Sino–Japanese and Sino–Western relations.

Muslims in China and Sino–Islamic relations

The period between 1911 and 1949 saw Muslims as active participants at the centre of political developments in China. Muslim leadership supported the nationalists, and split in its support of communists. It is reported that two of the twenty-four members of the Republican State Council were Muslims. Republican Muslim officials such as Bai Chongxi, China's Defence Minister, Ehmetjan Qasim, Provisional Vice-Chairman of East Turkistan, and General Ma Bufang were influential in the Republican government. During Mao's March, some Muslim leaders resisted communist rule and were exterminated by Chinese communists and their Soviet allies. Muslim communities under communism were subjected to the same restrictions imposed by the communist regime on minorities, and freedom to practise their faith was extremely limited.

In the early years of the PRC, the Communist Party dispatched a series of ethnologist missions around the country. The goal was to collect information on the Chinese people, to classify them according to *minz* or ethnic groups and assess their suitability to the process of modernization according to Marxist principles. One of the missions' goals was to investigate the Huis' so called 'cultural backwardness.' The studies traced the origins of the Hui to the Ming Dynasty, a mixture of Arab, Persian and Central Asian roots. The findings established that they possessed an inherited predisposition for commerce, and that, although 'culturally backward', illiterate and poor when the PRC was formed, 'the Hui have made great progress under the PRC's guidance and assistance.'[27]

During this period, Muslims were subjected to forcible assimilation into communist structures. The Hui had to constantly combat stigmatization and stereotypes that classified them as 'primitive, feudal, exploitative, and backward.' As Gillette states, 'These Chinese Muslims combated the racial sterotype that the Hui people were "feudal" and poorly equipped for modernization. They showed themselves to be more "civilized" than their Han neighbors or the local government. They turned "tradition" into economic asset, and challenged the CCP's monopoly on "progress" by appealing to an alternative set of criteria for evaluating society.'[28] The Hui built on their ancestral accomplishments as merchants, endowed with a disciplined faith and a morally driven conduct. The deeply rooted values of hard work, discipline and patience inspired Muslims in China to endure communist pressure and its brutal structures, to survive the Cultural Revolution and later to benefit from domestic peace in the post-Mao era.

The status of Muslims in China was certainly a major concern to Muslims around the world after WWII, especially in the Middle East. They were alarmed to learn about the mistreatment of Muslim communities across China at the hands of communists, the closing of mosques and the brutality in Xinjiang. Given that the predicament of this minority was exploited by China's opponents, China determined to project a better image of its Muslims. When it celebrated its national diversity, it included them and, generally speaking, it geared more of its foreign policy towards the Middle East and the Islamic world. Some Chinese Muslims became envoys for China to the Islamic world, assisted significantly towards securing diplomatic recognition for China and improved Sino–Arab and Sino–Islamic relations.

Sino–Middle Eastern relations post WWII

Mao, Chou En-lai, Lin Biao and senior communist comrades showed significant interest in the Middle East during the communist Long March and afterwards. They closely followed political events in the region, especially WWII developments. Their fears, at that time, were based on the possibility that a collapse of the Allies in Europe and elsewhere would allow Germany to extend its influence to the Middle East, and eventually to the Far East. Their fears nearly materialized when France collapsed and the Vichy government took over. Syria, under French control, declared loyalty to Vichy rule. Iraq's pro-British government collapsed, and Rashid Ali Al-Kelani, a pro-Germany prime minister, took over. German forces showed stiff resistance in North Africa. This scenario meant that, if the Allies were unable to stop the Germans from advancing, the Far East would not be spared from Japanese wrath. Unpredictably, towards the close of 1943, the direction of the war changed when Germany decided to invade the Soviet Union.

Mao and Chou En-lai, in particular, were fully aware of the national liberation movements across the Middle East and developments in Egypt in particular. Mao understood the consequences of colonial rivalry over the region as well. He also predicted that the collapse of the old colonial powers – Britain and France – would lead to the emergence of new imperial powers, namely the US and the USSR, both of which would make the region the centre of their antagonism. The Middle East has, in fact, become the centre of world politics and the primary arena for superpower rivalry. As Yitzhak Shichor (1979) affirms, Mao divided the world into zones: to him, the Middle East lies in the intermediate zone. 'The control of this area by a hostile power would not only precipitate a third world but also endanger the survival of the PRC.'[29] Therefore, the PRC viewed developments in the Middle East as a matter of national security and regime survival.

Mao attributed the problems of the region to external intervention and imperial rivalry. He advocated that 'local problems would be settled by the local peoples alone, and that no Middle East problem could be settled thoroughly before outside intervention, which had caused or sustained it, was liquidated.'[30] Shichor affirms that 'these Chinese attitudes have never changed but China's policy has undergone several changes since 1949.'[31] Even on major issues such as the Arab–Israeli conflict, China continued to believe that Arabs and Israelis are capable of resolving their differences should the imperial powers cease their intervention in the internal affairs of the Middle East. China's hope of ending such intervention was placed in the hands of Middle Eastern liberation movements. It invested heavily in building such movements, provided them with light arms and diplomatic and political support in international forums, but all fell short of China's expectations, with one single exception, the National Liberation Front of Algeria.

The first major and direct interaction between China and Middle Eastern countries was at the Bandung Conference in 1955 in Indonesia. The Chinese and Israeli delegations conducted 'trade' talks which explored diplomatic recognition, given the fact that Israel was the first Middle Eastern country to recognize China in January 1950, while the majority of Arab countries recognized the Republic of China as the sole representative of China. Shichor maintains that China had sent repeated messages to the Israelis signalling its interest in establishing diplomatic relations. Some signals were explicit, but all of them were misread, misunderstood or totally ignored.[32] Had the Israelis been able to recognize China's diplomatic gestures, China could have been an active participant in managing and resolving the Arab–Israeli conflict as early as 1955.

In fact, the Bandung Conference and the Non-Aligned Movement provided China with an international forum from which it engaged extensively in international politics. It also provided China with the opportunity to secure diplomatic recognition especially in the Arab world, extract support from Third World countries, engage in trade talks and resolve some of its own problems, especially those that dealt with territorial disputes with India, Vietnam, Burma and other neighbouring countries. Chou En-lai's diplomacy, charm, sharpness and commitment to the causes of Third World nations made China exceptionally influential and a successful participant in the non-aligned movement.

Mao's intermediate zone theory

Mao's aforementioned theoretical paradigm on classifying the world into zones guided China's international relations. Shichor states that 'Mao's intermediate zone theory was to become the cornerstone of China's Middle Eastern policy.'[33] According to Mao's paradigm, 'the main contradiction in the post-war world lay not between Moscow and Washington but between US-led Western imperialism and Asian, African, Latin American, and even some capitalist countries.'[34] His understanding was totally rejected by the Soviets who advocated that contradictions on the world scene centred between Moscow and Washington; hence, the socialist world should rally behind Moscow in its anti-imperialist battle. But China continued to perceive the conflict as a confrontation between imperialism and Third World countries in particular, and American advances in the Middle East were viewed as a threat to China's national interest and regime survival. In the postwar period, Chinese foreign policy concentrated its efforts on preventing a wholesale American takeover in the Middle East by strengthening its relations with governments in the region, as well as providing generous support to national liberation movements.

China resisted American military pacts, or Western-sponsored pacts in the Middle East, especially the Baghdad Pact. It coined the term 'military crescent':

> allegedly an American military alliance [that] stretched from Japan to the Middle East and included South Korea, the Ryukyus (Nansei Islands), Formosa (Taiwan), Indochina (Indonesia), Pakistan, Persia and Turkey, as a direct act of hostility not against the Soviet Union and Eastern Europe but against China, and even more so against the countries of the 'crescent' themselves.[35]

Although China devoted remarkable efforts and resources to creating a home-grown Middle Eastern awareness of the American threat in the intermediate zone, the Chinese 'were disturbed by the submissive attitude of Middle Eastern countries and their lack of resistance to Western encroachments. But above all, it was the perception of potential threats to their security, not to mention the war in Korea and Indochina that put the Chinese on alert.'[36] China's only partial success in the Middle East did not deter it from expanding contacts and influence across the region. Following WWII, it continued to conceptualize its foreign policy goals towards the region, and sharpened its ideas and skills in dealing with the imminent threat of American and Soviet expansion in the Middle East. Its policy revolved around its anti-imperialist agenda promoting trade, cultural contacts and diplomatic recognition. 'Trade relations were always regarded by China as an avenue to better mutual understanding that might lead to normal relations.'[37]

China supported the Arab national liberation movements and the right of the Arab people to self-determination and freedom from Western colonialism. Its support of the Algerian Revolution was a milestone in this regard. At the beginning, China co-ordinated its policy towards the Middle East with its closest ally, the USSR, but the friction between the two communist giants since 1963 complicated China's foreign policy towards the region. Nevertheless, China made significant strides in the Arab world in the areas of trade and diplomatic recognition. It supported Egypt in its struggle against Israeli, French and British aggression in 1956. At the time, Egypt was leading Arab, African and Third World countries in their anti-imperialist struggle. China extended a hand of friendship to Egypt and other Arab countries such as Syria, Iraq, Yemen and Algeria, and Arab countries reciprocated, although not at the pace expected by China, especially in offering diplomatic recognition.

Towards resolving the ongoing Arab–Israeli conflict, China consistently advocated a peaceful solution. Although China was not a member of the United Nations, it supported UN Resolution 181 in 1947, the Partition Plan that divided Palestine into an Arab and a Jewish state. The UN was acting on a resolution introduced by the Soviet Union, China's closest ally then, and approved by the UN General Assembly and then by the Security Council. China's enthusiasm for the Partition Plan, which was passed 2 years before the establishment of the PRC, also stemmed from the fact that it was the Soviet Union who designed it, mobilized support for it and secured its passage at the General Assembly in co-ordination with other countries such as the United States. The US supported the plan, but the leading role was courtesy of the Soviets. They hoped that Israel would be a bastion for socialism in the Middle East, given that early Israeli institutions such as the labour unions (Histadrut), Kibbutz (agricultural settlements) and Knesset (people's assembly, parliament) had their roots in socialist and communist thought.

The Arab–Israeli conflict

The Arab–Israeli conflict dominated Sino–Arab relations from 1949 to 1976. All along, China maintained impartiality and advocated a peaceful resolution to the conflict. According to Shichor, China understood the conflict within a two-dimensional approach: a strategic and a tactical one. He maintains that 'whereas the strategic Chinese interpretation of the conflict has remained fundamentally consistent to this very day, attitudes towards the parties concerned have changed considerably according to circumstances.'[38] China perceived the struggle as an imperial power conflict between external antagonists who created the conflict, nurtured it, sustained it and benefited from its continuation. Albeit, China did not deviate from the dominant narrative of the conflict at that time, that the origins of the conflict lay within post-WWI settlements, with incompatible promises issued by Britain to Arabs and Jews and continued colonial rivalry in the Middle East region. When the mandating power, Britain, found out that its occupation was unsustainable in Palestine and turned to the United Nations for a solution, the Soviet Union pushed hard for Resolution 181 to divide Palestine in two.

Although the Israelis gladly received the resolution and were successful in declaring their state, the Palestinians failed. Britain, as a colonial power occupying Egypt, pushed the Egyptian army to confront Israel while the US was secretly arming the Israelis. Therefore, the Anglo-American struggle in the Middle East post WWII strengthened the conflict, and the intervention of the Soviets, who were later on the side of Egypt and the Arab people, prolonged the conflict. Shichor maintains that:

> in tactical terms, the Chinese originally maintained a neutral and balanced stand on the Arab–Israeli conflict, slightly inclined, until the 1950s, in favor of Israel. Peking held the Arab governments no less responsible than Israel for the 1948 war, and for the fact that the Partition Plan's provision for an Arab state in Palestine had not even been implemented: places inhabited by Palestinian Arabs were part of what had been occupied by Jordan, Egypt and Israel.[39]

Therefore, China reiterated the fact that the Partition Plan would be the only solution to a lasting peace in the Middle East.

The emergence of the Non-Aligned Movement provided China with a new forum to express its views on regional and international relations, given that China was absent from the United Nations deliberations. China's goal was to use this forum to secure diplomatic recognition and curb any potential recognition of Taiwan as an independent state, or the sole representative of the Chinese people. Chou En-lai, who represented China in such forums for over 20 years, showed some support of the Arab views on the conflict, and intervened for the Soviets to sell arms to Nasser in 1955. Simultaneously, Chou En-lai was meeting Israeli delegations and diplomats exploring the establishment of diplomatic relations between Israel and China. While Israeli sources emphasized Chinese impartiality in dealing with the Middle East conflict, Arab sources tended to exaggerate China's support of the Arab side and the Palestinian Resistance Movement.[40] It is true that Chou En-lai reiterated China's support for Egypt, but China never gave significant military support to the Arabs to alter the direction of the wars, and neither did the Soviet Union.

China also provided the PLO with light weapons in its resistance against Israel and Jordan. Chinese, Soviet and Socialist support for Egypt was incomparable by all standards to the quality assistance provided by the US to Israel. The Arab side seems to have misread Chinese diplomatic statements on the Arab–Israeli conflict, and ignored the impartial Chinese attitude towards the conflict. The Arabs were desperate for a third party to intervene in the conflict, hoping that it would be China. Psychologically speaking, the Arab side was absolutely devastated by American military of Israel, disappointed with the nature of Soviet backing and unable to convince China to intervene in the conflict wholeheartedly. While China continued its calls for peace, direct talks and a regional solution to the conflict, the Arabs wanted material aid such as quality military reinforcements to turn the tide in the conflict. It is as if the Arabs were drowning in a sea of conflicts and looked to China as a saviour, but the latter ignored the calls for rescue.

Either way, at the same time that China gave the Arabs diplomatic and light military support, it tried to keep good relations with Israel. But the immense burden of managing the Arab–Israeli conflict was entrusted to the Soviet Union not only by China, but by the entire communist world. When the regional alignment materialized from 1957 onward, Israel was clearly on the Western side, and Egypt was on the Eastern bloc's side. Therefore, each received disproportionate support from their camp. While the United States provided Israel with quality military support, the Soviets provided Egypt with symbolic political and military support leading to a disparity in the balance of power in the Middle East in favour of Israel. The same unequal assistance was extended to other Soviet allies in the region, such as Syria. The outcome was utter defeat of the Arab side in military confrontations with Israel in 1948, 1956, the 1967 War, the 1973 War and the Israeli invasion of Lebanon in 1982. The only relative exception was the 1973 October War, in which Egypt and Syria made some gains at the beginning of the war and then lost them completely to Israel at a later stage. The relative gains made by Syria and Egypt were not an indication of a change in the quality of Soviet armament made available to them; rather, they were a reflection of a national determination to attain some kind of military gains on the ground.

The ultimate goal of the 1973 War was also political in nature. In its aftermath, a momentum for peace gathered strength as the combatants, including Arabs, Israelis and their respective allies – the US and the USSR – were convinced of the futility of a continued war and the necessity to pursue a peaceful settlement to the conflict. The Roger Plan, the Kissinger Shuttle Diplomacy and later the Camp David agreements in 1978 and 1979 represented this trend. When peace gathered momentum, China felt vindicated, as it had advocated direct talks and peaceful settlement of the conflict all along.

China joined the United Nations in 1971. This step represented a very important development as its permanent status in the organization provided China with unlimited global opportunities to express its foreign policy goals and flex its muscles in international relations. While China continued its diplomatic support of the Palestinian cause, it was dismayed by the lack of unity among Arab countries towards the Palestinian question in international organizations. Such inconsistency on the part of the Arabs puzzled the Chinese, causing them to judge issues related to the conflict on their own merit without necessarily co-ordinating or consulting with Arab countries. Furthermore, China had to master the game of being a permanent member of the Security Council, and simultaneously manoeuvring its way among conflicting interests, namely, the animosity of both the US and the Soviet Union towards China.

China welcomed the newly established Palestinian Liberation Organization in 1964, and connected with it directly. It also strongly condemned 'reactionary' regime interventions such as Jordan in Palestinian affairs. China received Arafat repeatedly in Beijing, and supported the rights of the Palestinians to self-determination. Similarly, China supported the Israeli Communist Party, Maki, and hoped it would gain a significant role in Israeli politics and advance the cause of peace between Palestinians and Israelis.

Algeria co-sponsored the admission resolution with Albania for China's membership in the United Nations in 1971, and Arab support 'was favorable: eleven for, four abstentions (Bahrain, Jordan, Lebanon and Qatar), while only Saudi Arabia voted against.'[41] The rhetorical war waged by China against 'reactionary' monarchies and lack of Chinese understanding of Saudi foreign policy prompted Saudi Arabia to oppose China's membership in the United Nations. Its objection and its 'no' vote on the resolution came as no surprise. It was a reaction to China's support of Nasser in his war in Yemen, and to his aerial attacks against the kingdom. It was only after the oil embargo in 1973 that China began to understand the role of Saudi Arabia when King Faisal demonstrated his ability to make independent foreign policy decisions away from 'imperialist' countries such as the US, to quote Chinese terminology. China became more practical in its foreign policy, liberating itself incrementally from the confinements of the communist dogma. Later on, it mastered pragmatism in foreign policy, which proved to be rewarding for its foreign policy goals. Jordan abstained to protest China's support of the PLO in its war against the monarchy and against the Jordanian armed forces, while Bahrain's vote was motivated by Saudi pressure.

The 1967 War and its aftermath

The Six Day War of 1967 was a critical factor in Middle Eastern politics. The utter loss Nasser suffered in the war led to the discrediting of Arab nationalism in general and to Egypt losing its prestige among Arabs, Muslims and Third World countries. China held the Soviets responsible for such a loss, charging them with pushing Nasser into a war for which he was not prepared, and failing to provide Egypt with the quality military support necessary to achieve victory. Instead, the Soviets provided Egypt with negligible and non-military-related support that led to its utter defeat. China had previously advised Nasser that self-reliance was the best method for developing his national military capabilities, but Nasser believed in his allies' military support (the Soviet Union and the Socialist bloc). China counselling Egypt in this way must not be confused with its enduring belief that the conflict in the region could only be resolved peacefully. In the wake of the Six Day War, calls for a peaceful settlement, and once again dominated international debate over the Middle East. Once again, China advocated a peaceful settlement of the Arab–Israeli conflict. 'This Chinese formula remained intact throughout the later years, despite the tactical shifts in China's Palestine policy.'[42] In fact, China held both the US and the USSR responsible for prolonging the conflict. China felt that Arabs and Israelis were willing to accommodate each other's existence and interests, whereas the US and Soviets were unwilling to settle the conflict for reasons that dealt with their global rivalry, ignoring the needs of the people of the Middle East at the same time.

In the 1970s, the Vietnam War topped the list of some other major shifts in international politics that drastically affected the Middle East. The war weakened the US presence in the Far East; therefore, the US felt it needed to recover from its catastrophic consequences and quell, at least temporarily, the conflict in the Middle East. Kissinger led the process of realignment of both Egypt and China to the American camp. After Nasser's death in 1970, Sadat, a pragmatic head of state, re-examined the nature of Soviet–Egyptian relations and reasoned that Egypt's national interests would be better served by realigning them with the Western camp. Sadat was also more willing than his predecessor to compromise and enter into direct peace negotiations with Israel, which far exceeded the wildest Israeli expectations, especially his visit to Israel and his speech in the Knesset on 22 November 1977. The Soviets' loss of Egypt was significant in that it was the first step towards the decline in Soviet influence in the region.

Another stumbling step that led to a direct confrontation between the Arab-Islamic world, on one side, and the USSR, on the other, was the Soviet invasion of Afghanistan in 1979. The invasion led to an epic encounter in which Islam and communism collided. Arabs and Muslims were stunned by the reports of massive civilian casualties and unjustified loss of human life during the invasion. The nature of the Soviet occupation of Afghanistan and the weaponry used against unarmed civilians triggered a sense of resistance across the Islamic world that led to an alliance between Islam and the West. The goal was to make the Soviets' presence in Afghanistan as costly as the American presence in Vietnam. Therefore, a new generation of Jihadi Muslims emerged, who dedicated their lives to evicting the Soviets from Afghanistan. The war consumed the Soviet Union for 10 years, and finally forced it out in 1988. The Soviet invasion of Afghanistan turned out to be one of the most defining events in modern history. Its consequences are still unfolding, and the subsequent instability in Afghanistan, the civil war and the current War on Terror originated from that point. It first led to a confrontation between the Islamic world and the Soviet world, and later to the current confrontation that pits the US and the West against the Islamic world, between the Clash of Civilizations and the War on Terror paradigms.

When China was awarded a permanent seat at the UN and Taiwan was evicted from it in 1971, US–Sino relations began to improve. China's rapprochement culminated in Nixon's visit to Chairman Mao in 1972, which once again altered international politics and established diplomatic relations between the two countries in 1979. China facilitated the withdrawal of American forces from Vietnam, kept North Korea and Burma in check, supported the US against the Soviets in Afghanistan and reduced tensions in the Far East.

Other elements that added to shifts in the region were the political developments in Iran that led to the resumption of diplomatic relations with China in 1971. The scope of the relationship was fairly limited, but the eruption of the Islamic Revolution in 1978–79 brought about unprecedented changes on the Iranian, the regional and the international scenes. The Shah's regime collapsed after a popular uprising against the oppressive policies of the Iranian secret police, known as the SAVAK. Imam Khomeini assumed leadership in Iran, and a new resurgent Shi'ism was ushered in regionally and globally. The reaction of the Sunni world was resistance to and rejection of revolutionary Iran, much like the resistance against the expansion of Shi'i influence after the US invasion of Iraq in 2003. In order to put an end to the emerging Iranian threat, Saddam Hussein declared war against Iran in September 1980. His goal was primarily territorial and regional dominance as he sought to crush the Iranian Revolution in its early stages. While Iraq made significant territorial gains at the beginning of the war, it was unable to sustain them because of territorial overstretch and lack of supply lines. Iran mobilized itself to meet the Iraqi threat.

Contrary to what Saddam Hussein had believed and hoped for, the Iraqi invasion of Iran led to the consolidation of the Islamic Revolution and the strengthening of its internal front. The Iranian army and the Revolutionary Guard reassembled, and a Revolutionary Militia known as Basij regained its strength after absorbing the first wave of the Iraqi advancement. Iraq realized that its decision to wage war was not well thought out. Iraq's strategy was built entirely on miscalculations: Saddam Hussein believed the West, the Arab countries and basically the entire world would rally behind Iraq in the war, but that never materialized. Iraq was willing to accept a ceasefire in the second year of the war, but Imam Khomeini rejected the offer and insisted on toppling Saddam Hussein. Both countries were locked in a war that consumed each other's strength for 8 years but, during that time, both nations solicited external support. In all this, China supplied both Iran and Iraq with arms. Iraq needed Chinese weapons to resist Iranian conventional superiority, whereas Iran needed Chinese anti-aircraft missiles to counter Iraqi aerial superiority. Ultimately, when the war ended in 1988, China gained the favour of both combatants.

China and the peaceful settlement of the Arab–Israeli conflict

Prior to 1976 and as part of China's media campaign of anti-imperialism, the Chinese media rhetorically opposed 'imperialist' schemes to resolve the conflict, allegedly at the expense of the Palestinian people but, after that time, Chinese media outlets reduced their 'anti-imperialism' rhetoric towards the Middle East. *The People's Daily*, the New China News Agency or Xinhua 'refrained from explicitly condemning the political solution approach to the Arab–Israeli conflict'[43] and began positive coverage to boost the efforts of China's support for a peaceful settlement to the Arab–Israeli conflict. Curiously, Israeli scholarship maintains that China never deviated from its belief that the Arab–Israeli conflict could only be resolved through peaceful means. Arab sources were led to believe, or wanted to believe all along, that China was supportive of the military option, and misunderstood China's support for the Palestinian and other Middle Eastern national liberation movements. China neither advocated an elimination of the state of Israel nor believed in it. When China supported the Palestinians' rights, it meant the right of self-determination in the already recognized parts of Palestine after Resolution 181, i.e. the Partition Plan that was accepted and supported by Israel itself. The promulgation of Israel as an independent state was an explicit admission by the Israelis of the legitimacy of the Partition Plan that recognized both Israel and Palestine as separate states.

China was also as harsh in its criticism of Jordan as it was in reference to the lack of awareness of Palestinian national aspirations, but it refrained from criticizing its ally, Nasser, for the occupation of Gaza. China condemned Jordan's control of the West Bank and its reliance on 'imperialist' countries and their military support. The Chinese media also unleashed its wrath on Jordan, holding it fully responsible for Black September, a manoeuvre by the Jordanian army to suppress and oust guerrillas in the Palestinian Resistance Movement from their camps in Jordan. China was aware of the potential threat that the Palestinian organization represented to the exiting regime in Jordan; it was fully aware of the intentions of Fatah, the Popular Front for the Liberation of Palestine and other Palestinian organizations, which stated clearly and publically that their goals were to topple the monarchy of King

Hussein in Jordan and replace it with a puppet government sympathetic to the Palestinian cause.

China repeatedly called Jordan a 'reactionary' monarchy, a puppet of Western imperialism. It also condemned the declaration of King Hussein, in March 1972, that established the United Arab Kingdom (UAK) with two provinces: Palestine and East Jordan. China's views were identical to those of Fatah, PLFP and other Palestinian organizations that the goal of the UAK was to do away with the existence of a Palestinian state. However, King Hussein's vision was a federation in which the UAK would be composed of two provinces, the East Bank and the West Bank, each with its own parliamentary structures and administration, while defence and foreign policy would be conducted by the UAK's central government in Amman. This solution was acceptable to Israel, as it refused to negotiate with or talk to the Palestinians during that period. The US, European and some Arab countries supported the proposal as well. The UAK could also have led to the realization of some Arab goals after the 1967 War, such as the restitution of the West Bank.

China's opposition to the plan and its continued criticism of Jordan over Black September were well grounded in its support of the PLO. As a result, Jordan abstained from China's admission to the United Nations in 1971, but relations between the two countries improved significantly when Jordan consolidated its sovereignty over its territory, resumed its leading role in the Middle East and international politics and improved its relations with the PLO.

China was not yet a member of the United Nations when resolutions for peace plans were under way during the passing of SC Resolution 242 in 1967, but abstained from voting on SC Resolution 338 in 1973, which basically reiterated the proposals found in the Roger Plan, and Resolution 242 as well, calling for a peaceful settlement to the Arab–Israeli conflict. SC Resolution 338, which passed 14 to 1, invoked a ceasefire to end the 1973 War. China's abstention should not be understood as opposition to peace but as resentment towards the continuing role of the Soviet Union and the United States, a role viewed by China as escalating the conflict rather than genuinely attempting to resolve it. In fact, what complicated China's voting pattern in the United Nations and its organs is the fact that there was no Arab consensus on major issues facing the region. Therefore, China voted according to its interests and its understanding of regional and international relations governing political and military developments on the scene.

Kuwait's declaration of independence

One of the major crises in Sino–Middle Eastern relations during this period was the Kuwaiti declaration of independence on 19 June 1961, which continues to have ramifications on the region's politics to this day. The declaration caught many nations by surprise, and Iraq in particular as it did all it could to prevent it. To avoid a possible Iraqi invasion, 11 days later, Kuwait asked for British military assistance to safeguard its process of independence.

'China was the first communist country to recognize Kuwait' on 28 June 1961, confused by the developments, but ambitiously hopeful of its corollaries.[44] The step proved to be exceptionally successful as it brought hefty dividends later as Kuwait and China developed cordial diplomatic, trade and political relations. China utilized the Kuwaiti route to infiltrate gulf markets and encourage diplomatic recognition from Saudi Arabia in particular.

Relations between Kuwait and China continued to flourish in spite of the interruption of the Iraqi invasion of Kuwait in the summer of 1990 and the ensuing Gulf War in which China maintained its support for Kuwait's independence. However, it abstained from voting on SC Resolution 678 in 1990, which authorized the use of force against Iraq. China's abstention was considered to be tacit support for the resolution (given that it could have vetoed it), and was not sanctioned by Kuwait or the United States and its coalition. On the contrary, its vote was highly appreciated and considered by Kuwait and its allies a significant step towards support for the UN's resolution on Iraq and its eviction from Kuwait by force. In the aftermath of the war, Chinese–Kuwaiti relations were reinstated and intensified as Kuwait's sovereignty was temporarily interrupted. China contributed to the rebuilding of Kuwait, strengthened its bilateral trade relations and, in doing so, secured major oil exploration contracts in the country. China's upstreaming, exploration and production of oil in Kuwait are critical to China's energy security and strategic partnership with this Middle East country.

Post-Mao era

The death of Chairman Mao and Deng Xiaoping's consolidation of power ushered in a new era in China's foreign and domestic politics. Xiaoping made economic modernization the centrepiece of China's domestic and foreign policy, extended its trade relations with the Middle East and partnered with the region, especially in the area of energy. So the Middle East occupied an important position in this project. At that time, China's energy production was sufficient to meet its domestic needs, but the acceleration of its industrialization process made the Middle East the primary destination for energy supply. Subsequently, China's primary goal was to establish diplomatic relations with states in the region. Jordan recognized China in 1977, Kuwait in 1978, Lebanon and Oman in 1983. Other countries followed suit while China enhanced its quality relations with Turkey, Iran, Israel and other Arab states, culminating with Saudi Arabia extending its diplomatic recognition of China in 1990. In fact, Chinese–Saudi relations developed in an unprecedented fashion to the extent that the two countries forged a strategic partnership later on.

China's economic modernization process promoted a constructive foreign policy towards the Middle East based on friendly relations with all nations and a strict commitment to non-intervention in their internal affairs. Previously alarmed by China's support for leftist insurgencies in the region, conservative Middle Eastern countries now welcomed the commitment. It led to encouraged co-operation so that the Middle East currently identifies more with China than with the US or Europe, the traditional allies of the region. The nature of China's involvement is also understood in pure commercial terms rather than ideological, hegemonic or imperial. Observers note that:

> there appears to be an equal amount of enthusiasm from Middle Eastern countries to take advantage of the world's fastest growing market. China's presence is largely perceived as non-ideological, economically oriented and pragmatic. Furthermore, there is little concern that China's increasing status as a world power will constitute a security threat. Hegemony, domination, and imperialism are associated with the United States and Europe. China is not seen that way.[45]

It offers something different to the region: 'at various times, many welcomed the example China provided of national autonomy; its identification with oppressed nations; its demand for greater equality and justice within the world system; its model of discipline and frugality; and its moral, financial and technical support, usually little or nothing expected in return.'[46]

One of the major developments in Xiaoping's period and the China–Middle East rapprochement was the unprecedented Saudi–Chinese engagement in the mid-1980s. Saudi Arabia and China had not been friendly towards each other. Saudi Arabia, as stated above, voted against China's membership of the United Nations and continued its recognition of the ROC (Taiwan) as the sole representative of the Chinese people up to 1990. However, the past 25 years have witnessed unprecedented progress in reciprocal relations. Moreover, China mended its relations with Oman, and the latter became the first Arab country to export oil to China in 1983. It is vital to mention that China had strongly supported the leftist guerrillas in Oman in their war against the Sultan, but the processes of resolving the conflict and the subsequent reconciliation in Oman made it easier for both sides to build strong relationships based on mutual interests. China retracted its support of leftist forces in the Arab Gulf region as well as the Middle East; therefore, Middle Eastern countries accepted China's pure economic interest approach as the basis for mutual and multilateral relations between the two sides.

The collapse of the former Soviet Union in 1991 also provided an opportunity for China to exercise leadership. While the demise of the Socialist bloc in 1989 represented a challenge to China, it was obvious that it would not allow itself to follow the same path. It began its economic reforms at least a decade earlier and managed its economic affairs much better than the former Soviet Union and other Eastern bloc nations. The 1990s represented a challenge to Sino–American relations as well. China continued to improve its rapport with the US until the Tiananmen Square massacre occurred in 1989. This put a major damper on US–Chinese relations, but China managed to weather the storm successfully by constructively engaging with the Clinton Administration in the 1990s. Sino–American relations improved substantially as China followed a less confrontational path towards the United States, concentrated on trade relations and showed support for US foreign policy in the Middle East, especially its support for the peace process and the disarmament of Iraq. China benefited from the existing American energy arrangements in the region and its needs were accommodated by the US as well as Western countries. When George W. Bush was elected President in 2001, China was optimistic about the future of Chinese–American relations as it had previously had strong relations with the Administration of George Bush Sr, and in particular with James Baker, the Secretary of State.

The pressing issues on China's agenda in the 1990s were to continue to demand an end to economic sanctions imposed on Iraq and Libya. Simultaneously, China supported the UN and the IAEA's efforts to disarm Iraq. It opposed the emerging calls within the administration to invade Iraq, although China did not make any significant efforts to prevent the Bush and Blair alliance from invading the country in 2003. On the contrary, China voted in favour of SC Resolution 1441 on 22 October 2002, delivering an ultimatum to Saddam Hussein to open up Iraqi nuclear facilities for inspection or risk international military reaction. Furthermore, China showed its willingness to take an active role in dealing with Middle East affairs; it appointed a permanent envoy to the Middle East in 2002, established the Chinese–GCC Forum in 2003 and the Chinese–Arab Forum in 2004 and concluded unprecedented levels of bilateral co-operation with Middle East countries in the areas of energy, trade and even arms sales.

China and the War on Terror

The 11 September 2001 terrorist attacks that befell the United States shocked China as much as the rest of the world. In their aftermath, the world showed unprecedented sympathy for the US, and offered unconditional support towards combating international terrorism. China's Minister of Foreign Affairs sent a cable of condolence to the American people the very same day, as did President Jiang Zemin who spoke to President Bush on the day after the tragic events. He reiterated the deep sorrow of the Chinese leadership, the people and its government, and offered support in the US war on international terrorism. The United Nations also discussed the terrorist attacks thoroughly, passed several resolutions in support of the US, offered sympathy to the American people and unlimited support to the American government. Envoys to the United Nations expressed their nations' support as well, and supported Security Council's resolutions, especially Resolution 1368/2001, which was adopted unanimously on 12 September.

The international community determined that the attacks represented a threat to international peace and security, recognized the right to respond and combat by all means threats to international peace and security, expressed deepest sympathy to the United States and called on all nations to work together to bring the perpetrators to justice and co-ordinate to eradicate international terrorism. Usually, China abstains or vetoes resolutions that carry a threat or the use of force or advocate intervention in the internal affairs of other nations as it has done recently in the Syrian case. However, a veto or an abstention was inconceivable, so China fully supported the resolution.[47] The United Nations and the international community continued to support the US, passing SC Resolution 1373 on 28 September 2001 which confirmed the content of Resolution 1368, the right of the United States and the international community to intervene militarily in Afghanistan to deal with the Taliban government and its Al-Qaeda allies. The Security Council reaffirmed 'the inherent right of individual or collective self-defense as recognized by the Charter of the United Nations as reiterated in resolution 1368 … the need to combat by all means, in accordance with the Charter of the United Nations, threats to international peace and security caused by terrorist acts.'[48] Shortly afterwards, the US assembled an international force that toppled the Taliban government in Afghanistan and captured, killed and denied safe haven for Al-Qaeda members.

The terrorist attacks provided China with an opportunity to go after East Turkistan's dissidents unchecked. As Rob Gifford highlights, 'the US provided, and still provides, a blank check for Beijing to do what it wants in suppressing any kind of dissent in Xinjiang, under the guise of combating terrorism, without fear of any criticism from Washington.'[49] Gifford states that the Uighur Muslims belong to a 'moderate, mystical branch of Islam called Sufism, and during the 1990s the US government had championed their freedom of religion as part of its criticism of China's human rights record.'[50] However, in the Afghanistan War, the US captured few soldiers from Xinjiang fighting with the Taliban. Therefore, to secure China's continued support for the War on Terror, the Bush Administration 'agreed to put a previously unknown Uighur group called the East Turkistan Islamic Movement on its list of terrorist organizations.'[51] China utilized the global atmosphere resentful of terrorism and used it to root out dissidents in Xinjiang. Gifford reiterates that 'the global discourse of the war on terrorism is now commonly used by authorities to rationalize the violent handling of conflicts in Xinjiang.'[52] Human rights organizations condemned the US blank cheque given to China, and ridiculed Bush's appraisal of China as a 'partner' in the War on Terror. However, international support for the United States in its War on Terror began to change when the Bush Administration invested most of 2002 drumming up war in Iraq, and mobilized world support for regime change in Baghdad that materialized on 19 March 2003.

Muslims in contemporary China

There are around 25 million Muslims in China. They belong to one of the ten recognized Muslim minorities in the country: Hui, Uyghur, Kazak, Dongxiang, Kyrgyz, Salar, Tajik, Uzbek, Bonan and Tatar. The Hui are the largest, estimated at 9.8 million, and their native language is Chinese, whereas other Muslim minorities speak several languages: Turkic, Persian, Mongolian and a mix of Indo-Persian languages. Culturally, the Hui are closer to the majority Han than any other Muslim minority, although they differ from the Han on issues related to faith and food habits. They are also scattered around the country whereas other Muslim minorities are concentrated in certain parts of China, such as the Uyghur in Xinjiang. In terms of Muslims' religious freedom, or lack thereof, they are governed by what China calls Document No. 19, drafted by the China's Communist Party's (CCP) Central Committee in 1982, entitled the 'Basic Viewpoint and Policy on the Religious Questions during Our Country's Socialist Period.' The document was forwarded to the entire country after an in-depth study by the Secretariat of the Central Committee of the religious question. It summed up in a more systematic way the positive and negative historical experiences of the CCP with regard to the religious question since the founding of the PRC.[53] The Central Committee instructed all concerned 'to undertake conscious investigation and discussion of the religious question, and should increase supervision and promote inspection of the implementation of each item related to this policy.'[54] The document also went on to explain the existence of religion 'as a historical phenomenon' that 'has its own cycle of emergence, development, and demise.'[55] It recognized Buddhism, Daoism, Islam, Roman Catholicism and Protestantism as religions in China, and traced back Islam's emergence in China to 1,300 years ago, estimating the number of Muslims at 10,000,000.[56]

Furthermore, Document 19 discouraged the building of new religious structures in which normal religious activities were to be held; all places of worship were to be under the administrative control of the Bureau of Religious Affairs, and no religious propagation outside designated places or inciting arguments among believing masses were permitted. It stated that religious institutions famous for their charming architectural beauty were to serve as cultural facilities in addition to places of religious worship, but that religious activities were not to interfere in production. Religious patriotic organizations were to be fully supported to implement the policy, training and educating young generations of patriotic religious personnel in a planned way. This meant that the religious policy was only meant for citizens, but members of the CCP were not free to believe in religion. It was a determined crackdown on what is called 'criminal and antirevolutionary' activities that hide behind the façade of religion, severely punishable by law. Realizing the importance of religion in international relations, religious communities were to actively develop friendly international religious contacts, but also firmly resist infiltration by hostile religious forces.[57]

Obviously, the document is severely restrictive towards religious practices, especially towards Islam, as most of the prohibitions in the document are major pillars of faith, such as congregating, propagating beliefs, charity, fasting, pilgrimages, contact with the Muslim *Ummah*, etc. It falls short in comparison to the drastic shifts that occurred in China's economic, social, political, regional and international policies. Scholars and human rights activists are heavily critical of the document, which basically added nothing new to China's understanding of religion since 1950. As Veselic put it, 'Many Chinese researchers of religion, too, are heavily critical of the current policy, and I have heard various scholars lament on several occasions that despite the tremendous political, economic and social shifts China has undergone in the past three decades, only ethnic and religious policies still remain the same as in the 1950s.'[58] Where Islam is concerned, the government not only restricted religious practices, but also embarked on the process of reinterpreting Islamic scripture. The project began in earnest in 2001, and it is directed by the Steering Committee of Islamic Affairs of the China Islamic Association.[59] Veselic reports that a leading Muslim imam indicated to her that:

> the interpretation was guided by the principles of loving one's country and loving one's religion, unity, adherence to the middle way, auspiciousness of the two worlds (this world and the other world), respect for tradition and drawing on positive concepts from Islamic schools of thought internationally.[60]

Document 19 is very restrictive of religious freedoms, especially in Xinjiang. The authorities restrict religious practices, prohibiting government employees from fasting during Ramadan and imposing restrictions on minors attending religious activities. They restrict religious education in religious schools, control Friday prayers, the texts of sermons and criminalize possession and import of religious materials and their reprinting and dissemination. The ultimate goal of state policy towards Islam is to fight what is called the 'three evil forces: international terrorism, ethnic separatism, and religious extremism.'[61] As Veselic points out, 'religious issues are inextricably tied up with ethnic-political ones.'[62] Clearly, China's policy towards religious freedom, especially in Xinjiang, is preoccupied with the security dilemma.

Aside from religious freedoms for Muslims, political expression is severely restricted, especially in Xinjiang. All sorts of resistance to Chinese dominance are met with extreme force from Chinese authorities. Probably, the passing of the Olympic torch through Kashgar in Xinjiang Province on 18 June 2008 sums it all up.

> Windows are forbidden to be opened, curtains drawn and shops closed temporarily. One hour before the torch relay, roads are blocked and people are not allowed onto the streets. Security is tight and police are on patrol. Owing to security considerations, local residents are asked to stay at home to watch the torch relay on TV. Compared to other cities, the number of people watching the relay along the streets is much smaller. During the relay Internet services in hotels are also disconnected.[63]

Conclusion

This chapter highlighted some of the major events that occurred between China and the Middle East since the early days of the Silk Road. This unique commodity, in addition to the swift Arabian horses, promoted trade relations between China, Central Asia, the Middle East and Europe. The advent of Islam enormously advanced Sino–Islamic relations that were characterized overall by close co-operation, albeit at times with some minor military confrontations such as the Talas Battle in 750. According to Islamic law, animosity ended on the battlefield, and afterwards the Abbasids pursued friendly relations with China based on trade, and China reciprocated by opening up its land to Muslim immigration. Muslim communities became influential in China, but their success provoked jealousy among the Han majority who carried out some bloody massacres against them in 878 AD. Muslims recovered from these massacres, rebuilt their communities, strengthened their presence and extended trade relations into East Asia.

During the decline of the Islamic Empire, Muslims collaborated with the Yuan Dynasty which formed the Mongol Empire. Their co-operation distorted their image, and the Han retaliated against the Muslim presence in China. Muslims rebelled against ethnic discrimination in the country in the eighteenth and nineteenth centuries. In the early years of the twentieth century and during the Republican era, Muslims were active in politics and occupied key positions in the state. However, under PRC rule, they suffered like any other religious community in China. The mistreatment of Muslims was the subject of debate by Muslim governments around the world who intervened on their behalf as early as 1955. Since then, Muslims' conditions have improved somewhat, but not significantly. The religious freedoms of some Muslim minorities such as the Uyghur are severely restricted, whereas Hui Muslims enjoy a relatively wider range of religious freedoms. China embarked on a process of reinterpretation of Islamic scripture, the Holy Quran, to suit its socialist and economic agenda.

2 A five-dimensional paradigm

Energy, trade, arms sales, cultural relations and political co-operation

Introduction

The rapid pace of China's involvement in the Middle East in the areas of energy, trade, arms sales, culture and politics has generated substantial research interest. Scholars scramble to explain such involvement, matching it with existing theoretical frameworks, developing their own representations and attempting to predict its future course vis-à-vis the dominant powers in the region, i.e. the United States and Western powers. They also wonder if such vigorous involvement aims at dislodging the US and its allies from the Middle East, or if it is pure business transactions that seek a steady source of energy to sustain China's economic prosperity. The objective of this chapter is to examine the depth of China's involvement in the Middle East and, in so doing, I develop a five-dimensional approach that takes into account the complexity of China's presence in the Middle East in terms of oil imports, trade relations, arms sales, political co-operation and cultural relations. These five dimensions are inextricably intertwined. Theoretically, three schools of thought are competing to analyse China's involvement in the region: the realist, the liberal institutionalist and the constructivist. Some of China's policies in pursuing its goals, or at least some of them, in the region allude to the fact that China might be following a realist approach in defending and promoting its interest in the Middle East. However, China also seems to be working within the existing 'Western liberal' system and institutions to meet its energy needs and pursue a wide agenda of bilateral and multilateral relations with Middle Eastern countries. From a constructivist point of view, the region and its people are much more attuned to China's narrative, historical experience and deep-rooted civilizational contacts with the Middle East than to Western powers, as we will see in the subsequent sections.

A five-dimensional approach: oil, trade, arms, politics and culture

Through its modern politics, the Chinese government has given unprecedented priority to the Middle East. At the core of this multifaceted engagement is its perpetual quest for energy security, in addition to trade, arms sales, culture and political co-operation. At times, its focus has shifted according to its interests and necessities and to regional and international developments. While China sought diplomatic recognition, its interests were political and diplomatic in nature from 1949 to 1976, but the focus shifted to arms sales in the 1980s, and deepened into trade and energy from 1993 onwards. Currently, Middle East oil accounts for 45 percent of China's crude, as this country becomes increasingly reliant on the region. In fact, China is projected to import 70 percent of its oil needs from the Middle East by the year 2020. In return, China exports consumer goods and services and arms to Turkey, Saudi Arabia, Libya, Iran and Syria and imports modern weapons from Israel. China is either the first or second trading partner of Middle Eastern countries, surpassing both the US and Japan. It has overtaken Japan as the world's second largest crude oil importer from the region since 2003, and it is second only to the US, soon topping the list of oil-importing countries from the Middle East. Finally, cultural Sino–Middle Eastern relations have become crucial over the past ten years, sustained by growing cultural contacts that have rapidly intensified. For instance, China is becoming a major tourist destination and a source of education and knowledge for Middle Eastern students.

Among China's strategic political engagements in the Middle East are its appointment of a Special Envoy to Syria in February 2012, a permanent envoy to the Middle East in 2002, the establishment of the China–Gulf Cooperation Council (GCC) Forum in 2003, its active role in the UN peace missions in the Middle East and its current involvement in crises related to the Arab Spring. At times, Chinese diplomacy has seemed to be proficient in creating a balance between competing interests in the Middle East and in striking a balance between adversaries in the turbulent region, as seen in its views on the peace process and the Arab–Israeli conflict. At other times, it has seemed reactive, inefficient and confused, as in its current response to the developments of the Arab Spring in Syria, Yemen, Bahrain, Jordan and Egypt. Nevertheless, the Sino–Middle Eastern strategic partnership provides a vibrant Chinese economic model to be replicated by the region.

By all standards, China's miraculous economic growth, industrialization and near dominance in world markets is unprecedented in modern history. The country seems to have gone from a rural society and agriculture-based economy to a high-tech society and industrialization in less than three decades. Its spectacular modernization has lifted hundreds of millions from poverty into the middle class in record time. The same process took 300 years to develop in the West and over 150 years in Japan. Other parts of the world, referred to as Third World nations, have been lagging behind for the past 400 years. The transformation has altered China in unrecognizable ways in less than 30 years, making the twenty-first century appear to be the century of the 'dragon.'

Over the past two decades, China's economic growth rate has ranged between 7 percent and 11.40 percent, which has overcome the current economic tsunami very well compared with other major economic powers. It hosted the most successful Olympic Games ever in 2008 and has managed to send a man into space. In addition to launching its ambitious space programme to be utilized for its economic development and boost its national security, the Shenzhou-9 spacecraft was launched successfully in mid-June 2012; it docked with 'China's orbiting space laboratory, making the nation the third after the United States and Russia to complete a manned space docking'[1] and safely returned to earth. China seems to be consistent in pursuing an ambitious global agenda to sustain its economic growth. This is very realistically attainable as 'China is on track to become the world's largest economy sometime between 2025 and 2035.'[2]

Oil and China's energy security

The primary objective of China's heavy involvement in the Middle East is oil. This diligent pursuit prompted observers, practitioners and scholars to expand the scope of their debate over China's active involvement in the Middle East to include the Chinese global quest for energy security and its economic reach worldwide. At the heart of such scope is the fact that Southeast Asia is becoming the centre of the emerging global economic order, and the Middle East is becoming its primary source of energy. Gökay maintains that 'a closer look at the extraordinary economic expansion of the Southeast Asian region for the last twenty years can give some insights into the remarkably new kind of global economic order that may be emerging at the edges of the current systemic crisis.'[3] Douglas et al. illustrate how China's quest for energy security has drastically altered its relations with the Middle East,[4] whereas Yetiv and Lu provide an in-depth analysis of China's global quest for energy security. They also offer pivotal policy-oriented recommendations for China and the US to avoid confrontation in the region. They advise that both the US and China should reduce their reliance on Middle Eastern oil. They note that, as China builds strategic oil reserve facilities, it should be admitted to and actively involved in the International Energy Agency talks. They also advise China and the US to carry out joint business ventures in the oil sector and bilateral dialogue over energy policy. China is to avoid a nationalist approach to its energy security and any posture of building military capabilities in the region as well.[5] Beng and Li examine China's overdependence on Middle Eastern oil and its preoccupation with 'the stability and security of its energy supply, especially from the Middle East which currently supplies up to 57 percent of China's overall oil usage imports.'[6] Zha concludes that China's heavy reliance on Middle Eastern oil is projected to continue because it is deepening its economic relations with the region and following a balanced approach towards Middle Eastern conflicts.[7] Taylor expands the scope of the debate over China's tireless quest for energy security to the greater Middle East. He projects that China's demand for oil will increase 130 percent by 2025 to 12.8 million barrels per day (mbd).[8] Figure 2.1 illustrates China's oil consumption for the period from 1965 to 2020.

Mawdsley deals with the anxiety generated among Western states and businesses as China becomes a major player in the region,[9] whereas Chen

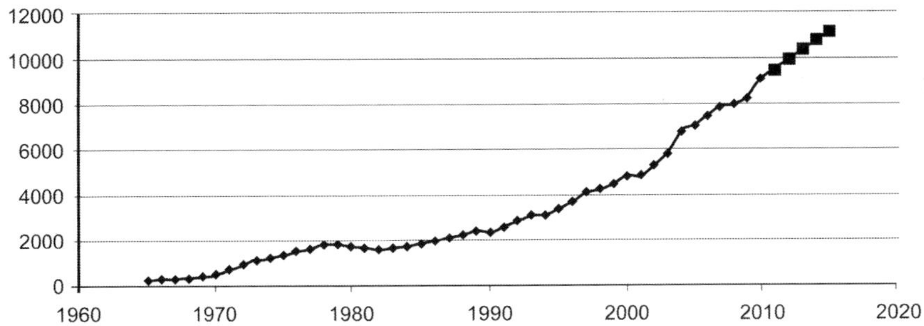

Figure 2.1 Increasing oil consumption in China from 1965 to 2020 in mbpd
Source: The figure is constructed from PB's Data Base for the period from 1965–2012 at: http://www.bp.com/statisticalreview
Figures from 2010–2020 are authors forecast at: http://smoothforecast.com/Smooth-Forecast/index.jsp

attempts to quell such anxiety by providing a Chinese perspective on the motivation behind China's quest for equity in foreign oil. In its efforts to secure the energy necessary for its economic growth, he identifies three options for China: trade, oil diplomacy and force. He notes that a consensus on trade and oil diplomacy has developed thanks to two major considerations: 'first, there is little likelihood that China can develop naval capabilities that can overtake the US Navy and effectively protect China's oil supplies. Second, the supreme objective of the People's Liberation Army is to prevent Taiwan's independence and resist against a possible US intervention.'[10] Chen defines the concept of oil diplomacy as 'the foreign activities with explicit involvement of the central government aiming to secure foreign oil and gas resources or promote interstate oil and gas business cooperation.'[11] Although China and other Asian countries realize the necessity to diversify their source of oil imports, it is becoming increasingly difficult to move away from the Middle East given the uniqueness of the region in relation to oil sustainability, geographical proximity and strategic location.

Wu and Fesharaki maintain that 'the Middle East is Asia Pacific's largest energy supplier, satisfying a demand on oil that must keep pace with the region's continued economic growth. This dependence on the Middle East has caused Asia Pacific to join the United States and other Western nations in the hunt for alternative suppliers.'[12] Central Asia was identified as a potentially major oil supplier, but the limitations of the region make it nearly impossible as a substitute for Middle Eastern oil. Central Asia is landlocked and suffers from major political instability, although the countries of the region strive to be part of the world energy supplier club. Wu and Fesharaki conclude that 'Central Asia is eager to join the Middle East in fueling Asia Pacific's growth, but a solid energy triangle between Asia's Pacific, the Middle East and Central Asia would be difficult to form in the coming decades. Central Asia's potential may be great, but it is not another Middle East.'[13] The enduring conflicts between India and Pakistan, the instability of Afghanistan and the vulnerability of Central Asia to security threats complicate any regional potential for energy co-operation, although China has been exploring alternative routes and making substantial progress in this regard. Sino-Kazak and Sino–Russian pipelines are a testament to China's determination to tap into oil reserves in Kazakhstan, the Caspian Sea region and as far as Siberia. The pipeline accomplishment is a clear indication of China's determination to exploit Central Asia's energy potential and to overcome distance and costs.

The issue of reliability of Middle East supplies has been a primary concern for consumers and observers. Bubalo and Thirlwell highlight the fact that the Middle East is the only consistent energy source globally. They also maintain that 'much of the increase in global oil demand in coming years will come from Asia, and specifically from China and India, the bulk of the supply response is likely to come from the Middle East.'[14] In dealing with energy insecurity, neither economic giant is 'willing to rely on market mechanisms. Both see their reliance on oil imports as a strategic and economic vulnerability',[15] but they so far have no alternative but to rely on the Middle East. For China, in particular, 'energy security has already become a key foreign policy priority, while for India it is quickly becoming one.'[16]

Other energy observers approach the complexity of the energy issue in China's foreign policy towards the region from a security perspective. For instance, Russell maintains that China has developed a body of strategic interests in the greater Middle East. Among these are security ties with Saudi Arabia, Iran, Pakistan and other states in the region. Oil is at the heart of such a strategy.[17] However, he notes that China is increasingly becoming a 'good international citizen' and does not follow a policy of indifference towards the non-proliferation regime. Grumbine emphasizes a major concern over China's rapid development and the prospect of global energy sustainability. He states that 'China's rapid, ongoing development is deeply influencing global patterns of resource production and consumption and their associated environmental and geopolitical impacts.'[18] Grumbine identifies three key drivers in China's rise: the sheer scale of China's population, its rapid urbanization process and globalization. In fact, China's demand for oil is associated with the massive urbanization process in which 600–700 million Chinese, or 50 percent of the population, will live in cities. The growing middle class will eventually transform China's economy from export oriented to a home-based consumer economy. China will not only be the 'factory of the world', but a consumer-based society and a leading force in the current international economic recovery effort.[19]

China's increasing demand for oil has made it the second oil importer and the second consumer of oil and gas worldwide. In the coming decade, it is expected to surpass the US by a substantial margin (Figure 2.2).

Energy security: destination and obstacles

China seeks energy security, and its foreign policy is geared towards utilizing its external relations to serve its economic growth. Energy security is defined as

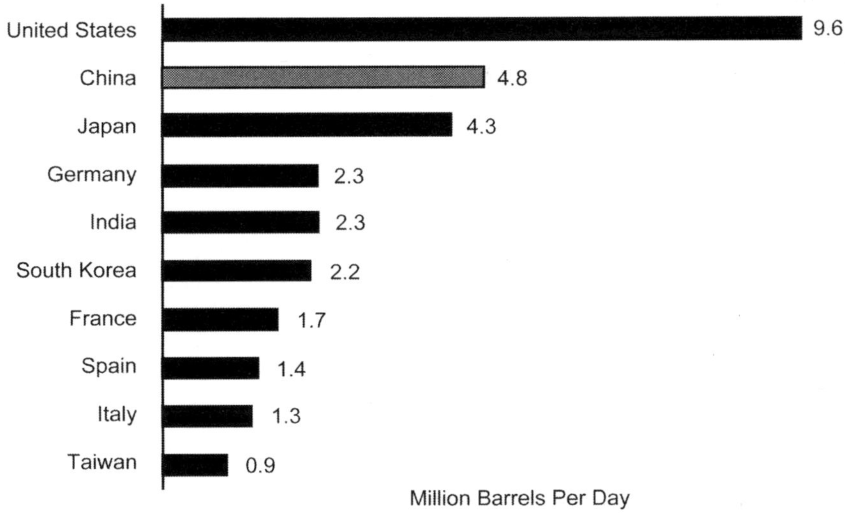

Figure 2.2 Top ten oil importers in 2012
Source: EIA, Short-Term Energy Outlook, (April 2012), reprinted with EIA's permission.

'guaranteeing and securing oil supplies from abroad as essential to China's continued economic growth and modernization.'[20] The nation has established three oil corporations to reach energy security, the China National Petroleum Corporation (CNPC), China Petrochemical Corporation (Sinopec) and the China National Offshore Oil Corporation (CNOOC), each of which has a distinctive role to play towards the materialization of such a far-reaching goal. Unquestionably, the primary aim of China's global engagement is to ensure a steady flow of oil to maintain its economic growth, which has averaged between 7.0 percent and 11.40 percent in the past decade while its oil consumption grew by 7.5 percent, seven times faster than the US market. For China to maintain such a level of economic growth, its energy needs are projected to increase from 130 percent to 150 percent by 2020. China's current oil production stands at 4.07 mbd, while its consumption reached 9.57 mbd in 2010, second only to the United States. China imports 5.5 mbd.[21] Beng and Li report that, according to some sources in the International Energy Agency (IEA), 'China will import 5.9 to 6.9 mbd in 2020, constituting 63 percent to 70 percent of total consumption',[22] most of which will be imported from the Middle East. In fact, China will exceed this level of imports much sooner, given the fact that, this year alone (2012), China's imports are estimated at 5.98 mbd. Table 2.1 illustrates China's growing oil consumption since 1965. The trend accelerates exponentially with China's industrial growth, urbanization and modernization.

The Middle East seems to be the chief focus for China's energy security. James Kynge makes a comparison between the growing need for oil in America in the early years of the twentieth century and China's appetite for

Table 2.1 China's oil consumption in thousand barrels per day (000 bd) from 1965 to 2015

Year	*000 bd*	*Year*	*000 bd*	*Year*	*000 bd*	*Year*	*000 bd*	*Year*	*000 bd*	*Year*	*000 bd*
1965	216	1975	1,346	1985	1,820	1995	3,394	2005	6,944	2016	11,323
1966	277	1976	1,539	1986	1,934	1996	3,722	2006	7,437	2017	11,776
1967	274	1977	1,630	1987	2,055	1997	4,120	2007	7,817	2018	12,230
1968	299	1978	1,823	1988	2,203	1998	4,216	2008	7,937	2019	12,683
1969	402	1979	1,831	1989	2,338	1999	4,452	2009	8,201	2020	13,136
1970	556	1980	1,690	1990	2,320	2000	4,766	2010	9,057		
1971	755	1981	1,612	1991	2,520	2001	4,859	2011	9,510		
1972	867	1982	1,597	1992	2,736	2002	5,262	2012	9,963		
1973	1,061	1983	1,638	1993	3,047	2003	5,771	2013	10,416		
1974	1,220	1984	1,695	1994	3,115	2004	6,738	2015	10,870		

Source: BP Statistical Review of World Energy, 2011, from 1965 to 2010 at www.bp.com/statisticalreview
Note: Figures for 2010 to 2020, author's calculations and forecasting

oil in the twenty-first century. While the US relied on oil deposits within its borders such as those in Oklahoma, California, Alaska and Louisiana, the question remains as to where China's thirst for oil can be met.[23] The answer is the Middle East. This need for oil and gas, along with the growing gap between China's oil production and consumption, has made the Middle East the centre of China's attention. Figure 2.3 illustrates this gap, met by oil imports primarily from the Middle East since 1993.

China's demand for oil is not only driven by its economic growth rate, but also by the unprecedented number of vehicles in the country. In proportion with income increase, a greater number of Chinese can afford cars, and the number of vehicles increases. Nearly a decade ago, the number of cars in China was around 1 million. Currently, China has more than 22 million cars. By 2020, it is projected that China will have 140 million vehicles, most of which will be energy inefficient, fuelling the increasing demand for oil.[24]

While China follows a global strategy to meet its energy needs, its main source seems to be the Middle East. Table 2.2 illustrates the growing importance of the Middle East in China's energy security and China's growing reliance on the region. Figure 2.4 illustrates the difference between China's domestic production, consumption and net imports. China's oil imports peaked in 1998 reaching 61 percent, declined for some years, but still remains exceptionally high. China attempted to diversify its energy sources in Africa, Canada and Latin America, although the Middle East remains the most reliable source. This trend explains future projections, which expect China to rely on the Middle East for 75 percent of its oil needs in the coming two decades.

As China's demand for oil increases, and with an international environment characterized by rising economic powers such as India, the competition between existing powers such as Japan and the US would escalate tension on the world scene. Some scholars have termed China's energy security as

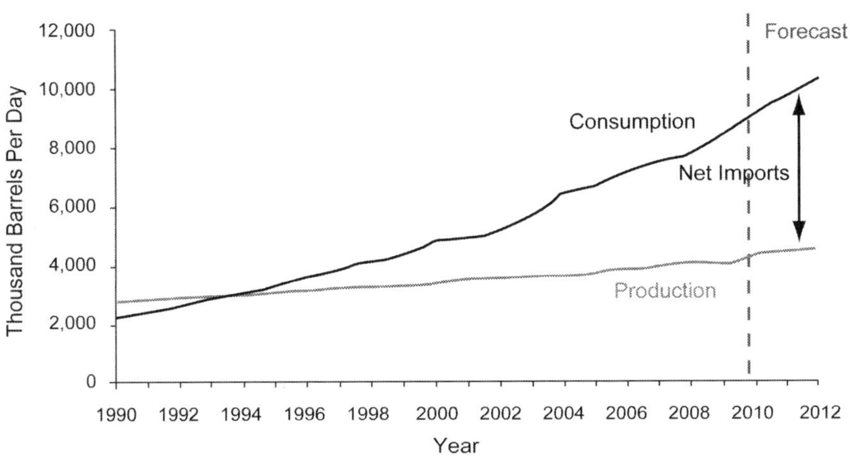

Figure 2.3 China's oil production and consumption from 1990 to 2012
Source: EIA, Short-Term Energy Outlook, (April 2012), reprinted with EIA's permission.

Table 2.2 Growth rates, oil production, consumption, net imports and oil import percentages from the Middle East

Year	*Growth rate*	*Oil production (mbd)*	*Oil consumption (mbpd)*	*Net imports (mbd)*	*Oil import percentages from the Middle East*
1993	13.40	2,903,463.00	2,959,491.00	56,028.00	34.70
1994	11.80	2,957,310.00	3,160,605.00	203,290.00	39.70
1995	10.30	3,059,620.00	3,363,155.00	303,530.00	45.50
1996	9.70	3,211,280.00	3,610,085.00	398,780.00	52.90
1997	8.80	3,284,550.00	3,916,270.00	631,720.00	47.30
1998	7.80	3,301,740.00	4,105,835.00	804,090.00	61.00
1999	7.00	3,317,028.00	4,363,601.00	1,046,573.00	46.20
2000	8.00	3,377,527.00	4,795,715.00	1,418,188.00	53.60
2001	7.30	3,434,535.00	4,917,882.00	1,483,347.00	56.20
2002	8.00	3,529,761.00	5,160,714.00	1,630,953.00	49.60
2003	9.10	3,559,006.00	5,578,111.00	2,019,105.00	50.90
2004	9.10	3,657,452.00	6,437,484.00	2,780,031.00	45.40
2005	9.90	3,781,760.00	6,720,000.00	2,939,240.00	47.20
2006	10.50	3,844,870.00	7,201,278.00	3,356,404.00	40.22
2007	11.40	3,900,958.00	7,817,000.00	3,677,000.00	39.95
2008	9.60	3,725,000.00	7,937,000.00	4,212,000.00	46.00
2009	9.20	3,995,620.00	8,537,860.00	4,210,000.00	52.00
2010	10.30	4,071,000.00	9,057,000.00	4,986,000.00	47.00
2011	9.20	4,100,000.00	9,510,000.00	5,505,900.00	46.00
2012	8.10	4,300,000.00	9,963,000.00	5,980,000.00	45.10

Source: Dunn, Candace, US Department of Energy. *China's Crude Oil Imports by Source*, 2006 and 2007; *Facts Global Energy*, 2008; *2010 China Statistical Yearbook*; BP, *2012 Statistical Review of World Energy*, 2011; US Energy Information Administration (EIA) and author's calculations and forecasts.

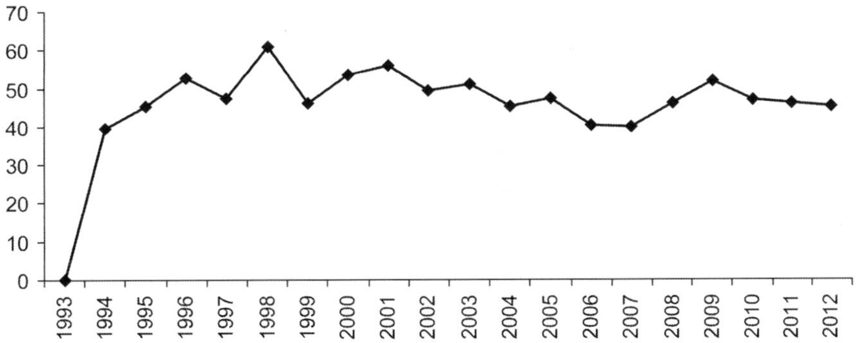

Figure 2.4 China's oil imports from the Middle East as a percentage of its total imports for the period from 1993 to 2012

'provocative.' Navarro warns that the increasing demand for oil will lead to lingering global inflation and recession due to the rising price of oil which continues to shock the world's economy. He maintains that:

> despite the serious impacts of inflation and recession that may result from China's increasing participation in world oil markets, it is China's highly provocative energy security strategies and their far-ranging geopolitical effects that may ultimately prove to be most dangerous to global economic and political stability.[25]

It becomes apparent that the two biggest oil consumers, the US and China, are competing largely in the same region: the Middle East.

Impediments to energy security

There are three major impediments to China's energy security: insufficient domestic oil production, price fluctuations and the lack of control over oil transport routes, both sea and land. China achieved oil self-sufficiency between 1963 and 1983. In 1983, China began importing oil from Oman, although its domestic production was still sufficient to meet its needs for 10 years. However, a decade later, it was apparent that its domestic production was insufficient to meet its rapidly increasing demand for oil to fuel its spectacular economic growth. Although it has been rehabilitating its existing oil fields, and exploring and developing new fields in mainland China and offshore, its domestic production is less than half its consumption. China produces 4.071 mbd,[26] but the bulk of its oil imports comes from the Middle East. The countries of the region seem fully supportive of China's involvement, but the West differs greatly with China on the instruments of energy security. China seeks joint equity, whereas Western countries seek to compel China to abide by the rules of supply and demand as dictated by the international energy market. The latter is fully under Western control, a source of discomfort to many players, not only China, but also India, Turkey, Russia, Brazil, South Africa and other countries. Contrary to alarmist Western voices against China's potential hegemony in the region, the Middle East is eager to diversify its consumer base and free itself from Western dominance, which has proven to be threatening to regional development, especially in the area of prices and vulnerability. Not only do Middle Eastern countries greatly welcome Chinese involvement in oil exploration and refining, but also deem such presence vital in the creation of balance in international energy markets.

The second impediment deals with the fact that China lacks control over two major oil routes: 'seaborne oil imports, largely through the strategic choke-points of the Straits of Malacca and the South China Sea, are beyond Chinese reach, while the land based pipelines through Kazakhstan can easily be held hostage to adversarial elements and antagonistic policies of other countries.'[27] The Malacca Straits, which lie between Indonesia, Malaysia and Singapore, are the main route for Asia's oil imports from the Middle East; they are congested waterways about 2.5 km wide at the narrowest point, and incapable of meeting the growing demand for passage of oil tankers. 'The Malacca Straits currently handle 11 million barrels of oil per day, a figure which on current oil demand trends would need to double by 2030. Yet, the Straits are already close to capacity in terms of shipping traffic.'[28] Dependence on a single supply route is an endless concern for China, with all the risks and the uncertainties associated with it. This vulnerability represents a strategic deficiency in China's energy security. Any tension with regional powers surrounding the Straits, or with global powers such as the United States will definitely jeopardize China's well-being, stability and development. This concern explains China's continued attempts to develop a strategy with multiple routes. In fact, in addition to traditional oceanic transportation, in a quest to reduce its reliance on the Malacca Straits, China has begun the construction of three major pipelines.

The Sino–Burmese oil and gas pipeline

Although the pipeline's construction process began in June 2010, the Sino–Burmese oil and gas pipeline began in October 2010 at the Chinese end. CNPC, the largest Chinese oil company, owns the project, which will be run by its subsidiary, PetroChina. It is expected to be finished in 2013. The oil and gas pipeline begins at the West Burmese port of Kyaukryu, enters China through the city of Ruili and ends in Kunming, the capital of Yunnan Province. The distance is 2,380 km. It is expected to carry 22 million tons of crude oil annually, coming from the Middle East and Africa. It will be refined in the An'ning refinery, which is under parallel construction with the pipeline. However, the natural gas pipeline extends to Guizhou Province in southern China, with a distance of 2,806 km and a capacity to transport 12,000 million cubic metres of natural gas to China annually.[29]

The Sino–Kazakh pipeline

In 1997, China negotiated the Sino–Kazakh pipeline, reaching an agreement in 2003 and beginning construction in 2004. 'The Sino–Kazakh pipeline, with a total length of over 3,000 kilometers, would be able to deliver up to 20 million tons of Caspian Sea crude oil annually to western China.'[30] In 2005 the pipeline was partially functional and was fully completed in 2011, at a cost of $3,000 million. It begins on the Caspian Sea in the Kazakh city of Atyrau and enters China at Dushanzi, Xinjiang; it connects with China's west-to-east oil pipeline. In 2010 the pipeline met its expectation of delivering 10 million tons of crude oil, and it is gradually increasing to reach its ultimate goal of transporting 20 million tons of crude oil by 2013. In addition to the pipeline, CNPC managed to acquire a 50 percent share in the Kazah North Buzachi field in 1997, believed to contain 1,000 million–1,500 million barrels of oil. In 2005, CNPC also gained control of the South Kumkol field and part of the North Kumkol and Kazgermunai fields in a deal with the Kazakh government worth $4,200 million, thus solidifying Sino–Kazakh energy relations.[31]

The Sino–Russian pipeline

The Sino–Russian pipeline transports oil from Russia's far east oil fields of Skovorodino, enters China through the city of Mohe and ends in Daqing in Heilongjiang Province. It extends over 1,000 km and transports 15 million tons of Russian crude oil annually (from 2011 to 2030, according to the Chinese–Russian agreement). The pipeline became operational in 2011, and its effectiveness exceeded expectations, although it passes through rough terrain. The project is exceptionally beneficial to both sides. As Russia seeks to diversify its consumer base, it has been switching gradually to Asian oil markets instead of West European ones. In fact, Russia seems to be more ambitious in Asian markets than China, and seeks to make China's territory a transit to Asian oil consumers. Russian (then) Prime Minister Vladimir Putin said in August 2011 that 'Moscow aims to provide 30 million tons of crude oil to the Asia-Pacific region per year, and plans to raise that amount to 50 million tons per year in the future.'[32] China is also a leading Asian powerhouse in refining oil, marketing it and marketing oil products and related petrochemicals as well.

Railways and oil imports

In addition to oceanic shipping and pipelines, China continues to import oil from Russia by rail. However, the ambitious Sino–Russian pipeline project will reduce China's reliance on railways. The pipeline is faster, provides a sustained volume of transiting oil and is more reliable and economically more efficient. The Gwadar Port of Pakistan is another source of oil shipped by rail. Owing to the strategic partnership between Pakistan and China, the latter has been developing the port on the Indian Ocean and building a naval base.

This port faces the Arab-Persian Gulf and the Strait of Hormuz. The idea is that oil tankers will empty their loads at the Gwadar Port, and the oil will be shipped via Pakistan to China's borders by three methods: railway, pipelines and trucking. This is one of the most efficient contingency plans China has been pursuing in dealing with the potential closure of the Strait of Hormuz.

Price fluctuation

The third impediment to China's energy security is the fluctuation in oil prices. In the summer of 2008, the spike in the price of oil to $147.50 per barrel was astounding to China, as the country struggled to meet its growing demand for energy and cope with increasing oil prices (Figure 2.5).

Achieving energy security in a climate of price fluctuations appears to be challenging not only to China, but to other global powers, especially the United States. China's active involvement in the Middle East to secure its oil needs aims to reduce the impact of price fluctuations through equity ownership in oil fields in the region. However, such extensive involvement alarms Western rivals who view it as contributing to price hikes, and potentially contributing to the escalation of current and future crises in the region. China views equity shares as a shield from price fluctuations, and the West views it as a deceptive practice seeking to place Western consumers in a less favourable position. Equity shares also complicate the process of dealing with current security challenges in the Middle East in the sense that China shields its oil equity partners from international criticism. The prolonging of the Syrian people's suffering, the prolonging of the standoff between Iran and the international community over Iran's nuclear programme and holding the Sudan responsible over the genocide in Darfur are examples of the impact of equity shares on security matters in the Middle East. While China may have a case

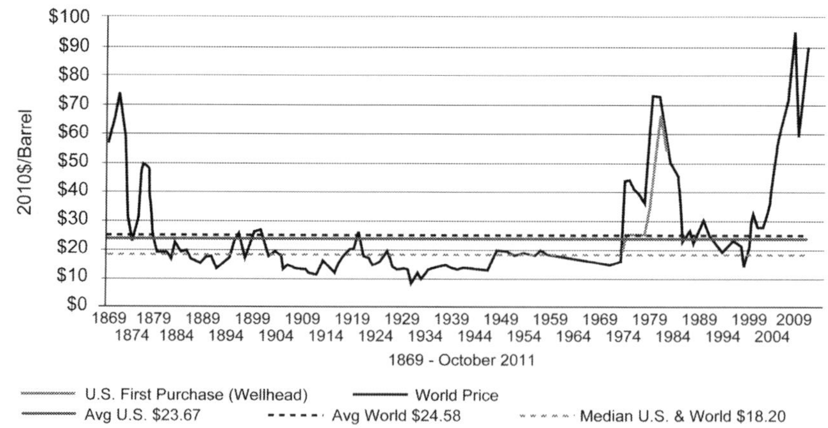

Figure 2.5 Crude oil prices from 1869 to 2010
Source: WTRG Economics at: http://www.wtrg.com/oil_graphs/oilprice1869.gif

to make, so far, it has not been successful in explaining the rationale behind its equity share policy in Middle East oil markets. However, the oil-producing countries see it in a prism closer to China than to the West. They view it as contributing to diversifying production efforts; this explains their eagerness to involve Chinese, Indian and Malaysian oil companies in oil exploration and production. Although Western countries continued to be distressed by China's determination to obtain more equity shares in oil markets in Iran, Saudi Arabia, Algeria, Libya, Iraq, Sudan, Syria, Kuwait, Oman and Yemen, China's rationale is that it seeks to minimize the impact of price fluctuations, which threaten its economic growth and create unmanageable levels of uncertainty in its industrial sector. Moreover, China's inability to provide a convincing argument for its oil equity policy only increases uncertainty, suspicion and unpredictability in the future of oil markets. Paradoxically, China pays a great deal of attention to equity. For instance, 'in 2005, over 80 percent of China's imported oil was purchased under some type of bilateral arrangement.'[33] Some observers maintain that China's resentment towards the dictates of the free market stems from the fact that:

> Beijing tends to regard it as an unfair and unsafe arena for latecomers … meanwhile, China has come to realize that other countries in the world hold misgivings that its energy security problem may turn into a security issue. This realization, in turn, may help it conduct more energy cooperation with the U.S. and other consuming countries.[34]

Navarro termed it a Chinese zero-sum game approach, which differs from other players such as the US. 'China has adopted a bilateral contracting approach in which it seeks to lock down the physical supplies for themselves, China essentially locks out other nations.'[35]

Whereas Middle Eastern countries seem willing to accommodate China's needs, the West finds itself increasingly in fierce competition with China over energy resources. At any rate, dealing with China's oil security dilemma is a necessity. The US, in particular, could choose to follow a policy aimed at excluding China from the Middle East, or accommodating China's needs. Although the US views China's presence in the region with some apprehension, so far it has no exclusionary policy towards China. A positive step in this direction is to understand China's energy needs in pure commercial, rather than 'security', perspectives. Both approaches, however, seem to be challenging to the US. The latter is particularly alarmed by Sino–Iranian relations as they make total isolation of Iran an unattainable goal. On the other hand, even if the US had a clear policy of excluding China from the Middle East, neither its traditional allies nor its foes in the region would enforce such a policy as they are all racing to cut lucrative deals with China and enhance its involvement in the region. Saudi Arabia is just as desperate for a partnership with China as Iran, the US number one foe in the region. After 11 September 2001, Saudi Arabia's security cannot be perceived in the same prism as before the terrorist attacks, as the US no longer views this country as a 'strategic ally.' At this point, Saudi Arabia is eager to liberate itself from Western hegemony in the oil sector by enhancing its trade relations with China and increasing its arms imports.

Given the complexity of China's exclusion process, some observers advise that the US should assist China in its quest for energy security by keeping sea lanes open to Chinese vessels from the Arabian-Persian Gulf to the China Sea, via the Straits of Malacca. They also highlight the importance of assuring China of America's understanding of its energy security needs – a shared interest approach in the region, rather than exclusionary – and refraining from any efforts to contain China.[36] China understands well the sensitive nature of its involvement in a region where the US has its lead interests; therefore, it continues to reduce its vulnerability to American supremacy in the Middle East via bilateral partnerships, particularly with its neighbours, Russia, Kazakhstan, etc.[37] So far, China enjoys the 'free-ride' protection of the US Navy for its oil tankers that roam the region; at this time, China lacks the naval capability to protect its fleet against piracy off the Horn of Africa, in the Gulf of Oman and in the Indian Ocean. In comparison with China, other rising powers such as India have made substantial progress in developing their naval capabilities, but China is determined to catch up sooner rather than later (Figure 2.6).

Two dominant schools of thought in the field of international relations, the realist and the liberal institutionalist, promoted some scholarly debates on the pursuit of Chinese energy security. Realists advocate the idea that, in its

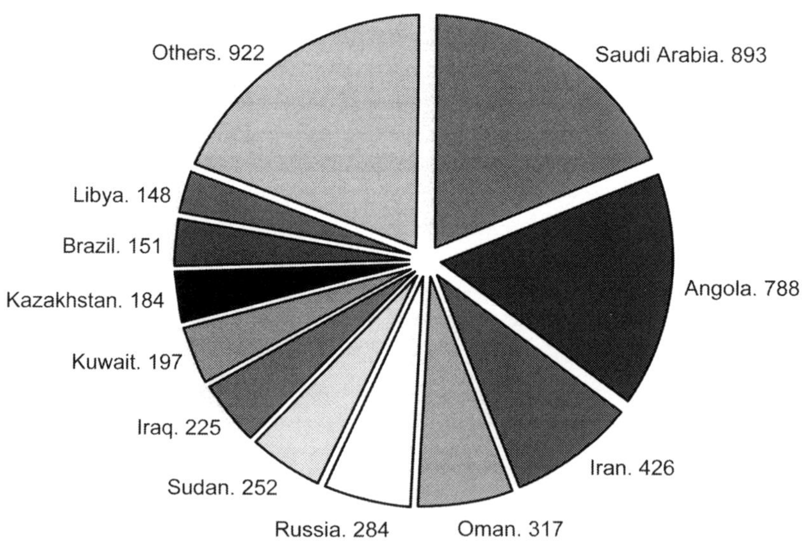

Figure 2.6 China's crude oil imports by source in bd (000) in 2010
Source: US Energy Information Administration, China-Country Report at: http://205.254.135.7/countries/cab.cfm?fips=CH

efforts to secure necessary oil shares in the Middle East, China will develop a militaristic exposure which would include a naval build-up to rival American maritime presence, exchange oil for arms, promote and exploit turbulence in the region, continue in its equity share oil policy and an exclusionary oil approach and strictly follow a national interest approach in its foreign policy towards the region, free from any moral consideration.

> China will try to use its growing influence to reshape the rules and institutions of the international system to better serve its interests, and other states in the system—especially the declining hegemony—will start to see China as a growing security threat. The result of these developments, they predict, will be tension, distrust, and conflict, the typical features of a power transition.[38]

Realists and 'analysts within the realist persuasion foresee the emergence of China as a revisionist, if not a belligerent state. They speculate that China's oil needs could prompt it to pursue destabilizing policies such as naval arms build up and oil for arms exchange.'[39] Probably the most distressing aspect of the realist understanding is its assumption that China would follow a confrontational foreign policy towards rivals in the Middle East, rather than working within existing institutional frameworks to ensure its energy security. That is, China is on a collision course with the US, Britain, France and other Western and non-Western countries, such as India. Some doomsayers have identified what they termed 'threatening Chinese' policies in the region, such as equity shares, an indicator of China's realist approach to its oil needs from the region.[40] Some of China's energy policies are well grounded in current energy institutions which are Western in nature.

The realist approach tacitly assumes a level of coercion in Sino–Middle Eastern relations. However, in examining the relationship between the two sides, one would find that oil-producing countries are much more eager to engage China in the region's oil markets than China itself. The coercion, then, seems to be Western in nature rather than Oriental, i.e. Western countries and Western oil corporations exercise coercive measures to secure their oil interests in the region. The most apparent manifestation of such coercive Western approach is the US invasion of Iraq in 2003, an American–British joint business venture that went critically wrong. Its main goal was to control Iraq's oil wealth by installing a pro-Western government; neither goal has been attained so far. It has created an unprecedented level of instability in Iraq and the region at large. Iran, Saudi Arabia, Algeria, Oman, UAE and other countries are racing to strengthen their energy and trade ties with China of their own will. Their goal seems to be freedom from Western dominance in oil markets. Middle Eastern countries are welcoming China's involvement in both upstreaming and downstreaming (exploration and refining) of oil. In exchange, China is opening its territory to Middle Eastern investment in oil, gas, petrochemicals and other sectors. The Saudi SABIC and the Kuwait

National Petroleum Co are leaders in petrochemicals and refinery building in China. Oil producers do not see China as threatening to their national sovereignty, territorial integrity or exploitative of their national wealth in the same manner in which they view the United States, Britain, France or even Italy and the Netherlands. While China and the US in particular disagree on some aspects of China's oil policy in the Middle East, namely equity sharing, the US is also not fully convinced that China represents a threat to its national interest in the region, as realists assume. For instance, although the US resents China's relations with Sudan and its current policy towards the uprising in Syria, it seems to be accommodating China's oil needs. China is reciprocating by being sensitive to American interests in the Middle East. An expression of such understanding is the US approval of the renewal of oil contracts with the Iraqi government signed by CNPC and the former Government of Saddam Hussein in 1997. Most recently, in the United Nations, China abstained from blocking a resolution to use force against the Gaddafi regime in Libya; however, China and Russia blocked a similar resolution dealing with the Syrian crisis on 4 February 2012.

China seems to be following a liberal institutional approach, in that it works within existing institutions to secure steady access to energy resources at reasonable prices. The current mechanisms of oil exploration, processing, marketing and consumption are Western in nature, built in the early years of the twentieth century, but China did not participate in their construction. While Western observers continue to criticize China's equity policy as an unfair practice, China begs to differ. Unfairness in oil prices stems from the fact that current world markets submit newcomers to the dictates of the free market economy, which are designed to fully serve the interests of the West, rather than China or any other newcomer, such as India. Additionally, China's equity policy is neither an indication nor a vindication of realist tendencies in the sense that China shares such equities with other countries, and works closely with other players to ensure a steady flow of energy to all, i.e. energy security. The best example is the establishment of the Greater Nile Petroleum Company (GNPOC) in Sudan as a joint venture with several countries: the Sudan (5 percent), CNPC of China (40 percent), Petronas of Malaysia (30 percent), Oil and Natural Gas (ONGC) of India (25 percent). The GNPOC produces over 300,000 bd. The reason why no American or Western oil corporation is involved directly in the joint venture is that the US government banned American companies, especially Chevron, which was the very first to invest in the country's oil sector, from dealing with the Government of Sudan, and also discouraged European corporations from co-operation with that Government. When Chevron was pressured to sell its shares, the ONGC of India rushed in to close a deal. Although CNPC could have had the priority to buy Chevron's shares, it did not object to ONGC's partnership, even though India is a formidable competitor for China. Consequently, if China were pursuing a realist policy towards the region, it should have excluded GNPOC of India and other countries from the joint venture. If

China had chosen such an option, the Sudan would not have objected to it in any way. Moreover, as Ikenberry claims, the uniqueness of the current 'Western system' is that it is accommodating to emerging powers, and

> China in short, is increasingly working within, rather than outside, the Western order. ... What separates China from other states, and indeed previous global powers, is that not only is it 'growing up' within a milieu of international institutions far more developed than ever before, but more importantly, it is doing so while making active use of these institutions to promote the country's development of global power status.[41]

China's foreign policy trends reflect what Ikenberry maintains: China is growing and learning, and fulfilling its international obligations as a responsible stakeholder. It exercised some pressure on the Sudanese government in reference to Darfur, and contributed to resolving the Iranian–Western standoff, but failed to deal with the current Syrian Revolution. China's veto of the 4 February 2012 Security Council Resolution only prolonged the suffering of the Syrian people. Its opposition to the military option against the regime seems to be totally losing ground and becoming costly to all parties, China included. In dealing with Iran's nuclear programme, China continues to prefer 'quiet diplomacy' and states that it understands Iranian security concerns, whereas the West seems to be confrontational, motivated by Israeli calls for war against Iran. Some Western observers have noticed that 'in recent years, China has diplomatically and publicly postured as an international "good citizen" on the array of norms and agreements that constrain the proliferation of weapons of mass destruction and ballistic missiles.'[42] On the other hand, the complexity of dealing with the Iranian nuclear project has to do with the fact that China views US efforts at non-proliferation towards Iran as a regime change-oriented policy, rather than a strict commitment to the non-proliferation regime. China has no trust in the American nuclear assessment of the Iranian nuclear project. A similar assessment exaggerated Iraq's nuclear capabilities and led to the occupation of Iraq and the current fragmentation of the country.

US inconsistency in this aspect weakens the non-proliferation regime in several parts of the world. For instance, US strategic partnership with India on nuclear co-operation is a clear violation of the Non-Proliferation Treaty (NPT), which India refuses to ratify. Also, America's opposition to the Iranian nuclear project is understood as part of the enduring animosity between Iran and the US since 1979. On 1 May 2003 the world was alarmed when former President Bush, shortly after declaring 'mission accomplished' in reference to the 'American triumph' in Iraq, began to prepare the ground for regime change in Iran and entertained the idea of territorial modification in Saudi Arabia and other parts of the Middle East. As it turned out, the only impediment to such a scheme was America's fumble in Iraq. Had America been successful there, the map of the Middle East would be reconfigured, and Iran would have been the next target of America's wrath (although Iran was originally expected to be the first target). As Baker and Kessler assert, 'although administration officials do not use the term "regime change" in public, that in effect is the goal they outline as they aim to build resistance to the theocracy.'[43] However, the insurgency in Iraq and Iran's role in complicating the American occupation of Iraq made the administration think deeply before initiating any military attack against Iran.

Although the momentum for a military confrontation between the US and Iran waned in the first two years of the Obama Administration, it remains an option. Recently, in fact, President Obama has been under tremendous Israeli and Saudi pressure to curb the Iranian nuclear project. China continues to adhere to its belief that the US opposition to Iran's nuclear programme is a matter of regime change, rather than strict American commitment to the non-proliferation regime. China also seems to be aware of security concerns with Middle Eastern countries, and realizes the importance of a regional security system that provides all with security and guarantees territorial integrity. In so doing, China invokes its strict devotion to the principles of non-intervention in the internal affairs of nations – territorial integrity, sovereignty, peaceful co-existence, a harmonious foreign policy and a peaceful rise being the main principles that guide its foreign policy. Neither Iran's national security nor the national security of Arabs or Israelis is guaranteed under the current conditions prevailing in the Middle East. The region is in dire need of a regional security arrangement in which the US, China, Russia and other players can advance in co-operation with regional players. However, as China's demand for oil increases, with an international environment characterized by rising economic powers such as India, the competition with existing powers such as Japan and the US will escalate tension on the world scene.

Trade and trade diplomacy

Building on the Silk Road's rich tradition of trade relations that spans over 2,000 years with the Middle East, China is vigorously pursuing an ambitious market agenda in the region. Its trade links in post WWII followed several trends that can be identified. For the period between 1950 and 1971, 'political' trade or 'trade diplomacy' was an instrument in China's foreign policy utilized to secure diplomatic recognition. Chou En-lai and Chen Yi led China's foreign policy for over 20 years, during which time they utilized the Non-Aligned Movement, the Bandung Forum and bilateral and multilateral Chinese relations with Middle East and Third World countries to promote China's foreign policy goals. China first approached Egypt and bought cotton five years before Egypt recognized the PRC in 1956. Meanwhile, trade talks with Israel began in 1952 even though Israel recognized the PRC in 1950 and diplomatic relations were officially established four decades later in 1992. Other countries such as Syria, Algeria, Libya, Tunisia, Somalia, Sudan and South Yemen enjoyed significant attention from the Chinese leadership, although trade volumes were marginal. In addition to diplomatic recognition,

China's 'trade diplomacy' and trade relations in this period were ideologically based and entrenched in anti-imperialist rhetoric. Chinese trade policy highlighted trade solidarity relations with fellow Third World countries as a method of resisting neocolonial infiltration. It was strong in its anti-imperialist posture, but weak in substance. Bilateral and multilateral arrangements were also constructed to resist the neocolonial economy within the 'Third World family.' However, four decades later, the anti-colonial economy, central planning, autarky and isolationism proved to be economically disastrous. It had failed in achieving development, the long-sought goal in the Third World. Therefore, China realized that it had to change course, a step that proved to be one of the wisest decisions ever made in China's history.

Other powers that rejected change or were unable to adjust their economies collapsed. Therefore, what was called the 'imperial economy' or Western 'liberal' economy has become the main vehicle for growth, prosperity and development. China completely abandoned its rhetoric and, since 1978, has vigorously engaged in the world economy under the far-sighted leadership of Deng Xiaoping. When he consolidated his power that year, he examined China's economic backwardness and recognized the unlimited opportunities on the global scene in the post-Mao era. China embarked on a process of national recovery by looking outward, opening up to the world, exploring economic opportunities and building partnerships worldwide. Japan provided the technical knowhow needed for China to begin its most ambitious economic recovery programme ever. Preoccupied with their own crises of imperial overstretch and economic stagnation, the US and USSR provided China with the necessary political space to brilliantly manoeuvre its interests worldwide. The USSR was embroiled in a devastating conflict in Afghanistan that depleted its resources and fragmented its domestic front, leading to its demise in 1991.

The US was also recovering from the devastating Vietnam War in the 1970s, its domestic upheavals during the Civil Rights movement and the consequences of the Watergate scandal. The US was more than willing to continue détente not only with the Soviet Union, but also with the PRC to normalize relations and resume economic co-operation, to open up its markets to Chinese products and grant China the 'most favoured nation' status at a later stage. China took advantage of such an atmosphere conducive to its economic recovery and wasted no time. In a few years, it assumed the role that Japan had held in the 1970s to produce consumer goods at competitive prices, and relaunched a complex network of new Silk Road trade with the entire world. The Middle East was a primary destination within this scheme. In the 1980s, Chinese construction corporations competed with Korean, American, French, British and Italian companies over contracts for the construction of highways, ports, shopping malls, multipurpose buildings, etc. They managed to carry out ambitious projects and gain the confidence and trust of Middle Eastern countries. Chinese labour also found its way to markets in the Gulf region and North Africa, in Libya and Algeria in particular. Even though economic co-operation at the beginning was in the construction sector, it expanded soon after to commodities, energy, high-tech industry and services.

China's new approach is greatly welcomed in Middle Eastern countries, and its involvement in the region has become a major feature of its international relations. Post-Mao China abandoned its leftist fervour, confined its relations to pure business and refrained from any support of Maoist or leftists movements in the region. China strictly followed the principle of non-intervention in the internal affairs of the countries of the region. As a result, the new China, Red Capitalist China and the Dragon invasion of the Middle East can be noticed in every corner of the region. China's trade with the Middle East is driven primarily by its increasing demands for oil, gas and raw materials as well as markets. For this reason, China has strengthened its political, trade, military and investment relations with the countries of the region since the early 1990s. Table 2.3 illustrates China's growing trade volume with Middle Eastern countries from 2001 to 2010.

The economic boom in the Middle East and North Africa (MENA) has also motivated China's heavy involvement in the region.

> The MENA region is enjoying strong economic growth for the fifth year in a row, almost 6 percent, driven by high oil prices, acceleration in market-oriented reforms, and deeper integration in the region and with the rest of the world. The rise in oil prices from about $25 in 2002 to almost $147 in mid-2008 has brought an unprecedented windfall to the resource-rich countries. With a large part of the oil revenues invested abroad, particularly through sovereign wealth funds, net financial outflows have tripled since 2002. The region has also experienced a record increase in Foreign Direct Investment (FDI) flows, accounting for more than 4.7 percent of world FDI inflows in 2006, up from an average of 1.8 percent in 2000–2004. Oil-producing nations have intensified their efforts to diversify the economy. In the six resource-rich countries of the Gulf Cooperation Council (GCC), the non-oil sector now accounts for a remarkable 60–70 percent of GDP and a massive program of infrastructure and social spending is underway.[44]

In its latest review of the world economy in January 2012, the IMF stated that, 'economic activity in the MENA is expected to accelerate in 2012–13, driven mainly by the recovery in Libya and the continued strong performance of other oil exporters.'[45] The economic outlook for China and the Middle East (Table 2.4) seems promising in comparison with other parts of the world, thus increasing the prospects of bilateral and multilateral trade with the region.

There are several factors that motivated both sides to enhance bilateral trade relations. Accumulated oil wealth caused by the rising price of oil was greatly welcomed in China and East Asian countries; economic declines in the Euro-American trade zone also prompted capital to turn to the East instead of the West, its traditional direction over the past century; post-11

Table 2.3 China–Middle East trade volume in millions of dollars from 2001 to 2010

Country	*2010*	*2009*	*2008*	*2007*	*2006*	*2005*	*2004*	*2003*	*2002*	*2001*
Algeria	5,177.32	5,127.46	4,601.13	3,866.41	20,906.4	1,768.15	1,239.6	745.15	433.81	292.34
Bahrain	1,051.42	686.5	786.39	487.15	3,487.3	255.94	212.97	135.28	109.68	129.77
Egypt	6,958.9	5,845.02	6,303.2	4,672.53	31,922.7	2,145.18	1,576.37	1,089.58	944.77	953.21
Iraq	9,864.96	5,147.95	2,652.83	1,453.18	144,474.1	823.79	469.8	56.38	517.06	469.99
Iran	29,391.08	21,219.09	27,757.62	20,589.65	11,444.3	10,083.27	7,045.46	5,622.52	3,739.57	3,312.89
Israel	7,644.44	5,178.07	6,049.82	5,309.94	38,757.2	3,027.88	2,484.85	1,831.3	1,417.09	1,315.91
Jordan	2,053.61	2,070.65	1,949.31	1,181.36	10,309.8	910.68	710.76	524.81	358.03	274.29
Kuwait	8,556.95	5,043.54	6,790.12	3,629.26	27,853.1	1,648.97	1,248.11	1,188.24	727.33	642.49
Lebanon	1,346.73	1,065.84	1,096.72	717.34	5,080.4	476.23	493.56	370.1	280.27	238.24
Libya	6,576.92	5,178.66	4,229.44	2,410.07	23,980.5	1,302.22	671.74	215.68	112.75	95.18
Morocco	2,937.5	2,504.84	2,809.98	2,586.11	19,289.3	1,483.88	1,157.56	856.76	573.41	384.23
Oman	10,723.72	6,158.73	12,421.36	7,270.29	64,690.2	4,329.9	4,389.51	2,067.72	1,506.65	1,676.32
Palestine	26.37	24.32	41.03	37.65	280.7	23.83	9.92	6.93	4.48	4.95
Qatar	3,311.28	2,253.87	2,385.79	1,208.88	9,987.9	676.39	437.78	354.88	223.55	408.61
Saudi	43,195.49	32,548.39	41,846.17	25,366.97	20,1403.7	16,070.14	10,298.1	7,319.12	5,106.89	4,075.19
Syria	2,483.26	2,220.59	2,303.22	1,876.74	1,4062.1	906.37	720.67	506.28	371.08	223.19
Tunisia	1,119.8	818.66	787.17	512.23	4,080.8	339.63	279.22	200.89	182.41	109.37
Turkey	15,110.58	10,094.75	12,569.25	11,768.02	80,692.4	4,875.47	3,412.67	2,597.81	1,377.83	905.02
UAE	25,686.89	21,226.88	28,256.94	20,035.65	142,015.3	10,775.44	8,145.61	5,810.46	3,896.26	2,824.99
Yemen	4,002.94	2,405.95	4,394.46	2,708.34	30,348.1	3,214.79	1,916.25	1,899.23	731.1	661.05

Source: National Bureau of China Statistics, *2010 China Statistics Yearbook*, at www.stats.gov.cn/tjsj/ndsj/2008/indexee.htm (accessed 19 March 2012)

Table 2.4 World economic outlook projections

Country/region	*2010*	*2011*	*2012*	*2013*
China	10.4	9.2	8.2	8.8
United States	3.0	1.8	1.8	2.2
Germany	3.6	3.0	0.3	1.5
India	9.9	7.4	7.0	7.3
United Kingdom	2.1	0.9	0.6	2.0
France	1.4	1.6	0.2	1.0
Japan	4.4	–0.9	1.7	1.6
Brazil	7.5	2.9	3.0	4.0
Middle East and North Africa	4.3	3.1	3.2	3.6

Source: table constructed from data provided by World Economic Outlook Update Global Recovery Stalls, January 24, 2012 http://www.imf.org/external/pubs/ft/weo/2012/update/01/index.htm

September 2001 restrictions imposed on the freedom of movement of capital and people diminished the prospects of trade with the Euro-American markets. The Middle Eastern business community suffered greatly from travel restrictions and the harassment of Western security agencies; in contrast, it found the gates eastward wide open for them. Reciprocally, China increased its trade volume with the Middle East, Central Asia and the Asian continent at large.

Some Sino–Middle Eastern trade institutions

In their quest to enhance Sino–Middle Eastern trade relations, China and Middle Eastern countries created countless numbers of formal, informal, private and civil society institutions, forums, offices and bureaus to supervise and manage their economic and trade relations. For its part, Chinese diplomacy is geared towards a singular objective: to employ political and diplomatic relations to enhance trade in the region. The following section highlights a few such entities.

The Arab Chamber of Commerce and Industry

The Arab Chamber of Commerce and Industry is based in Hong Kong, and is considered to be one of the pillars of Sino–Arab economic co-operation. It has established the Hong Kong Islamic Index, a list of Shari'ah-compliant corporations that encourage investment and avoid forbidden types of trade in Islam, such as manufacturing and selling alcohol, processing pork products or practising usury. It has also established an international Islamic mediation and arbitration centre to resolve conflicts according to Islamic tenets of dispute resolution, in addition to an Institute of Islamic Studies, a Mosque Fund and the *Amwal* Credit Union. The chamber also provides information, convenes conferences and workshops and promotes Sino–Arab trade relations across China and the Arab world.[46]

The Arab Business Club

The Arab Business Club, China branch, is one of the leading Arab associations that promote bilateral business relations. The club is a 'business network specialized to develop trade relations and investment between China and Arab countries.'[47] It also provides services to entrepreneurs, business people and investors in both markets.

The China–Arab Co-operation Forum

The China–Arab Co-operation Forum was established in 2004 as a comprehensive approach to Sino–Arab relations. Politically speaking, the forum highlights the necessity of regional stability and the peaceful resolution of regional conflicts. In the economic sphere, the forum's main goal seeks to promote co-operation in the areas of investment, commerce, quality inspection, technical co-operation, oil and gas, tourism, environment, taxation and customs and agriculture.[48]

China–Gulf Co-operation Council

The China–Gulf Co-operation Council was established in 2008. The council's objective is to co-ordinate between China and the six members of the Gulf Co-operation Council, Saudi Arabia, Bahrain, Kuwait, Oman, Qatar and the United Arab Emirates, in the areas of trade, energy, tourism, technology and investment, and enhance mutual understanding and friendship.[49]

The Saudi–Chinese Business Council

The Saudi–Chinese Business Council was founded in 2000 to promote bilateral Sino–Saudi relations in the areas of trade, energy, petrochemical industries, railways, pharmaceuticals, motor industry, minerals, construction, tourism, education and culture.

Association of Chinese Companies in Saudi Arabia

The Association of Chinese Companies in Saudi Arabia was established in March 2012 under the supervision of the Chinese Embassy. Its main goal is to manage over 100 major Chinese enterprises, over 20,000 entrepreneurs in Saudi Arabia, promote trade and facilitate co-operation between Chinese and Saudi enterprises.

The Kuwait–China Investment Company

The Kuwait–China Investment Company was founded in 2005 by the Kuwaiti Investment Authority, Kuwait's sovereign wealth fund, 'as a key investment vehicle in Asia, to take advantage of growing trade flows and investment opportunities in the fields of agribusiness, energy, real estate, infrastructure, and financial services. In 2008 Sino–Kuwaiti trade volume hit a record high of $6.78 billion, up 85 percent from the $3.67 billion of 2007.'[50] The company also builds on a rich tradition of co-operation between China and Kuwait since 1962. China was one of the very first countries to recognize the independence of Kuwait, to support its reconstruction and aid in the restoration of its sovereignty after the Iraq invasion. Trade relations between the two sides include Kuwait's investment in Chinese markets, China's oil imports and export of consumer goods and services to Kuwaiti markets.

China–Israel Business Forum and China–Israel Joint Committee of Trade and Economy

The China–Israel Business Forum and the China–Israel Joint Committee of Trade and Economy aim to promote trade between Israel and China. The two entities, in addition to several other associations and friendship organizations, build on a rich tradition of co-operation between Israel and China that dates back to the 1950s. While Israel exports weapons and high-tech products to China, the Chinese side exports consumer goods, electronics, petrochemicals and services.

Turkey–China Economic Co-operation Forum

China and Turkey, two rapidly growing economic powers, have intensified their trade. Senior Chinese and Turkish leaders have been exchanging visits to strengthen Sino-Turkish economic co-operation. Currently, the value of bilateral Turkish–Chinese trade 'is estimated at $24 billion, to be raised to $100 billion over the coming eight years.'[51] China needs Turkish support to deal with its Xinjiang separatist movement and to recognize the One-China policy. In his latest visit to Ankara, Xin Jingping, the vice-president of China, extracted commitments from the Turkish leadership to refrain from supporting the East Turkistan Liberation Movement and to support the One-China policy in reference to Turkish–Taiwanese economic co-operation. In exchange, China would intensify bilateral trade relations to exceed $100 thousand million over the coming 8 years and provide Turkey with ballistic missiles and other types of military needs. Turkey is also interested in opening up Turkish industries to Chinese markets.

Forum on China–Africa Co-operation

In addition to their membership of the China–Arab Forum, Sino-North African relations are managed through the Forum on China–Africa Co-operation, established in 2000. It includes Arab countries in North and East Africa: Mauritania, Morocco, Algeria, Tunisia, Libya, Sudan, Egypt, Somalia,

Comoros and Djibouti. In the first ministerial meeting, the attendees signed the Beijing Declaration, which highlights the commitment of each side to promote co-operation in trade, finance, investment, culture, agriculture, education, health care and science and technology.[52]

Iran–China Joint Economic Commission

Economic and trade relations between China and Iran are deeply rooted in history. Currently, Iran is the third largest supplier of crude oil to China. The annual value of oil imports from Iran stands at $30 thousand million annually. In addition to co-operation in the areas of oil and natural gas, Iran is a major importer of Chinese goods and services, given the embargo imposed on Iran by the US and Europe because of its nuclear programme.

Cultural relations

A third major area of co-operation between China and the Middle East is cultural relations. In fact, cultural interaction has been a major theme in Sino–Middle Eastern relations since the 1950s. China signed cultural agreements with several countries even prior to its openness policy. China's successful trade and oil co-operation since the 1980s has enhanced cultural ties between the two sides. The spectacular Olympic Games opening and closing ceremonies in 2008 captivated the hearts and minds of millions across the region to the point that they sparked interest in learning more about China and its culture, history and civilization. China is responding to this growing interest by pursuing several ventures, including opening Confucius centres across the region, establishing student exchange programmes, teaching Chinese and learning Arabic, Persian, Turkish and Hebrew. In fact, an important area of co-operation between China and the Middle East is education. Previously, China was not a main destination for Arab students seeking higher education because the fear of indoctrination was widespread. Currently, even conservative Arab monarchies do not shy away from sending students to study and train in China. For example, there are 10,000 Arab students, 1,500 of whom are Saudi Arabian, studying in Chinese universities and colleges. Besides these cultural exchanges, Chinese cuisine has also become very popular in the region, and tourists flock in both directions to see and taste the marvels of each country.

Confucius Institutes in the Middle East

There are twelve established Confucius Institutes in the Middle East. The institutes are cultural institutions affiliated to the Chinese Ministry of Education with goals similar to the British Council, the US AMIDEAST Center, Goethe Institute of Germany and the Italian Dante Institute. Their main goal is to promote the teaching and learning of Chinese language, history and culture. Chinese official figures maintain that 'more than 500,000 foreigners have taken Chinese language courses' made available by the institutes.[53] Their mission is to instil an appreciation of Chinese culture, history, customs, cuisine and music; to disseminate information on China's development and trade; to organize workshops, Spring Festivals, Chinese New Year, etc. Appreciation of Chinese culture has also increased because of China's rising economic and political clout. 'Chinese culture is no longer rusty antiques on display in quiet museums around the world, or imaginative descriptions in books for foreign readers. A more lively and diverse China, with a delicate mixture of old and new, tradition and modernity, is approaching foreign audiences.'[54] Middle Eastern countries are warmly receiving the Confucius Centres as a symbol of Chinese cultural co-operation and wisdom (Table 2.5).

Arms sales

Sino–Middle Eastern military co-operation goes back to the 1950s, the early years of the PRC. Shichor illustrates China's indirect role in facilitating the first arms deal between Egypt and the Soviet Union in 1955, known as the Czechoslovakia arms deal.[55] China also sold or provided free of charge light weapons to national liberation movements in the Middle East, especially the PLO. However, since the late 1970s, China has noticed the monetary and non-monetary value of arms sales to the region and significantly increased its arms transfer, although it is not one of the top five military exporters to the Middle East, and the latter remains one of the largest recipients of arms transfer. Shichor also states that, between the late 1970s and the late 1980s, the Middle East 'became Beijing's leading arms market (primarily Iraq and Iran, but also Egypt), absorbing over 90 percent of the total valued at the end of the 1980s at around US $20 billion.'[56] Figure 2.7 illustrates the fact that

Table 2.5 Confucius Institutes in the Middle East

Country	*Institution*
Egypt	Cairo University, Suez Canal University
Iran	University of Tehran
Israel	Tel Aviv University
Jordan	Ammen Talal Abu-Ghazaleh Organization
Lebanon	Saint-Joseph University
Morocco	University of Mohammed V-Agdal
Sudan	University of Khartoum
Turkey	Bogazici University, Middle East Technical University
UAE	University of Dubai, Zayed University

Source: Confucius Institute website at http://college.chinese.cn/en/node_1979.htm

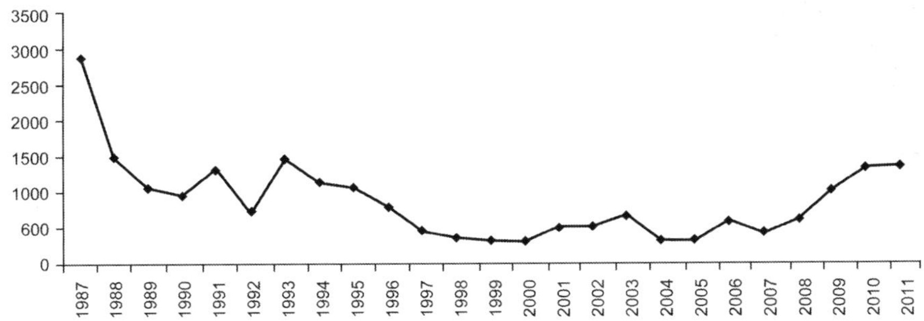

Figure 2.7 China's arms exports to the Middle East and North Africa in millions of US dollars from 1987 to 2011
Source: SIPRI's data set at: http://www.sipri.org/databases/armstransfers/background

China's arms transfer to the region peaked in the 1980s, declined drastically and then picked up again in 1993 and between 2008 and 2011.

The budget created 'extra budgetary resources used perhaps to import advanced military technology and sophisticated weapons and defense equipment, ironically from Israel.'[57] Israeli–Chinese military co-operation began in the early 1980s when Israel transferred arms and military technology to China. 'These arms sales and deliveries were made without US objection and Washington's knowledge and possibly even tacit approval. In those years, before the unexpected collapse of the Soviet Union, Washington had considered Beijing an ally, (though) undeclared, and a partner in the fight against Moscow, mainly in Afghanistan.'[58] However, since 1991 China's rapid rise has changed American strategic tactics towards China. Its rise is viewed as controversial to say the least, and potentially threatening to American interests worldwide. Consecutive US Administrations and the US Congress have been continuously pressuring Israel to curb its military co-operation with China, and demanding that Israel cease the transfer of American military technology to China, but repeated calls and even 'non-binding' congressional resolutions have made limited impact on the Sino–Israeli strategic military partnership. China realizes the value of Israeli military technology and has invested heavily in Israel's high-tech industry, of which the military is the main beneficiary. China also has close military relations with Israel's military corporations, three of which made it into the top 100 worldwide military producers: Elbit Systems, Israel Aerospace Industries and Rafael.[59]

The current Saudi–Chinese partnership was built on the first successful arms deal concluded by the two sides in 1988. Saudi Arabia purchased fifty DF (Dongfeng or east wind), 3A (CSS-2) conventional warhead intermediate-range missiles from China. The deal paved the way for the establishment of diplomatic relations between the two sides two years later.[60] Since then, Saudi and Chinese co-operation has expanded to the oil and gas, trade, petrochemicals, railway, construction, tourism and culture sectors. Turkey is another

Middle Eastern country that has had significant military co-operation with China. Shichor affirms that, although trade relations are increasing between the two sides, military co-operation has been more significant in Sino-Turkish relations since the late 1990s. Military co-operation between China and Turkey 'focused on multiple launch rocket systems, based on the Chinese WS-1A/B (Turkish designation: kasirga, Whirlwind or tornado, or TR-300) and on tactical missiles based on the Chinese B-611 (Turkish designation: yildrim, thunderbolt or lightning) similar to the DF-11 (M-7 or CSS&).'[61] Turkish–Chinese military transfer is a matter of national security to China, as Turkey is viewed as a traditional supporter of Uighur separatists in Xinjiang. In exchange for military co-operation, transfer of Chinese weapon systems to Turkey and strengthening trade relations between the two sides, Turkey has agreed to restrict the activities of the East Turkistan liberation movement on its territory. At the same time, it also recognized China's unequivocal sovereignty and territorial integrity, including East Turkistan (Xinjiang), and fully submitted to the One-China Policy. Table 2.6 illustrates China's arms exports to a selected number of Middle Eastern countries from 1987 to 2011, in millions of dollars.

China also has strong military co-operation with Algeria, Syria, Yemen, Iraq and Sudan. These oil-producing countries have provided major economic concessions for China in the area of equity share in their oil fields, access to raw materials, natural resources and precious metals in exchange for arms sales. China's military co-operation with Iran was first established during the Iran–Iraq War (1980–88). Iran was one of China's main importers of ammunition, tanks, missiles, landmines, jetfighters and even weapons of mass destruction (WMD).

Table 2.6 Chinese arms exports to the Middle East and North Africa for the years 1987–2011 in millions of dollars

Country	*1987–1990*	*1991–1994*	*1995–1998*	*1999–2001*	*2002–2005*	*2005–2008*	*2009–2011*
Algeria	50	80	5	23	15	61	18
Egypt	104	112	26	18	264	91	70
Iran	1,002	779	502	216	310	251	222
Iraq	1,211	0	0	0	20	0	0
Jordan	0	0	0	0	8	8	0
Kuwait	0	0	0	46	41	0	0
Oman	0	0	0	0	12	0	0
Saudi Arabia	450	0	0	0	0	33	33
Sudan	115	52	54	0	133	46	0
Tunisia	0	27	0	0	0	0	0
Turkey	0	0	6	12	8	24	0
UAE	0	14	0	0	0	0	0
Yemen	0	0	0	0	0	150	150
Total	2,932	1,064	593	315	811	664	493

Source: SIPRI's data set, at www.sipri.org/databases/armstransfers/background.

> China rebuffed international criticism of its transfer of WMD equipment and technology abroad, its large sales of conventional weapons in the 1980s to Iran and Iraq, and its sale of several dozen intermediate-range ballistic missiles to Saudi Arabia. China sometimes denied transferring or selling weapons and equipment despite overwhelming evidence to the contrary.[62]

Owing to domestic and regional instability concerns, China will continue to be a source of arms for some countries in the Middle East such as Syria, Algeria, Sudan and Yemen. At the same time, international security threats to the countries in the region carry an implicit but ignitable potential for wars. Finally, China's economic pre-eminence, the increase in its military budget, the expansion of its naval presence on the high seas and its concentration on the high-tech military industry are expected to revolutionize its arms transfers worldwide.

The Long March for diplomatic recognition and political co-operation

As stated in Chapter 1, Sino–Middle Eastern relations are deeply rooted in history. Post WWII, China's political engagement in the region led to diplomatic recognition, although the march for diplomatic relations was even longer than The Long March itself. Israel was the first Middle Eastern country to recognize the PRC in January 1950, and the last country in the region to establish diplomatic relations with China in 1992. Table 2.7 provides some information on China and the Middle East in terms of the date of diplomatic recognition of China, population, GDP rates and GNIP.

In between, China not only managed to secure diplomatic recognition, but also to build strategic partnerships with the region in the areas of security co-operation, trade relations and energy. It is deeply involved in the management of the current pace of the Arab Spring, by slowing it down and attempting to break its momentum, as we see in the Syrian Revolution. It hais also been involved in reviving the peace processes and dealing with the Iranian–Western standoff over Iran's nuclear programme. China is also following in the footsteps of India, Pakistan, Jordan, Bangladesh and other UN-contributing countries to peace missions around the world. In addition to its Foreign Affairs Ministry and its diplomatic and economic missions, the PRC has established several forums to promote its ties with the region. The two most notable that currently deal with the political developments in the region are the office of the Special Envoy to the Middle East and the office of the Special Envoy to Syria.

In 2002, China appointed a Special Envoy to the Middle East. The mandate of the office was to co-ordinate China's political involvement in the Middle East, especially its efforts towards resolving the Arab–Israeli conflict. Recently, the envoy Wi Sike has been very active in explaining China's

Table 2.7 China and the Middle East: country, date of diplomatic recognition, GDP, GNIP and GDP growth rate

Country	*Date of diplomatic recognition*	*Population*	*GDP/$million*	*GNIP/$*	*GDP growth rate*
Algeria	20 December 1958	35.5	161,979.4	8,100.0	3.3
Bahrain	18 April 1989	1.3	30.4	28,169	4.1
China	NA	1,338.3	5,926,612.0	7,640.0	10.4
Egypt	30 May 1956	81.1	218,894.3	5,269.0	5.1
Iraq	20 August 1958	32.0	82,150.3	3,370.0	0.8
Iran	16, August 1971	74.0	906.2	11,490.0*	3.2
Israel	24 January 1992	7.6	217,332.7	27,660.0	4.7
Jordan	14 April 1977	6.0	27,573.5	5,800.0	3.1
Kuwait	22 March 1971	2.7	141.7	40,700	4.2
Lebanon	9 November 1971	4.2	39,006.2	14,090.0	7.0
Libya	9 August 1978	6.4	92.62	16,880.0*	6.4
Morocco	1 November 1958	32.0	90,804.6	4,600.0	3.7
Oman	25 May 1978	2.8	66.8	25,190.0	4.4
Palestine	20 November 1988	4.2	12.79*	2,656	7.0*
Qatar	5 July 1988	1.8	173.2	107,721	18.7
Saudi Arabia	21, July 1990	28.08	434,666.1	22,750.0*	3.8
Syria	1 August 1956	20.4	59,147.0	5,120.0	3.2
Sudan	4 February 1959	43.6	62,045.8	2,030.0	4.5
Tunisia	10 January 1964	10.5	44,290.8	9,060.0	3.7
Turkey	4 August 1971	72.8	734,364.5	15,530.0	9.0
UAE	1 November 1984	7.5	297,648.5	50,580.0*	1.4
Yemen (N)	24 September 1956	24.1	24,799	2,213.0	8.0
Yemen (S)	31 January 1968				

Source: World Bank, Country Profiles, at http://data.worldbank.org/country
UNDP Country Profile of International Human Development Indicators, at http://hdr.undp.org/en/data/profiles/
Note: *2009 figures.

perspective on the Syrian uprising and the related Arab Spring developments across the region. He was also keen on reviving peace talks between the Israelis and the Palestinians, a vital step for the promotion of trade and development in the Middle East.

China adopted a peaceful resolution to the Arab–Israeli conflict as early as the 1950s, soon after the conflict erupted, and soon after the Partition Plan was proposed by the Soviet Union and approved by the United Nations in 1947. Given its strategic partnership with both Arabs and Israelis, China is in a much better position than the US, Russia, France, Britain or Germany to intervene in reviving the peace process, and to contribute to resolving the Arab–Israeli conflict. China is also currently involved in dealing with the Iranian–Western standoff over Iran's nuclear programme, supportive of a peaceful settlement to the Yemeni crisis, and supportive of peaceful negotiations between the Sudanese and South Sudan governments. However, the region has been generating tremendous levels of resentment and unpopularity towards China ever since its vetoes against the UN's condemnation of the Syrian government and its close co-ordination with Russia in the Syrian Revolution. Both Russia and China are held responsible for prolonging the suffering of the Syrian people.

Conclusion

This chapter has highlighted the five-dimensional framework of co-operation between China and the Middle East in terms of energy co-operation, trade, arms sales, culture and political co-operation. China became a major Middle East oil importer in 1993. Its dependence on the region is increasing rapidly and, in 2030, it is expected that 70 percent of China's oil imports will come from the Middle East. China is also extending its trade relations to every country in the region, to every city, town and village in the Middle East. Trade volumes between the two sides are expected to increase rapidly, as China floods Middle Eastern markets with cheap consumer goods. Both sides are also carrying out ambitious investment projects in heavy industries such as petrochemicals, refineries, cement and phosphates. To this end, both sides have established several economic organizations, forums, corporations and agencies to supervise their trade, industry, agricultural, technology and tourism relations. Cultural co-operation is also evident with Confucius Institutes spreading across the region, and Chinese cuisine and cultural appreciation increasing across the Middle East. Both sides are also working closely in the areas of security, military transfer and arms sales: this is mutually beneficial, as China sells arms to Saudi Arabia, Algeria, Iraq, Syria, Libya, Yemen, the Sudan, Syria, Iran and Turkey and imports high-tech military software and hardware from Israel.

3 Walking on thin ropes

A tridimensional perspective

China has been skilfully navigating the treacherous waterways of the Middle East in a quest to pursue its interests, identified in terms of oil, arms sales, trade, cultural and political relations, although the task has proven to be challenging on many occasions. China seems to be walking on thin ropes and playing soothing music to the liking of all parties. The goal is a 'win-win' situation, a phrase repeatedly used by Chinese senior officials in bilateral and multilateral relations. The political economy of Sino–Middle Eastern relations and the political landscape of the region appear to be triangular, that is, the result of interaction between three major players. Of course, the approach does not diminish the importance of bilateral relations. As Dittmer states, the triangular logic of relationships among political actors in the international arena applies to any situation meeting certain criteria: '(a) it circumscribes the possible relationships among three rational, autonomous actors, (b) the bilateral relationship among any two of these actors is contingent on their relationship with the third, and (c) each actor actively seeks to engage one or the other or both to forestall its defection or hostile collusion and advance its own interests.'[1] Within this triangular paradigm, and in relation to China's foreign policy towards the Middle East, there are sixteen dimensions that can be identified in the following sections.

The Chinese–Israeli and Arab dimension

To strike a balance between Sino–Arab and Sino–Israeli affairs is one of the most challenging aspects of Chinese–Middle Eastern relations. Although China has been viewed as traditionally supportive of the Palestinian cause on issues related to the Arab–Israeli conflict, it has a growing strategic partnership with Israel that dates back to the 1950s, even though the 'secret military ties between the two countries date back to the 1980s, and various reports estimate that Israel has exported between $1 and $3 billion worth of arms technology to the PRC.'[2] China needs Arab oil, and urgently needs a route to American top military technology that can only be accessed through Israel. The latter realizes its strategic and comparative advantage and has shown tremendous pragmatism in its relations with China. In fact, Israel seems to be willing to pass along American military hardware and technology to China in exchange for trade, military co-operation and political support.

China's active involvement in the Middle East is pivotal. Arabs believe that it would create a sort of balance in the peace process, which traditionally tilts in favour of Israel. In 2002, China responded to a direct request from Chairman Yasser Arafat to President Jiang Zemin that China appoint a Special Envoy to the Middle East, and considered the idea of joining the Quartet. The latter is an international committee of the United Nations (UN), the US, Russia and the European Union (EU) that shepherds the peace process. The accomplishments of the Quartet under the Bush Administration were negligible, as the US had complicated the work of the committee through its uncompromising policies towards the Palestinians. The Bush Administration also made it difficult for Israelis to realize the scope of opportunities provided by the Arab and European support to the process. Under the Obama Administration, the peace process died completely as the Israeli Prime Minister refuses to negotiate or compromise with the Palestinians. China's decision not to join the committee was over a disagreement with the Quartet in managing the conflict and its continued failure to resolve the Arab–Israeli conflict. China seeks to remain neutral and supportive of the process, rather than being associated with its failure. The credit in this regard went to the Bush Administration, to Netanyahu, the Israeli Prime Minister, and to Tony Blair, the Quartet's envoy. Overall, China seems to be making major strides in balancing its association with both Arab and Israeli sides: China relies heavily on Arab oil, minerals and markets, whereas it pursues strategic partnerships with Israel in the areas of technology, arms sales and agro-technology in particular.[3] The volume of China's trade with both sides is growing at a rapid pace, and it is only expected to proceed in this direction.

Chinese–Palestinian and Israeli relations

Equally challenging and closely related to Sino–Arab and Sino–Israeli relations is China's ability to strike a balance between its strategic partnership with Israel and its traditional support of the Palestinians. For the period between 1949 and 1976, it provided political backing and light military aid to the Palestinian organizations especially Fatah, the Popular Front for the Liberation of Palestine (PFLP), and later the Palestinian Liberation Organization (PLO) in support of their efforts for national liberation and independence.[4] China provided the PLO with diplomatic status, and supported the Palestinians in the UN upon assuming a permanent seat in the Security Council in 1971. However, Israel was also the first Middle Eastern country to recognize China in January 1950. China also supported the UN Partition Plan, the draft of which was introduced by the Soviet Union in 1947, China's major ally at the time. Therefore, China's views on the conflict have almost remained unchanged: it recognized both sides, the Palestinians and Israelis, and tacitly recognized their sovereignty, although diplomatic relations between China and Israel materialized four decades later. Throughout this period, China systematically supported the peaceful settlement of the Arab–Israeli conflict and highlighted the legitimate rights of the Palestinian people especially their right to establish a viable state in Palestine. However, China's involvement in national liberation efforts, especially in the Middle East, ceased in the post-Mao and post-Chou En-lai era. It was replaced by China's new foreign policy paradigm with new goals that include global engagement to accelerate economic development and technology transfer to China. Within this new prototype, China was struck by Israel's level of technological advancement. Since the mid-1970s, China has found in Israel a strategic partnership and a willingness to build a lasting partnership with China. The essence of their bilateral co-operation at the beginning was in the area of defence and technology transfer: Israel needs markets to export its defence products and weapons systems, whereas China needs Israeli expertise especially in the area of agro-technology, water systems, clean energy and information technology in general. On the other hand, China supported the growing Palestinian entity between 1991 and 2001 and the development of its state-like structures. However, the Palestinian National Authority (PNA) has to date failed to move from transitional to permanent state apparatus on account of Israeli counter efforts and inner conflict among Palestinian factions. The past 7 years saw near total failure on the part of the PNA to assume its responsibilities, but China's envoy remains supportive of the Palestinian People's rights and is ready to assist in building state infrastructure should conditions become stable in the PNA's territories.

China, Israel and the United States

Another challenging aspect of Sino–Middle Eastern relations is balancing its relations with the US and Israel. China has had a growing strategic partnership with Israel since the early 1980s centring around military co-operation and technology transfer. However, the US is Israel's traditional ally and its main supplier of advanced weaponry, economic assistance and political support since 1957. Israel is seeking markets for its advanced defence industry; China represents a reliable partner in this respect. There are over 200 Israeli arms-producing companies, and Israel exports 75 percent of its arms production. In fact, the American-based technical foundation of this industry makes the weaponry particularly attractive to China. In the area of military co-operation, Israeli–Chinese relations are governed by the nature of US–Chinese relations to a certain degree, and are limited by their scope and depth. Of course, it does not mean that Israel conducts its foreign policy in the shadow of the US or is deterred by American criticism. On the contrary, it has shown its ability to consistently defy the American will. However, to reduce tension with the US due to its opposition to arms technology transfer to China, both countries have learned to be more discreet in their bilateral military co-operation. The famous US opposition to the Phalcon radar systems and the drones prompted

China and Israel to wrap their defence co-operation in extreme secrecy. This explains the lack of credible information on their co-operation in this sphere in recent years. However, Israeli–Chinese bilateral areas of trade, agro-technology, irrigation systems, research and development and the energy sector have advanced beyond their initial expectations. China has also masterminded manoeuvring its interests with Israel with minimum levels of American opposition.

Chinese, Iranian and Saudi Arabian dimension

Another complicated dimension of Sino–Middle Eastern relations deals with striking a balance between Iran and Saudi Arabia. China understands well the theological and geopolitical dimensions that divide Iran and Saudi Arabia, and has no room for error in securing its interests with both powerhouses. Theologically speaking, Saudi Arabia represents the Sunni world, 90 percent of Muslims, whereas Iran represents nearly 8 percent of Muslims, the remaining 2 percent belong to smaller Muslims sects such as the Sufis, Ismailis, Bahá'ís, Ahmadiyya, etc. Among these sects, there are major differences on issues related to the principles of faith, governance and politics. Geopolitically speaking, Saudi Arabia and Iran disagree on nearly everything, which includes Iran's support for sectarianism in Syria, Iraq and Lebanon, Iran's support for Shi'a dissent in Bahrain, Iran's nuclear programme and Iran's occupation of the UAE's three islands of Abu Musa and Greater and Lesser Tunb. Iran also has a list of grievances against Saudi Arabia, with Saudi overproduction of oil to compensate for Iran's supplies due to the sanctions regime topping the list. Iran strongly condemns Saudi military intervention in Bahrain and accuses Saudi Arabia of attempting to annex Bahrain. Remarkably, China maintains strong relationships with both countries. Although the conservative Shah of Iran suspended diplomatic relations with China in 1949 but resumed them in 1971, there were few avenues of co-operation between this date and the beginning of Iran's Islamic Revolution in 1979.

Even though Ayatollah Khomeini disliked the fact that China resumed its diplomatic relations with the Shah's regime, he did not oppose dealings or even a partnership with China because Iran's friends were limited. Iran thought that China's assistance and mutual partnership was mutually rewarding. Yetiv and Lu summed up Iranian–Chinese ties neatly stating that the relationship 'revolves fundamentally around Iran providing China with crude oil and strategic minerals, while Beijing provides a growing quantity of technology and engineering expertise to Iran's industrial, mining, transportation, construction, and energy sectors.'[5] To some extent, Sino–Iranian relations resemble US–Saudi relations, which grew out of mutual interests first in the oil sector, then defence and other sectors since 1938. During the war with Iraq, China provided both Iran and Iraq with different types of conventional weapons. Yetiv and Lu pointed out that 'China's arms sales to the region expanded significantly during the Iran–Iraq War to the tune of over $12 billion.'[6] China provided Iran with the necessary weapons to counter Iraqi air assaults. 'From 1982–89 China sold Iran arms valued at $4.939 billion, 31.4% of all its arms sales in that period and over twice the value of Chinese arms sold to Iraq.'[7] In fact, 'China was exchanging arms for oil. This helps explain why arms sales to Iran were so important and why China resisted so tenaciously US efforts to restrict that trade.'[8]

China continues to be a major business partner and oil importer from Iran in spite of new waves of economic sanctions against Iran caused by its non-compliance with American, European and UN demands to put a freeze on its uranium enrichment programme.

> China views Iran as an important partner in China's plans to develop overland routes to transport oil from the Middle East. Moreover, a strong partnership with Iran has enhanced China's capacity to become an important player in Middle Eastern affairs. Although China recognizes its relationship with Iran may cost it international prestige and threaten Sino-U.S. relations, it has thus far shown unusual willingness to support Tehran.[9]

China is extensively involved in Iran's oil sector. It projects that investment 'in oil exploration and production, petrochemicals, and natural gas infrastructure in Iran could exceed $100 billion over the next quarter-century.'[10] China is also working with Iran to develop its natural gas field, a sector that is heavily underdeveloped. Iran is second to Russia in gas reserves, but its industry remains underdeveloped because of the sanctions regime imposed on Iran and the lack of interest from international gas companies in investing in Iran's natural gas sector, except for Chinese companies and, potentially, Russia's Gazprom.[11] South Korean companies recently withdrew from the Iranian market on account of American pressure on Korea to end its energy co-operation with Iran. The Iranian–Chinese partnership is not confined to energy or trade, but includes security. Iran's security is measured by territorial integrity and by preventing an American or Israeli attack on its territory and its nuclear installations. China and Iran co-ordinated closely in the 1990s to assist Iran in developing a nuclear deterrent; however, under pressure from the US, China reduced its assistance to Iran in this nuclear enterprise. China is actively seeking a solution to the current standoff between the world and Iran over its nuclear programme.

Iran's security dilemma, real or imagined, lies in the Persian/Arabian Gulf region and the Greater Gulf. Iran is surrounded by unstable governments in Iraq and Afghanistan. The US, Iran's traditional foe, is occupying Afghanistan, whereas the US withdrew from Iraq last year, but encircles Iran with military bases. It is also surrounded by unfriendly neighbours, Arabs, Turks, Kurds, Afghanis, Azerbaijanis and Pakistanis, in addition to existing or emerging nuclear threats originating from Pakistan, Saudi Arabia and Israel and, potentially, Turkey. Additionally, the enduring presence of the American ground, naval and air forces in the Gulf represents a major security threat to

Iran. The Iranian perception of security threats also stems from the fact that the US views the Arab/Persian Gulf as an 'American lake.'[12] The US is increasingly becoming a 'Middle Eastern' state as it maintains a substantial military and non-military presence in the region. However, the American wars in the region provided the greatest service to Iran. The removal of Iran's two Sunni enemies – the Taliban and the Ba'ath regime of Saddam Hussein – have brought unprecedented levels of opportunities, but also security challenges as it sits between Afghanistan and Iraq, now occupied or under US influence, so the fear of American encirclement is real. Added to Israel's growing influence in the region, intensifying its presence in Iraq via the infiltration of the Kurdistan Regional Government in northern Iraq, and the Baghdad–Tel Aviv trade relations. Israel is also deepening its strategic partnerships with Azerbaijan, thus increasing Iranian security anxiety. To shield itself from such threats, real or imagined, Iran has become more active in Middle Eastern affairs, and more adamant about its nuclear programme. Iran is the primary beneficiary of the misguided American invasion of Iraq; it provided Iran and Shi'ism with unprecedented opportunities. For the first time in history, Iraq is ruled by a Shi'i sectarian and dictatorial government led by Prime Minister Al Maliki, in close alliance with Iran. Thus, Iran's growing influence and assertiveness in the region has fuelled Sunni anxiety over the threat of the so called Shi'a Crescent.

As a defender of the Sunni world, Saudi Arabia continues to shoulder major security responsibilities towards the region. However, Saudi Arabia is not a match for Iran, and its efforts to counter the Iranian threat require close co-operation with the US and NATO. Recently, Saudi Arabia solicited China's assistance, which only highlights the importance of the role China is playing in balancing its interests with both Saudi Arabia and Iran, while simultaneously playing its role as a responsible country that seeks 'harmony', peace and prosperity in the Gulf region. China has been playing a pivotal role in bringing Iran to the negotiating table, and takes an active role in the ongoing P 5+1 negotiations with Iran over its nuclear programme.

Chinese, US and Iranian dimension

In a radical departure from the previous Administration, US President Obama sent a video message to Iran congratulating its people for the New Year (Nowruz) on 14 March 2009. His main goal was to establish goodwill towards Iran in attempting to resolve the ongoing confrontation between the two sides since 1979. Israeli President Perez followed suit. Both messages brought more anxiety to the Arab world as Arabs are fearful that the US is willing to compromise with Iran on its nuclear programme. In his message, Obama recognized the contributions of the Iranian civilization throughout history, and the contributions of Iranian-Americans to the cultural enrichment of the United States. He emphasized that the government of Iran earned national prestige around the world. However, he also recognized the strained relations between the two sides over the past 30 years, and urged the Iranian government to work with the US to resolve their differences through mutual respect and diplomatic channels. The president invited Iran to join the US in building on commonalities, rather than differences, between the two nations. He gracefully requested Iran to take its rightful place among the community of nations, which cannot be reached through terrorism or arms, but through peaceful engagement. He reminded Iran that its greatness can be realized through building not destroying, and invited the nation to take advantage of the promise of peace, partnership, trade and commerce with the US and other nations.[13] The key issue in the message was the US's willingness to provide security guarantees should Iran respond positively, thereby reducing tension in the region. While Obama's message had an electrifying impact on the people of Iran, the government reiterated its grievances towards the US without a clear response since 2009. Such a cautious response is normal in Iranian politics, given the fact that there has been fierce infighting among the different factions within the Iranian Government on how to manage US–Iranian relations. The clash between the hardliners, the reformers and the moderates is reflected in Iran's foreign policy, thus limiting Iran's room for manoeuvre with the US and the West in general.

The Obama Administration is willing to build on existing European–Iranian agreements in the area of peaceful nuclear energy development, which state that Iran is allowed to develop nuclear energy, but not uranium enrichment. Russia and China are also assisting in this respect. In fact, enriched uranium would be sent to Russia. This co-operation might lead to resolution of the Iranian nuclear standoff in the near future. However, Arabs and Israelis believe that any US compromise with Iran over its nuclear programme would be at their expense. Although Israel possesses nuclear capability and military superiority in the Middle East, Israel continues to view Iran's nuclear ambitions as existentially threatening. It remains to be seen how such a scenario would motivate some Arab countries such as Saudi Arabia or Egypt to pursue the nuclear option, and what China's role would be. In this arena, China and Russia are ready to assist Saudi Arabia in joining the nuclear club. The continued Saudi high-ranking official visits to Moscow should be understood within this framework. Russia and China are not only capable of assisting Saudi Arabia, but also willing to provide the Saudis with quality armaments, understood as knowledge of nuclear technology. Pakistan, Saudi Arabia's traditional ally, is also more than willing to assist Saudi Arabia in its future nuclear project. In fact, Pakistani nuclear capabilities owe a great deal to the generous financial support of Saudi Arabia.

China, Saudi Arabia and the United States

Post WWII, China viewed Saudi Arabia through the prism of nations under the enduring influence of imperialism. The Saudis also viewed China in a negative light as a communist, 'godless' country, therefore, it was deemed un-Islamic to extend a hand of friendship. Saudi Arabia was also a marginal country, and had no substantial weight in Middle East politics or international relations until the late 1960s. Whereas China was pro-Egypt and supportive of Nasser's agenda to promote national liberation, Saudi Arabia was a conservative, status quo-oriented monarchy. In fact, Egypt's military intervention in the civil war in Yemen in support of the revolution against the monarchy brought Egypt and Saudi Arabia into collision. Egypt bombarded southern Saudi urban centres repeatedly in the 1960s, and promoted division within the Saudi royal family. This division grew out of control, to the extent that the royal family deposed King Saud and installed his brother Faisal in 1964. King Saud accepted voluntarily exile in Greece until he died there in 1969, while King Faisal managed to reunite the royal family and confronted Nasser and Arab nationalism. His goal was to undermine the legitimacy of nationalists through the advancement of pan-Islamism instead of pan-Arab nationalism as an ideology. China began to take notice of the growing stature of Saudi Arabia, especially during the oil embargo imposed by King Faisal on the US and the West in support of the Palestinian Question in 1973. China admired the sense of independence King Faisal demonstrated in using oil as a weapon to advance the Arab cause, against the interests of Saudi Arabia's closest ally, the United States. The increasing price of oil provided Saudi Arabia with a distinguished status worldwide, and provided the Saudi government with the financial resources necessary to fund local and regional developmental projects.

Another factor contributing to the status of the Saudi government was the utter defeat of Arab nationalists in the 1967 War with Israel. After the war, Saudi Arabia took a leading role in Middle Eastern politics advocating pan-Islamism as an answer to the challenges facing the Arab-Islamic world. It called for the establishment of the Organization of the Islamic Conference (OIC), and led the organization to the point of weakening the institutions of Arab nationalism. Relations between China and Saudi Arabia developed gradually, and culminated in an arms deal in the 1980s. However, after the tragic events of 11 September 2001, the Saudi–Chinese partnership grew at a much faster pace proportional to the deterioration in American–Saudi relations. In one way or another, the US was responsible for the Saudi–Chinese strategic partnership. In the mid-1980s, Saudi Arabia sought the purchase of advanced American weapon systems to boost its security in the shadow of the Iran–Iraq war and Israeli military superiority.

Although the Reagan Administration was supportive of supplying Saudi Arabia with quality arms, the US Congress, acting under the influence of a strong Israeli lobby, opposed the sale of any advanced weaponry to Saudi Arabia, fearing threats to Israeli's security. At that point, Saudi Arabia sought military co-operation with China as the Soviet Union was not an option, given the epic confrontation between Islam and communism in Afghanistan in which Saudi Arabia played a central role. In conducting arms deals with China, Saudi Arabia sent a clear message that it had an alternative arms supplier and the US no longer had the monopoly over the supply of arms to Saudi Arabia. China sold Saudi Arabia some of the most advanced ballistic missiles in its arsenal: CSS-2 intermediate-range missiles, with a range of 1,500 miles and the ability to carry a payload of over 4,000 lbs.[14] This deal was enveloped in extreme secrecy as Saudi Arabia knew full well that the US would oppose it. As Russell frames:

> the Sino–Saudi CSS-2 missile deal was first publicly revealed as a *fait accompli* in March 1988. The first orders for the missiles were made in 1985, and a number of deliveries were made in 1987 and 1988 before news of the sale became public. The missiles delivered to Saudi Arabia came from an array of over 100 nuclear-capable IRBMs that were first tested by the PRC in 1969 and later deployed in 1971.[15]

The Saudis were also concerned that Israel might carry out a pre-emptive strike to destroy the infrastructure of the missiles before they became operational. Yetiv and Lu found out that,

> in the 1990s, Beijing improved its economic relationship with Saudi Arabia, culminating in the 1999 Strategic Oil Cooperation Agreement signed in Riyadh by then President Jiang Zemin. At its core, the relationship was struck on a simple quid pro quo. The Saudis opened their market to Chinese investment, and Saudi companies began to participate in China's downstream refining business, thereby winning a foothold in the Chinese market.[16]

The terrorist attacks on the United States on 11 September 2001 deeply debilitated the Saudi–American partnership. 'The discovery that many of the terrorists responsible for the attacks on the United States, including Osama bin Laden himself, came from Saudi Arabia created unusual tension in one of the longest-standing friendly relationships the United States has had in the Middle East – a relationship born from mutual interests in Saudi Arabia's rich oil fields.'[17] The fact that fifteen of the nineteen terrorists were Saudi citizens brought Saudi Arabia under unprecedented American scrutiny and pressure. The US had been committed to the stability and territorial integrity of Saudi Arabia since 1938 but, since the tragic events, the two countries no longer view each other as strategic partners. In fact, Saudi Arabia's Government began to view the US as a major security threat to Saudi territorial integrity and sovereignty. Shortly after the attacks, leading voices in American politics and the media demanded that the holy cities of Mecca and Medina be levelled using nuclear weapons, and urged the occupation of Saudi Arabia by taking over its oil fields and dismantling the kingdom into small fractions, reinstating the historical division of the country into Southern, Northern, Eastern and Western Arabia instead of a unified kingdom.

The complexity of the situation made it clear that Saudi Arabia never felt less safe and secure as it did shortly after the attacks. The drastic changes in Saudi–American relations compelled Saudi Arabia to search for partners capable of providing the country with a sense of security. China was eager to fill that void and, as Bubalo states:

> China's growing interest in, and engagement with the Middle East is occurring at a time when US relations with many regional states have reached their lowest ebb. The recent decision by Saudi Arabia to award the first foreign contracts for natural gas exploration to Chinese and Russian firms, at the expense of a US bid, raised eyebrows, though was hardly surprising given the residual strains in the Saudi–US relationship. Saudi Arabia is quickly becoming a key oil supplier for China, while the Saudi national oil company ARAMCO is investing in China's refining sector.[18]

King Abdullah of Saudi Arabia cultivates the Sino–Saudi partnership with special attention, making it the pinnacle of his foreign policy. His first visit as king in 2005 was to China, not to the United States. The partnership has expanded its security co-ordination, trade and oil interests far beyond expectations. Saudi Arabia not only exports oil to China, but is also actively involved in the downstreaming of the oil industry in China. In fact, it is building a US $5,000 million refinery in China's Fujian Province. In return, China is selling arms to Saudi Arabia, flooding Saudi markets with cheap industrial products, relieving Saudi Arabia from its reliance on Western oil markets and balancing the American influence in the region. Currently, Saudi Arabia is supplying 16 percent of China's crude imports. State-controlled Saudi Basic Industries Corp. is investing $4,000 million in a Chinese ethylene complex that will give the Middle Eastern chemical giant a solid foothold in the fast growing Chinese petrochemical sector.[19]

The Sino–Saudi partnership is understood but not welcomed by the US, who continues to express its intention to protect its interests in Saudi Arabia, and is willing to overcome some of the consequences of the tragic attacks, such as the visa restrictions on Saudis. In reciprocity, the government of Saudi Arabia has taken significant steps to respond to American demands in the areas of intensifying its efforts in combating terrorist organizations, regulating charity organizations, reforming its educational systems and monitoring financial transactions to ensure no funds will reach terrorist organizations. Saudi Arabia was also asked to show some significant support in resolving the Arab–Israeli conflict and support for the peace process. In a goodwill gesture towards the US and Israel, Saudi Arabia rallied the Arab world in a 2003 Arab Summit towards comprehensive normalization with Israel based on the land-for-peace formula. Although the Saudi peace initiative was driven by a feeling of guilt over the terrorist attacks and provided Israel with a historic opportunity for peace in the region, Israel never responded positively, a strategic mistake committed by Israeli Prime Minister Sharon, and continued by his successor, Netanyahu. Moreover, the Bush Administration squandered this exceptional 'peace moment' by declaring war on Yasser Arafat and invading Iraq. The Arab goodwill and sympathy for the American sorrow gathered after the terrorist attacks were soon replaced with more resentment towards America and its presence in the region. As far as China is concerned, the Saudi peace initiative is consistent with its views on the conflict all along. Namely, China has called for a peaceful settlement to the conflict consistently since the 1950s. It has also shown sensitivity towards US interests in Saudi Arabia and continues to avoid any potential confrontation with the giant, but proceeds undisturbed with its own agenda especially after the warm Saudi welcome.

The American–Chinese and Middle Eastern dimension

Perhaps the American, Chinese and Middle Eastern dimension is the most important triangle of politics in the region. Whereas Chinese–Middle Eastern relations date back to the early days of the Silk Road, the American presence and interest in the region goes back to the early days of the American Republic in the 1770s.[20] The broader Middle East has had much influence on America since its inception. The early American–Middle Eastern wars of the later seventeenth and early eighteenth centuries encouraged the US to build a strong navy to counter the threat from North Africa to its commerce with Europe. In the early years of the twentieth century, and up until the mid-1950s, the US was the most favoured, admired and respected great power in the Middle East. American partnership with the region was consolidated under the FDR Administration in his meetings with King Abdul Aziz Ibn Saud of Saudi Arabia in 1945. The meetings ushered in an American–Saudi partnership that lasted until the terrorist attacks on 11 September 2001. It was based on a simple principle: security in exchange for oil and, only later on did the two countries expand the range of their bilateral relations and co-ordination in international affairs; the US solicited Saudi support for the containment of the former Soviet Union. For seven decades, the partnership functioned well, and the US increased its presence in the region until the Middle East became the cornerstone of US foreign policy. Through its presence in the Middle East, the US managed to support Israel, contain the Soviets, secure oil fields, secure oil routes and ensured the security of America's allies and friends in the region.

Today, the question is whether the US is willing to share the bounty of the region with newcomers such as India and China, or if it would rather pursue a policy of exclusion of China, in particular, from the Middle East. A close examination of the current state of affairs between the two countries in relation to the Middle East underlines America's goals to isolate Iran and Syria and their proxies in the region, namely Hezbollah and Hamas, at a time when China finds it necessary to manoeuvre its interests with those of America. China cannot jeopardize its strategic trade relations with the US, while at the same time pursuing its own national interests in the Middle East. Its main objective is defined in terms of energy security, and this requires active engagement in the affairs of the region. Lately, China has been leading the opposition to sanctioning the Syrian regime over its atrocities against its people and, along with Russia, shielding Iran from a severe American–Israeli attack on its nuclear installations. The US, however, wants China to act responsibly in the Middle East in exchange for trade concessions and an active role in international trade organizations. There is considerable frustration, which can easily be deduced by examining Sino–American interaction in the Middle East. However, such frustration needs to be put in perspective.

American resentment of China in the Middle East is part of the overall US foreign policy confusion towards China and its rise, i.e. peaceful or coercive in nature. Alterman and Garver believe that the confusion stems from Americans concentrating on China's military spending and the potential Chinese naval build-up that might threaten American interests worldwide. It is obvious that the US is struggling to formulate a lucid foreign policy towards China.[21] China continues to present its 'peaceful rise' as non-threatening to any player, and states that it seeks co-operation and peaceful co-existence with all nations. That, of course, does not mean the elimination of potential conflict between China and the US in the Middle East or elsewhere. 'It is a fear for energy security, rather than a concern over energy adequacy itself that could fuel Sino–American tensions in the Middle East.'[22]

On the American intellectual scene, there are schools of thought debating the nature of the Chinese rise, whereas the Chinese intellectual scene is dominated by scholars who believe that US foreign policy is geared towards the 'containment of China' and limiting its potential global outreach. The realists led by Robert Kagan view China as a belligerent nation-state that 'wants to preserve its rule at home and expand its reach abroad.'[23] American realists advocate containment towards China, and preventing it from reaching its power potential on the global scene. On the other hand, Ikenberry and other liberal intuitionalists view China's rise as manageable within the existing framework of Western institutions in which China can be integrated and accommodated. In such a system, the US is to 'place itself at the center of a series of new global institutions where nations could come together and solve common problems.'[24] Ikenberry advocated a 'milieu-based approach'[25] to deal with China's rise, in which China is accommodated and included in international institutions. In return, China would develop a sense of a responsible stakeholder in international relations, which China has been learning to do over the past two decades, sometimes succeeding, while failing miserably at other times such as in the case of supporting the Syrian regime's oppression of its people.

Anxiety towards China also stems from the current state of the economy prevailing in the United States. Americans view China as a giant economic powerhouse that is purchasing American assets through its sovereign funds. The negative attitude towards China is heightened by the tense election rhetoric every two years in the US, in which China is regarded as a scapegoat in the failure of American economic institutions. Overall, the US and China have managed to pursue their national interests in the Middle East, sometimes co-operating, at other times competing and colliding with each other over some issues such as the Syrian crisis.

The Sino-Pakistani, US–Indian alliance and the Middle East

A less drastic, but vital, dimension is associated with the Sino-Pakistani alliance vis-à-vis the Indian–American partnership in relation to the Middle East. One of the ironies of the post-Cold War era has been the growing strategic partnership between India and the United States. While Pakistan has been consistently pro-US since the early years of the Cold War, India was under Soviet influence. Similarly for China, India is a growing regional and international powerhouse; it has its own strategic goals in the Middle East, which are identical to those of China. While US–Pakistani relations revolve around the war on international terrorism, US–Indian relations cover a wide range of issues that include trade, science and technology and nuclear co-operation. Both Pakistan and China feel threatened by the Indian–American alliance, and vehemently oppose it as both share traditional animosity towards India for various reasons, among which are territorial disputes. Consequently, China is maximizing its partnership with Pakistan.

An apparent aspect of such co-operation between the two sides is building trade, railways and the Gwadar military base in Pakistan. China's strategic goal is to monitor maritime movement in the Arabian Sea and the Hormuz Strait to ensure the flow of oil to China. Moreover, the Chinese presence in the Greater Gulf Region will enhance its partnership with Iran. China is optimistic about the prospect of building oil and gas pipelines from Iran, across Kazakhstan and Turkmenistan, and to China's western frontier province, Xinjiang. Such a pipeline will certainly assist China in its energy needs. China anticipates using the Pakistani port of Gwadar as a base for oil imports from the Gulf region, where oil tankers empty their loads to be shipped via pipelines, tankers or trains to China via Pakistan. Therefore, balancing Chinese interests with those of the US and India in the Middle East seems to be challenging, but China has masterminded the game of balance-making among contending players in the Middle East. An indication of its success is the Chinese partnership with the UAE, which has strong security and trade relations with both India and the US. The US is the UAE's major security partner, while India is the number one trade partner of the UAE. China is the UAE's second trade partner; however, China is balancing its interests well with those of the US and India. The same scenario applies to Saudi Arabia and Oman, both of which have strong security and trade relations with the US and India.

The US, China and Iraq dimension

During the Iran–Iraq War, China provided Iraq with the weapons necessary to resist Iranian conventional superiority. China opposed the Iraqi invasion of

Kuwait in the summer of 1990, and equally opposed the economic sanctions regime imposed on Iraq as well. In the mid-1990s, the sanctions regime impoverished Iraq and took a heavy toll on the population, prompting the UN to consider the Oil-for-food Programme (OFFP). China supported the OFFP and benefited from the programme, extending quality relations with Saddam Hussein's regime. However, when the US was making the case for war against Iraq in the autumn of 2002, China voted in favour of Security Council Resolution 1441 authorizing the use of force against Iraq if it failed to comply with the UN resolution on disarmament. The US invasion of Iraq occurred on 19 March 2003, and violence and instability ravaged Iraq for eight years. In voting in favour of the resolution, China violated the pattern it had established since 1971, whereby it opposes the use of force against member states. Usually, China abstains on similar resolutions, or vetoes them as it has done recently in the Syrian case in February 2012. For its support for the US policy towards Iraq, the Bush Administration allowed the Iraqi Government to honour oil agreements made between China and Iraq during the Saddam era. China was also permitted to take part in the reconstruction of Iraq. As a gesture of goodwill towards Iraq, China has also forgiven a debt of over US $4,000 million owed by the previous regime. Its goal is to maintain an active presence in Iraqi markets and boost its energy ties.

Currently, the Chinese mission of striking a balance in its relationship with Iran and Iraq is relatively trouble free, given the strategic alliance between the two Shi'ite governments ruling Baghdad and Tehran for the first time in history. High-ranking officials from both countries, China and Iraq, exchange visits regularly to validate energy agreements signed by the previous regime, reach new agreements and seek further co-operation in the area of trade. In fact, China has been very successful in renegotiating the Ahdab oil field deal signed by CNPC with the previous government in 1997. According to the revised agreement, the Ahdab oil field will produce 110,000 barrel per day (bd), up from the previous target of 90,000 bd for 20 years. CNPC would own 75 percent of the joint venture, while the Iraqi Northern Oil Company owns the remaining 25 percent. Within the same line of thinking and within the complexity of the Iranian–Iraqi–Kuwaiti triangle, China also managed to secure contracts with the Kuwait Petroleum Corporation (KPC). KPC and Sinopec are currently building the Guangdong refinery. The Guangdong refinery's cost is estimated at $9,000 million. It will be devoted to refining imported Kuwaiti oil, with a capacity of 300,000 bd. KPC is expected to supply several refineries in China with 500,000–700,000 bd by 2015.[26]

Sino–Iranian and US relations

In the period between 1953 and 1978, Iran was America's closest ally in the Gulf region and one of its close partners in the Middle East at large. Iran's military might was nurtured, developed and utilized by the US in the Gulf region. However, the oppressive nature of the Shah's regime mobilized a popular revolution that ended the Pahlavi's rule in Iran in 1979. During the era of the Shah's oppression, the Iranian people came to hold the US fully responsible for SAVAK's abuses. SAVAK (Iran's Organization of Intelligence and National Security) was the closest collaborator with the American Central Intelligence Agency (CIA) in the Middle East. When revolutionaries toppled the Shah's regime, America was identified as enemy number one of the revolution. Imam Khomeini described the US as 'the Great Satan' and used the terminology as a mobilizing force to ensure the survival of the revolutionary regime. Relations between the two countries have continued to deteriorate ever since. At times, the US and Iran confronted each other on land and at sea, an example of which is the latest American–Iranian confrontation in Iraq. Although Iran has emerged from the American occupation of Iraq and Afghanistan as the biggest beneficiary, tension continues to grow: Iran views American encirclement of the Islamic Republic as a security threat, and strives to minimize its impacts on the country. Under the Bush Administration, serious considerations were in motion towards regime change in Iran, following the Iraqi model. Shortly after Bush declared 'mission accomplished' on 1 May 2003, calls for regime change in Iran, Syria and, to some extent, territorial modifications in Saudi Arabia surfaced in political and media circles in Washington. Realizing the formidable nature of the threat, the three countries made the US mission in Iraq 'impossible.' Had the US been successful in its plan for Iraq, the political map of the Middle East would have been altered significantly.

Under the Obama Administration, a new approach towards American–Iranian relations is under way. Upon assuming the presidency, Obama made good on his promise to negotiate with Iran and resume diplomatic relations with it, should Iran reciprocate and act as a responsible member of the international community. Over the past four years, the US has engaged with Iran directly and indirectly over issues related to Iraq and to Iran's nuclear programme. While the Obama Administration has shown unprecedented levels of patience and flexibility in dealing with Iran, it has never ruled out the military option towards Iran's non-compliance with UN and IAEA's resolution on its nuclear programme. But so far, the administration continues negotiating with Iran through the P 5+1 Group, albeit keeping all options open.

The Obama Administration wants to build on European proposals in relation to the Iranian nuclear programme, but is also willing to accept a nuclear Iran that uses nuclear energy for peaceful purposes, not enriched uranium for nuclear weapons. Iran claims that its nuclear programme is meant to meet its growing energy needs, although Iran is a leading oil-producing country, but its refining capabilities do not meet its needs. There are very few countries worldwide who believe the Iranian claim that its nuclear programme is peaceful in nature. The world consensus is that Iran is developing a nuclear weapon, and all indications lead to this conclusion. The Arab countries and Israel are exceptionally alarmed by such a possibility, and they are willing to take all necessary steps to prevent it. While Israel has the military capabilities to carry out an attack on Iran's nuclear facilities, Saudi Arabia has encouraged the United States to carry out a surgical attack against Iran, and continues to push in this direction.

By examining the Iranian–American and Chinese perspectives on the current developments in the greater Middle East, one would find more commonalities than differences. China views the security of Iran and other states in the region as vital for the promotion of peace, commerce and trade. China is very supportive of efforts to rebuild Iraq and Afghanistan, a goal shared by other players as well. With regard to Afghanistan, Iran supports the idea of eradicating Sunni extremists, and the Taliban in particular, and is willing to facilitate the US mission to ensure that Sunni fundamentalists do not return to the country. China seeks to ensure the stability of Afghanistan as it hopes to build a future oil pipeline from Iran, passing through Afghanistan and ending in its western province of Xinjiang. Extremism in Afghanistan is threatening China's national security as it motivates Muslim Chinese in Xinjiang to revolt and provides them with training opportunities. Iran provided logistical support for the US mission in Afghanistan and is willing to expand in this sphere. The remaining part of the puzzle is an American–Iranian agreement in which Iran is permitted to pursue a peaceful nuclear programme, with uranium enrichment that does not exceed 20 percent. The US is ready to accept that, but Iran is uncompromising on its 'right' to a nuclear programme, a step that alarms Saudi Arabia and Israel in particular. Even if this 'limited' programme materializes, there is no guarantee that Iran would confine its activities to the peaceful aspect of nuclear energy. In fact, Saudi Arabia, Israel and other countries in the region are fully convinced that it means that Iran is developing a nuclear weapon, to which they must respond. Saudi Arabia would most certainly pursue the nuclear option, and Russia, China and Pakistan are willing to assist Saudi Arabia in joining the nuclear club.

China, the UAE and Iran

China has been steadily building a strategic trade partnership with the UAE, and already has a partnership with Iran built upon energy co-operation and deep-rooted civilizational ties. However, the growing tension since 1971 between the UAE and Iran over Iran's occupation of three islands that belong to the UAE has placed some strains on China, UAE and Iran relations. While China repeatedly reiterates its strict commitment to the territorial integrity of all nations, both sides expect China to support their claims over the islands of Abu Musa, Lesser Tunab and Greater Tunab. In early 2012 China's Premier Wen Jiabao visited the UAE and signed a joint communiqué with the UAE's Vice-President, clearly emphasizing China's support for UAE sovereignty and territorial integrity. The UAE understands it as supporting its rights over the islands, although the communiqué made no clear reference to the three islands by name. China has also reiterated its commitment to Iran's territorial integrity and sovereignty, but it opposes the escalation of the situation between the UAE and Iran. China repeatedly calls for a peaceful settlement to the conflict, but it does not seem to want to go further for fear it will receive similar treatment with its claims over the South China Sea and the disputed islands with the Philippines, Korea, Japan and Vietnam. The UAE has called on Iran to either accept the invitation for direct talks to resolve the conflict or take the dispute to the International Court of Justice. Obviously, the UAE has shown restraint and offered reasonable solutions, but Iran insists on escalating the situation, such as the provocative visit by Iran's President to the island of Abu Musa and the visit of the commander of the Revolutionary Guard in the spring of 2012. Iran has also stationed weapons systems on the islands, thus escalating and fuelling the conflict not only with the UAE, but also with the GCC and the Arab world.

Furthermore, Iran's threat to close the Strait of Hormuz because of its nuclear standoff with the international community adds more tension to the region. China has warned Iran about taking such a step as the bulk of its oil imports pass through the Strait, but China also wants to keep good relations with the UAE and Iran. If it decides to use its growing leverage towards ending the conflicts in the Gulf region, namely Iran's occupation of the UAE's three islands and Iran's nuclear standoff with the international community, then China will be making its greatest ever diplomatic accomplishment in the Middle East. However, should it refrain from providing any diplomatic initiative, continue its ties and maintain a balance without antagonizing either side, then China's diplomacy will score another accomplishment by navigating its own interests among contending forces in the Middle East.

China, Israel and Iran

The only type of relationship that exists between Israel and Iran is mutual threat and mistrust. Under the Shah's regime, Iran and Israel had a strategic partnership. Under the administration of Mohammad Khatami (1997–2005), Iran reciprocated positively towards the goodwill gestures it had received from Israel and the US. However, tensions between Israel and Iran escalated under the current Iranian president, Mahmoud Ahmadinejad, who made provocative statements against Israel, and the latter perceived Iran's quest to develop nuclear capability as existentially threatening. Israel resents Iran's support of Hamas and considers Hezbollah in Lebanon as a territorial extension of Iran on its northern borders.

Iran's support for Hamas, another declared enemy of Israel, complicates the Israeli–Iranian and Chinese relations. China needs Iran's oil and natural gas, and has a strategic partnership with Israel built around arms sales and technological co-operation. It highly values its ties with Israel, as mentioned before, as it needs advanced Israeli technology to modernize its armed forces, in addition to Israeli expertise in the areas of research and development, rural development, water technology, solar technology and agriculture. While reconciliation between Israel and Iran seems unlikely, China's primary goal is

to convince Iran and Israel that its relations with each side a
to diminish its relations with the other. Israel seems to trus
proceeding with its partnership, undeterred by the energy ties
and Iran. China has also ended its support of Iran's nucl
reduced oil imports since December 2011 and seems to be g
by the sanctions imposed on Iran. Simultaneously, it is an active participant in the P 5+1 Group that is negotiating with Iran with reference to its nuclear programme. The Group seems to be making some progress, and China once again seems to be successful in striking a balance between Iran and Israel.

China, the EU and the Middle East

China also has strong ties with the countries of the EU. The tension between China and the EU over the Middle East stems from some EU countries viewing China's energy practices and trade-dumping policy as unfair and threatening to their trade ties with the region. In order to strengthen their relationship with the Middle East and North Africa, the EU extended the Mediterranean Partnership to some countries in the region, therefore creating a sort of structure to facilitate trade, labour, tourism and political co-ordination with Mediterranean countries. Another source of tension between China and the EU that emerged recently has to do with China's stance on the Arab Spring. The EU condemned China's and Russia's double veto with reference to the Syrian crisis on 4 February 2012; it wants China to show some sympathy for the plight of the Syrian people and to stop blocking international efforts at the Security Council to curb the Syrian regime's transgression against its own people. China views such efforts as a regime-change policy and a step that undermines international law and the UN charter.

The EU also wants China to show some support for sanctions against Iran's nuclear programme, and encourages it to play a more active role in the UN's peace-keeping forces. While China wants to contribute to the UN's peace missions and wants to project the image of contributing to stability and world peace, it does not seem to be willing to contribute forces commensurate with its international presence and its economic strength. Its contribution remains symbolic, and its contingent suffered heavy losses when Israel bombed UN forces in Lebanon in 2006 during its war with Hezbollah. China appointed a Special Envoy to the Middle East prior to the eruption of the Arab Spring, but it remains reluctant to actively engage in the management of the Arab–Israeli conflict. It has advocated a peaceful settlement to the conflict for the past six decades, but seems unwilling to become a member of the Quartet and limits itself to encouraging both sides in an effort to revive the peace process. China neither wants to compete with the US or the EU, nor wants to be associated with the failed peace process. Rather, it wants to be viewed as a strategic partner for both sides: they understand China's position in the process, as well as its perspective and limitations. Massive trade imbalances and the EU's economic troubles provide leeway for China to manoeuvre its policies and interests relatively immune from the EU's criticism, and to strip the latter of any punitive or retaliatory policies against China across the Middle East.

China, India and the Middle East

Another triangular dimension of Sino–Middle Eastern relations is with India. Both countries have strategic interests and partnerships with Middle Eastern countries, but bilateral relations between the two rising Asian giants has been antagonistic at times and mired with mutual suspicion. Recently, China put its territorial dispute with India aside in favour of a more reconciliatory policy. Their bilateral trade is increasing, shaped by mutual interests and competition, and sometimes by conflict. Both India and China compete for trade partnerships with the Middle East. For instance, the UAE's first trade partner is India, followed by China. Although China is Saudi Arabia's major business partner, India is determined to increase the volume of its trade with Saudi Arabia, while China is determined to unseat India as the UAE's top trading partner. India influenced China in contributing forces to UN peace missions in the Middle East – an aspect in which India has been a pioneer since the 1950s.

Both India and China are major trade and energy partners with Iran, both are affected by sanctions imposed on it, and both are scrambling to find alternative energy providers. China seems to be more successful, although India has not suffered any oil supply shortage as a result of manipulation of the sanctions regime. For example, India pays for its oil in gold instead of US dollars or using banking institutions. Saudi Arabia on its own is capable of providing world markets with Iran's total share, estimated at 4.245 mbd.[27] Both India and China agree with Iran on its right to develop nuclear energy for peaceful use; both agree on the dangers of nuclearization of the Middle East and are willing to provide 'good offices' to ease the standoff between the West and Iran. China is in a much better position than India in this respect given that it is a member of the P 5+1 Group currently negotiating with Iran.

Both India and China are developing a strategic partnership with Israel with arms sales at its core, but both are viewed as supportive of the Palestinians' rights and the peace process. In spite of their support for the peace process, both countries seem to be reluctant to play a major role in reviving the peace process. India has similar reservations on the process and wants to be viewed as supportive from a distance, associated with the success rather than the failure of the process. Current conditions on the Israeli side do not seem to be conducive to peace as the current coalition governing Israel is pursuing policies designed to sabotage the process, not advance it. Therefore, both China and India realize their limitations and the limitations of the Quartet. Overall, although China and India are competing over trade opportunities, especially in the Gulf region, they seem to be accommodating each other's interests. China follows the 'all out' approach in markets such as the

UAE, Kuwait and Saudi Arabia; India leads in the Omani and UAE markets. The UAE market is highly competitive, and China views it as a primary hub for its external trade. India's advantage is in the labour sector. It is estimated that there are 1.5 million Indian workers compared with 200,000 Chinese expatriates in the UAE.

Sino–Algerian and Moroccan relations

An aspect of China's successful diplomacy is the balance it has established between Morocco and Algeria. The two countries are traditional foes feuding over the Western Sahara. While Sino–Algerian relations are deeply rooted in the War of Independence in the 1950s, Sino-Moroccan relations are still developing, but at a fast pace. China supported the Algerian Revolution and its War of Independence from France. It recognized the Algerian provisional government in 1958, four years before its official independence. Both countries maintained friendship during the Cold War and supported each other's causes: Algeria co-sponsored the readmission of China to the UN in 1971 and promoted China's economic co-operation with Africa. Their friendship prospered in the Openness Era, and trade grew steadily between them. In 2001, Sino–Algerian bilateral trade was estimated at $200 million, and grew steadily to $4.5 thousand million in 2010.

China is Algeria's second trade partner after France. It is also home to a prosperous Chinese community of merchants and construction workers, estimated at 45,000. There are 50 major Chinese corporations in Algeria, primarily working on construction and infrastructure projects. Algeria is a wealthy country free from international debt and endowed with $173,000 million in sovereignty funds, but lacking basic housing services, highways and sufficient health and educational services. The powerful Chinese construction companies have a lead in these sectors and are currently assisting Algeria in implementing its Five Year Plan, 2010–14, seeking to remedy the shortages in these sectors. Chinese oil corporations are also determined to compete strongly in the Algerian oil sector, even though it is dominated by American and European corporations.

China and Morocco established diplomatic relations in 1958, but the pace of trade relations has accelerated since the early 1990s. China is Morocco's third trade partner: while China provides consumer goods and services, it imports phosphates, citrus and other related products. China offers considerable expertise in infrastructure projects, fisheries and clean energy.

Sino-Turkish and Iranian relations

China has also been striking a balance between Iran and Turkey, both of which compete fiercely over dominance in the Middle East and Central Asia. Iran and Turkey clashed several times over issues related to Iraq, Syria and the Arab–Israeli conflict. Iran supports the Syrian regime in its oppression of its people, whereas Turkey supports the Syrian people and the Syrian National Council in its quest for regime change. Both countries are currently clashing over the situation in Iraq. Iran supports the sectarian Maliki Government, whereas Turkey supports the broader Iraqi coalition that includes Sunnis, Shi'a, Kurds and Turkmen. While Turkey is supportive of the peace process, Iran supports Hezbollah and Hamas in their opposition to the peace process. Both countries provide a different model of governance for the Middle East and Central Asia. Since 1991, Turkey and Iran have been in constant competition over influence in Central Asia.

Whereas Turkey provides a moderate model of government, Iran provides a hardline system inspired by the role of the clergy in politics. Given the complexity of Turkish–Iranian relations, China's relations with Iran centres around oil, natural gas, minerals and consumer products, whereas its relations with Turkey tend to have a much deeper perspective. In addition to trade, markets and investment, China needs Turkey's strict commitment to the One China policy. Turkey's ethnic ties with Xinjiang's Uyghur people makes Turkey of paramount importance to China. The Turkish people originated in Xinjiang and continue to honour their ethnic ties with their fellow Uyghur people, who are under China's direct rule. However, China has recently managed to extract a clear commitment from the Turkish government to its sovereignty over Xinjiang in the latest visit of China's Vice-President Xi Jingpin to Turkey in February 2012. In exchange, China pledged to provide Turkey with advanced missile systems, open its markets to Turkish industries and enhance cultural relations. Turkey needs missiles the US has declined a recent Turkish request to purchase a similar system. Turkey is also eager to find markets for its industries, and China's huge market is a great potential to Turkish industries to purchase similar systems.

China, the state and opposition in the Middle East

In the most recent dimension to Sino–Middle Eastern relations, China has been walking the thinnest rope of all to strike a balance between the state and the opposition in the Arab world, within the Arab Spring paradigm. Like many other countries, China was taken by surprise by the epic changes in the Arab world. Its reaction was marked by confusion, inconsistency and, at times, total support for oppressive regimes in the region. The challenge now is to find a neutral path. Through Special Envoys to the Middle East and Syria, and through other foreign policy apparatuses, China has proclaimed that it stands with the legitimate rights of the Arab people for reform, stability and development but, at the same time, it opposes the use of force against oppressive regimes, such as in Syria. It also shields itself behind principles of territorial integrity and non-intervention in the internal affairs of other nations, in accordance with the UN's Charter but, in doing so, it provides protection for dictatorial regimes in the Middle East and risks the wrath of the Arab people. In fact, for the first time, the Chinese flag was burnt in protest at China's use of its veto to block a resolution condemning the Syrian government on 4 February 2012. While China vetoed the resolution on several grounds (Chapter 4), and is unwilling to substantiate its proclaimed support for legitimate rights by removing the veto to UN resolutions against oppressive regimes in the region, the Arabs insist on China showing some sympathy to the plight of the Syrian people. Otherwise, they risk some economic consequences.

China fears that any posture in support of the Arab Spring will have ramifications at home; the revolutionary fever spreading across the region might reach China, something China will never tolerate. It is dealing with its own rebellious territories of Xinjiang and Tibet, which are threatening China's territorial unity. China risks damaging bilateral relations with the Arab world and its people–people relations. In fact, democratic and conservative forces in the Middle East have condemned China's policy towards Syria and called for a boycott of its products. China also risks destroying friendly relations with the new governments taking shape in Tunisia, Morocco, Egypt and, potentially, Jordan and Yemen. Such governments will not be forgiving if China exaggerates its support for dictatorial regimes. It already has difficulties in re-entering the Libyan market given that it provided the Gaddafi regime with weapons to bomb Libyan cities up to the very end of the conflict, and even after the passing of the UN's arms embargo on Libya. The Arabs are sympathetic to the Syrian people, and are bewildered by the level of violence committed by the state against civilians. China's interests require that it refrain from being sympathetic to dictatorships, particularly in view of recent indications that dictatorships are not best for business. Trade relations and economic development are the priority for new governments in the region. China should capitalize on this spirit and embrace change in the region, rather than oppose it and lengthen the suffering of the Syrian people in particular.

Conclusion

Against all odds, China is securing its interests among contending partners in the Middle East. China managed to build a strategic partnership with Israel, simultaneously building similar partnerships with the Arab side, and maintaining its traditional support for the Palestinian people. China manages its relations with the US in the Middle East skilfully as well. It provides the US with some support for its foreign policy in the region; the US reciprocates by providing security for Chinese oil shipments from the region. China has also maintained a remarkable balance with Iran and the Arab world. While China has strong bilateral relations with Iran revolving around oil, trade and arms sales, it has managed to deal with Arab concerns in relation to Iran. The Arab, American and Israeli sides are concerned about Iran's nuclear programme. Israel views such a programme as existentially threatening, whereas Saudi Arabia and other Arab countries view it as destabilizing to the volatile

Middle East. China is assuming an active role in bringing about and maintaining Iran's participation in the P 5+1 negotiations that have taken place over the past five years. In terms of the revolutions occurring in the Arab world since December 2010, China is failing to capture the depth of Arab resentment against the status quo in the region. To deal with such resentment, China appointed a Special Envoy to Syria, a Middle East Special Envoy and renewed its foreign policy apparatus. In spite of these political appointments, its support for the Syrian regime undermines any goodwill that China has towards the Arab people.

4 China's reaction to the Arab Spring

The upsurge of the Arab Spring caught China by surprise. China's foreign policy operates in the Middle East under the premise that authoritarian Arab regimes are immutable, especially the dictatorial regimes in Syria, Libya, Egypt, Tunisia and Yemen. For this reason, violent revolutions in these countries came as a shock to China. They reminded the nation of the massive Tiananmen Square protest in 1989 and the subsequent violence. It took China an entire decade to recuperate from this internal haemorrhage, although the scars of the massacre will be permanently present in the collective psyche of the Chinese people. This chapter proposes to examine China's reaction to the Arab uprisings, to open a debate on China's lack of a systematic approach to deal with the revolutions and to inquire about China's lack of a coherent policy towards the Arab Spring.

China's inconsistencies in its foreign policy stem from its repeated claims that it stands by the Arab people but, at the same time, it provides unlimited weaponry to their oppressors, the authoritarian Arab regimes across the region. This duplicity makes China the second most disliked country in the region after Russia. Its policy is reactive, as in the cases of Libya, Yemen and Egypt, and cautiously proactive and confrontational in the case of Syria, where China seems to have underestimated the reaction of the world towards its lack of support for UN efforts to protect Syrian civilians. In fact, the double vetoes cast by China at the Security Council on 4 February 2012, in solidarity with Russia in support of the Syrian dictator, incited the wrath and resentment of the Arab people.

China's failure to articulate a clear policy towards the ongoing developments in the Arab world also threatens China's growing economic and energy interests in the entire Middle East. Suddenly, religious edicts are issued by Muslim clergy to boycott China's products and to protest about its policies worldwide.

Arab Spring

The Arab Spring is a term widely used in the media and literature to refer to the revolutionary Arab momentum that gathered strength towards the end of 2010 and continues today. It accomplished major gains by toppling some dictatorial regimes in Egypt, Libya, Yemen and Tunisia. The peak of the Arab Spring was the demise of the Mubarak regime in Egypt on 11 February 2011, 18 days after massive demonstrations erupted in the country. After decades, if not centuries, of systematic humiliation, the Arab people demanded freedom and justice. The conditions that brought about the revolutionary momentum were similar to revolutions throughout history in Russia, China and elsewhere: a sense of humiliation and loss of dignity, corruption, repression, high unemployment rates, inflated prices of basic commodities, the spread of poverty, concentration of wealth in the hands of a few, cronyism and nepotism. The stacking of these conditions motivated younger generations to revolt but, unlike previous revolutions, the success of the uprising was mostly due to the quick, systemic organization of supporters accomplished only through effective current social networks.

The spark that ignited the Arab Spring came when Mohammed Bouazizi, a fruit vendor in the town of Sidi Bouzid in central Tunisia, set himself ablaze on 17 December 2010. Bouazizi's story expresses the abuse by security agencies of the Tunisian people, similar in many ways to widespread abuse across the Arab world. On the day of his immolation, Bouazizi prepared himself as usual before dawn and headed to the market pushing his fruit cart. Two police officers, including Fedya Hamdi, a female officer, stopped him, harassed him and began to help themselves to fruit from his cart. Bouazizi's story was widely reported, and neatly narrated by the *Washington Post* reporter Marc Fischer. According to Fischer, police forces were notorious for 'taking bagfuls of fruit without so much as a nod toward payment. The cops took visible pleasure in subjecting the vendors to one indignity after another – fining them, confiscating their scales, even ordering them to carry their stolen fruit to the cops' cars.'[1] Seeing his nephew in trouble from this harassment, his uncle spoke to the town's chief of police and asked him to intervene. In turn, the chief called the officers and ordered them to stop but, although they obeyed orders momentarily, they later came back to the market to punish the young man. Outraged by her chief's reprimand, Hamdi became violent with Bouazizi. She grabbed baskets of his apples and put them in the police car. Bouazizi tried to stop her but she pushed him and he fell to the ground. When he stood up, Hamdi slapped Bouazizi in the face in front of dozens of eyewitnesses and spat at him while he, angered and outraged, resisted and finally wept in front of over fifty vendors, mostly men. It was reported that he said in protest: 'Why are you doing this to me? I'm a simple person, and I just want to work.'[2] His humiliation by the female officer was beyond tolerance.

In Arab-Islamic culture, honour, dignity and pride reside in one's face, and violating the sanctity of these three principles is beyond anyone's tolerance. If being slapped is already one of the worst humiliations, for this to be done by a woman is even more insulting to a man's dignity and manhood. Bouazizi went to the City Hall to complain, but was told to leave because no one would talk to him, so he went back to the market and publicly announced that the whole world would soon hear about police abuse of vendors in that market and how corrupt the system was as a whole. He grabbed a container of petrol, walked to the municipality, poured the petrol on himself and set himself on fire. A video was taken of the whole incident, and later a blogger uploaded it to Facebook. *Al Jazeera* played the video on its major news broadcasts. His townspeople came to his assistance, protested and attacked government buildings, the symbols of oppression. As usual, the police's reaction was violent, but the protest had already spread all over the country. Bouazizi passed away on 4 January 2011, three weeks after the incident.

Widespread protests in Tunisia raised the ceiling of popular demands. No longer did the people ask for protection from police brutality, but for entire regime change. The massive protest forced Bin Ali, the dictator of Tunisia for 23 years, to flee to Saudi Arabia on 14 January 2011, only 10 days after Bouazizi's death. The wind of the Tunisian revolution began blowing in all directions. Neighbouring Libya, Egypt, Morocco and even the non-neighbouring countries of Bahrain, Jordan, Yemen and Syria erupted in massive anti-regime protests. Observing the success of the Tunisian revolt, the Egyptian masses were encouraged and gathered strength to mount a challenge against Mubarak's authoritarian regime. The Facebook and Twitter generation led the revolution, along with the organized Muslim Brotherhood and Salafis, and then the Christian minority, intellectuals, secular movements and political oppositions. After 18 days, a sustained massive campaign of demonstrations toppled the Mubarak regime. The price was exceptionally high when security agencies, especially the Secret Police, the Central Security Force of the Ministry of Interior, and *Baltajia*, their paramilitary troopers, shot over 800 demonstrators. The armed forces took over the Government and, because of their resistance and the resistance of the status quo forces in the country, Egypt has been going through a painful transition to stability on its long road towards democratization.

By comparison, the Tunisian revolution was successful in that it experienced a smooth transition of power with parliamentary elections and the swift, orderly and peaceful formation of a new Government. Other countries such as Syria, Yemen and Bahrain have been less fortunate as their revolutionary fervour continues to this day with much resistance and much bloodshed. The Syrian revolution has been by far the most tragic aspect of the Arab Spring. Syria is a country rich in its revolutionary history, endowed with an abundance of natural resources, but deprived of the minimum levels of freedom since 1969. Syria is '[O]ne of the most economically viable of the Middle Eastern countries, Syria has considerable arable land, reasonable water resources and a well-educated population.'[3] Syria was part of the Ottoman Empire from 1516 to 1918, when Arab revolutionaries established the short-lived Arab Kingdom of Syria from 1919 to 1921. The kingdom was destroyed by France, the mandating power over Syria and what is currently Lebanon as part of the post-WWI settlements.

For the period from 1921 to 1946, the Syrian people repeatedly revolted against French colonialism, resulting in their declaration of independence in

1946. In the post-independence era, several military coups occurred and Syria entered into unity with Egypt from 1958 to 1961. Hafez Al Assad, the Minister of Defence, led a coup in 1970 and ruled Syria with an iron fist until his death in 1991. In 1982, Hama, a major city in Syria, revolted against Assad's regime, to which Assad responded with an overwhelming level of force killing thousands of his opponents and bombarding the city with artillery and air attacks until it was subdued. His son, Bashar, succeeded him at the age of thirty-four. The Syrian people hoped that Bashar would be a reformer and bring substantial changes. However, Bashar followed the same abusive structures established by his father 30 years ago. Seeing the successes of the Arab Spring materializing in Tunisia, Libya, Egypt and Yemen, the Syrian people began demanding reform in March 2011. Their modest demands and the peaceful demonstrations were met by extreme levels of force similar to that used in Hama in 1982. The demonstration began in the city of Der'a on the border with Jordan and spread all over the country. Since March 2011, the UN estimates that over 15,000 people have been killed by the Government. All attempts to bring about a peaceful or a military solution to the Syrian crisis have failed so far, partly due to China's and Russia's opposition. Table 4.1 illustrates the number of casualties of the revolution for the period from March 2011 to 9 June 2012.

In addition to the massive number of casualties, Syria's security agencies have rounded up thousands of civilians, including women and children, subjecting them to torture. Table 4.2 illustrates the number of prisoners for the period from March 2011 to 9 June 2012.

China's reaction to the Arab Spring

The idea of massive protests in Tunisian or Egyptian style petrifies the authorities in Beijing. Immediately, and concomitant with the unfolding of events in Tunisia, Yemen, Libya and Egypt, in particular, Chinese policy circles articulated a sort of reaction that sought to downplay the happenings in the Middle East. Media outlets and state security apparatuses monitored the online flow of information, blocking some websites and the search for words related to the revolutions in Egypt and other Arab countries. The news on the Egyptian case in particular did not receive merited coverage. Media outlets were instructed to use the Xinhua Press agency's reports only. China also pursued a policy of diverting popular attention towards state efficiency in repatriating thousands of Chinese workers stranded in the Middle East and North Africa. The media highlighted China's accomplishments in the areas of economic growth, employment, keeping inflation in check, services, rising wages and generously provided education, health and employment services. Party officials regularly visited rural China, thus encouraging the policy of 'closeness' between the people and state officials. Furthermore, Chinese media highlighted China's distinguished model of development and efforts to achieve harmony, social peace and economic development. In juxtaposition,

Table 4.1 Number of people killed in the Syrian Revolution from March 2011 to 5 July 2012

City/province	*Number of deaths*
Damascus	356
Reef Damascus	1,664
Homs	5,236
Dera	1,503
Idlib	2,223
Aleppo	599
Deir Al-Zour	752
Al Raga	57
Al Swida	11
Hama	1,720
Lattakia	322
Tartous	36
Hasaka	98
Kenitra	21
Non-civilian	1,267
Civilian	13,332
Women	787
Men	12,563
Female child	366
Male child	983
Total at 5 July 2012	14,599

Source: Constructed from data provided by the Center for Documentation of Violations in Syria, at http://vdc-sy.org/index.php/ar/

Table 4.2 Number of prisoners of the Syrian Revolution from March 2011 to 5 July 2012

City/province	*Number of prisoners*
Damascus	3,078
Reef Damascus `	6,575
Homs	1,231
Dera	5,565
Idlib	1,594
Aleppo	1,239
Deir Al-Zour	727
Al Raga	522
Al Swida	209
Hama	1,781
Lattakia	712
Tartous	576
Hasaka	387
Kenitra	31
Women	327
Men	24,573
Female child	17
Male child	631
Total at 5 July 2012	25,553

Source: constructed from data provided by the Center for Documentation of Violations in Syria, at http://vdc-sy.org/index.php/ar/

security agencies eliminated any potential political assembly or sted potential political rioters and blocked their contacts. Media ...ited out that 'Western-style' institutions and norms ill suited the ..ople of Africa and the Middle East and 'colour' revolutions would not bring about real democracy.[4]

China struggled and continues to struggle to articulate a clear foreign policy towards the Arab Spring. The concern is both domestic and foreign. On the domestic side looms the possibility of massive popular protests similar to Egypt's that might threaten the stability of the communist regime. A related matter is the impact that Middle Eastern revolutions might have on the Xinjiang, Tibet and Taiwan issues. On the foreign side, the Middle East represents a 'national security' concern for China, given that China currently depends on the region for approximately 45 percent of its oil, and its economic growth and domestic stability are contingent to a large extent on these imports. Its growing reliance on natural gas and other types of materials is also a major concern should stability become a major issue in the Middle East. Therefore, it behoves China to have a clear policy towards the changes in the region to maintain peace at home and protect its interests in the Arab world. On principle, China opposes the Arab revolutions because they destabilize the region and potentially serve as motivational success stories to ethnic separatists and urban democratic forces in China. The following section provides some analysis of China's opposition to the Arab Spring, and discerns the reasons behind its support for dictatorial regimes in the Middle East.

Realism or confusion

China's opposition to the Arab Spring is well grounded in Realpolitik, that is in realism and its practical foreign policy implementation. Opposing it, China is defending its national interests and its interests in the Middle East as it perceives revolutions as threatening to its national security, domestic stability and prosperity. At home, the Arab Spring could inspire the Uyghur of Xinjiang and Tibetans in particular to revolt. This would be extremely threatening to China's national security. Urban democratic forces, student movements, disillusioned labourers, displaced farmers and the unemployed or laid off could be inclined to join demonstrations, and a revolution could potentially gather momentum in the country. To such a scenario, China's reaction would definitely be violent. The Chinese army, unlike the Tunisian army in its response to the uprising in its country, would not hesitate to use force against civilians, as it did in Tiananmen Square in 1989. In this sense, it is much closer to the Syrian, Russian and Belarusian model of armies in their use of force against unarmed civilians. If national instability should arise, and China become embroiled in civil strife, ethnic conflicts and regional wars, its economic growth, stability and prosperity would most certainly be affected, and the world economy as well. A violent crackdown similar to or much more violent than that in Tiananmen Square in 1989 would consume China for many decades to come, and its worldwide image as a rising nation that seeks peace, harmony and co-operation with all nations would be tarnished.

China has always opposed Western intervention in the Arab world, but was never as aggressive as it has been over the past year with respect to the Syrian crisis. Analysing its views on the entire project of change in the Middle East, analysts, observers and policy makers are puzzled by China's steadfastness before and after the double veto of the UN draft resolution on Syria on 4 February 2012 in defending the Syrian regime. China did not use its power of veto against a similar Security Council Resolution that authorized the use of force to halt state violence against the people in Libya on 17 March 2011. However, China first co-ordinated with Russia to use the veto and oppose a UN role in Syria, then modified its opposition towards mid-April 2012 to accommodate UN observers. China's Minister for Foreign Affairs, Yang Jiechi, stated that the abstention vote on the Libyan resolution was based on China 'taking into account the concerns and positions of the Arab countries and the Arab League and the special situation in Libya at that time. China joined some other countries to vote in abstention.'[5] However, the Arab League was far less involved in the Libyan case than in the Syrian crisis over the past year. In fact, the Arab League has never been so involved in any issue as it has in the Syrian case, except, of course, in the Palestinian question. Therefore, Jiechi's response reveals a deep fear of repercussions among Chinese leaders in the spread of revolutionary fervour from the Middle East to China and elsewhere.

China's veto underlines the claim that Security Council Resolution S/2012/77 and its subsequent General Assembly Resolution GA/11207 go far beyond the charter of the UN. However, a careful examination of the resolutions reveals that they are reasonable in calling for the government of Syria to halt violence and observe basic human rights in the country. Both Resolutions S/2012/77 and GA/11207 basically condemn human rights violations by the Syrian authorities, call on them to immediately end such violations and killings, cease violence, release prisoners, withdraw Syrian military and armed forces from cities and towns, guarantee the right to demonstrate, provide access to the Arab League and its advisers and an inclusive political process. Furthermore, the resolutions fully support the mission of the Arab League and demand that the Syrian authorities co-operate with the UN's High Commissioner's office for human rights, allow safe and unhindered access for humanitarian assistance and request that the Secretary General report to the Council in 21 days, in co-ordination with the Arab League and, in the event of non-compliance, to consider further measures.[6]

Chinese and Russian envoys, in addition to a few other countries supportive of the Syrian government such as Venezuela, Iran and Algeria, rejected the condemnation of human rights violations in Syria. They also demanded the inclusion of the opposition to the condemnation article in any future discussion on the Syrian crisis, to which supporters of the resolution never objected. The draft resolution clearly 'condemns all violence, regardless of its origin, and in this regard demands that all parties in Syria, including armed groups, immediately stop all violence or reprisals, including attacks against state institutions, in accordance with the League of Arab States' initiative.'[7] Iran, Algeria and Venezuela also rejected the Arab plan, as the League proposed a transfer of power from Assad to his vice president, similar to the Yemeni plan for power transfer as deliberated by the GCC.[8] Russia's manoeuvres in the Syrian crisis also have domestic and international dimensions. Domestically, aside from potential world criticism of Putin's continued crackdown on the independence movement in Chechnya and Daghistan, Russia hopes a confrontation with the West over Syria will boost domestic support for Putin's third-term presidency. Internationally, the reaction of the world was complete outrage towards Chinese and Russian rejection of such a basic, reasonable draft. It did not call for regime change, the use of force or for the fragmentation of Syria, as China and Russia claimed. However, from a Realpolitik perspective, China's options seem to have been limited to one choice: the veto.

Inviting change at home?

China is fearful of any mild, sympathetic or even neutral posture being interpreted as tacit support for the Arab Spring. Based on this fear, China reasons that, if it had supported the UN resolutions on Syria, it would have been inviting change at home and accepting international intervention in potential developments on Chinese soil, should an 'Arab Spring' materialize there. China objects to Article 15 of the draft resolution, which states that the Security Council 'decides to review implementation of this resolution within 21 days and, in the event of non-compliance, to consider further measures.'[9] Clearly, China views words such as 'to consider further measures' as a threat to use force against the Syrian government, given that similar language was used in UN SC/173 on Libya. Furthermore, after the 1989 Tiananmen Square massacre, China has vehemently opposed any language in Security Council resolutions that might hint at military intervention. A deviation from this rule was its support for the US draft resolution UNSC 1441 on 2 November 2002 authorizing force to compel Iraq to provide access to its nuclear installations for inspection. Usually, China has abstained on resolutions related to Iraq since 1990, and was less blunt in its opposition to SC/173 on Libya in 2011 by abstaining, not vetoing, it. China clearly views calls for human rights protection, freedom or democracy as calls for 'regime change'; therefore, any support for such movements in the Arab world tacitly implies undermining the communist system in China and its totalitarian allies in the region. This position of opposing such an agenda is non-negotiable to the ruling elites in China. Therefore, should China appear to be supportive of UN resolutions against dictatorial regimes or project the image of being supportive of Western agendas through abstention, it would undermine itself and its own regime.

Regime stability and continuity

The primary goals of both domestic and foreign policy are stability of the Chinese communist regime, territorial integrity and non-intervention in its internal affairs. To achieve such goals, China will not be deterred from using force at home and abroad. The Arab Spring clearly threatens all these principles in the following manner: for the first time in modern history, the Arab Middle East has inspired revolutionary, democratic change by defending freedom, justice and peaceful transition. Therefore, China fears that the contagious spirit of the Arab Spring will inspire ethnic separatists and urban opposition in the country. The violent uprisings of the Arab people and their willingness to sacrifice themselves for their freedom, as in the cases of Syria, Libya, Yemen and elsewhere, is seen from a Chinese point of view as an impetus for rebellious Xinjiang in Western China and Tibet. The Xinjiang-Uyghur people and the Tibetans see the Arab model as inspiring and transferable. The Uyghur, in particular, have a strong religious and cultural attachment to the Middle East through Islam and Central Asia, in particular, and are therefore viewed as receptive to influences from the region. The crackdown on separatist movements in those two regions in particular is a matter of national security to China. In the Middle East, democratic regimes after the revolutions will be much less committed to the 'One-China' policy in comparison with authoritarian regimes. Democratic governments across the Arab world will be sympathetic to the right to self-determination for Taiwan, Tibet and Xinjiang and support their quest for independence, whereas existing authoritarian regimes are entirely in support of the PRC's official views on this matter. It is hard to see a democratic government in Tunisia, Libya, Egypt, Jordan, Yemen, Iraq and elsewhere being supportive of China's subjugation of the Uyghur or the Tibetans, especially if these governments come from an Islamic or even purely secular background.

Politically speaking, China shields its foreign policy goals under claims of strict commitment to international law, which clearly prohibits nations from intervening in the internal affairs of other countries. However, China fears that any intervention in the domestic affairs of Syria and other Arab countries within the paradigm of the Arab Spring would be a precedent in international law to be potentially used as grounds for intervention in China's domestic affairs. It fears that international organizations and Western countries are embedding the seeds of intervention in China's affairs by smoothing the ground with Security Council resolutions towards the Middle East, given that China is vulnerable to similar interventions with respect to major internal issues such as Tibet and Xinjiang.

China also opposes the Arab Spring because it threatens the three major pillars of interest in the region: arms sales, trade and oil. Countries under pressure such as Libya, Syria and Egypt are consumers of China's weapons, and the latter does not wish to jeopardize its position in armament markets among tough worldwide competition. China competes with second layer arms producers such as Brazil and South Africa. China imports substantial quantities of oil, gas, minerals and raw materials from the Middle East, and exports consumer goods at competitive prices, but the Arab Spring is synonymous with instability, conflict, turbulence and uprisings. While China survived the economic crisis of the 1990s and global market turbulence over the past five years, it views change in the Middle East and North Africa as a personal affront from Western businesses and corporations, and believes that the advancements of Western dominance in the region could be threatening to its energy resources in particular. The triumph of the various revolutions is perceived in China as threatening to its energy and trade interests in the Middle East as well. However, there are no grounds for such perceived threats, as democratic governments will be eager to continue economic ties with China.

Nevertheless, the status quo is unsustainable from the Arab people's point of view. Arabs cannot be forced to live under authoritarian regimes simply because these serve external interests best, in addition to their own selfish interests. China's growing portfolio in the Middle East is measured against Western dominance in the region since 1950, but the Arab Spring might just prove to be a great avenue for the Arab people to build their own independence, and enter into economic and political partnerships on an equal footing with the rest of the world, China included.

Revolutionary agitation in China

There are several essential elements currently assembling in China that might sustain a momentum similar to the revolutions flaring up across the Middle East. They can create dissent and disruption, such as land seizure, unemployment, corruption and environmental degradation, in addition to struggles for human rights and political freedoms. Security agencies' harassment of Tibetans and Uyghur is another major destabilizing element. In fact, there are thousands of protests reported annually against the Chinese authorities. Adding to the complexity of China's ethnic situation and urban dissent, rapid economic growth is destabilizing by nature, but China seems to be dealing with high economic growth rates much better than Egypt, for example, which experienced a 5.4 percent growth rate in the past three years, although it is difficult to compare a country with a population of 1.3 thousand million people with Egypt's 80 million. Nevertheless, China is taking all the steps necessary to bring inflation under control, dealing with rising unemployment rates, cracking down on land seizure by corrupt political officials and business interests and, overall, showing more transparency in dealing with rampant corruption cases. It also provides generous support to expand educational facilities and admission to higher education institutions, and more access to health care and rural development. In spite of these efforts, revolutionary agitation cannot be totally ruled out. On its own, land seizure from poor peasants to be sold to developers mobilizes popular resentment towards party apparatuses that enrich only themselves; so the spirit of freedom and democratization is not far from Chinese popular conversation. The growing middle class, in particular, realizes that the level of freedom it enjoys is not commensurate with its economic accomplishments; therefore, the demand for freedom will only intensify.

Ethnic tensions destabilize. The Uyghur and the Tibetan regions are prime areas for revolutionary agitation. Xinjiang, in particular, seems to be highly flammable given that the Uyghur believe they are hopelessly under 'colonialism' and the imperial colonization of China.[10] The 2009 riots and ethnic tension between the Han and the Uyghur show that it is only a matter of time before western China explodes again. The resentment towards state assimilation has reached the point of combustion in Xinjiang. The continued tension in that province threatens China's foreign policy and bilateral and multilateral relations with the Muslim Middle East and Central Asia. China has strong economic relations with Turkey, a rising political and economic powerhouse in the region, and wishes to keep it that way, but the ethnic attachment of Turkey to the Uyghur in western China threatens Sino-Turkish relations should China find itself in a revolutionary situation in Xinjiang that requires a major military offensive.

American scholarship and policy circles have been keen on highlighting and not ruling out a Chinese revolution in the Arab Spring style, but such a tendency is heavily critiqued by China as intervention in its internal affairs. Last year, global media reported that John Huntsman, the US Ambassador to China, was present at a protest rally organized by some dissidents near Tiananmen Square in Beijing. Although Huntsman insisted that his presence was accidental – he was just strolling with his family and had nothing to do with inciting a rebellion or violence – the Chinese media strongly criticized his presence, calling on the US and its diplomats to refrain from intervening in China's internal affairs. The images of Huntsman surrounded by protesters could have been read in different ways: on the one hand, they could have signalled tacit US support for any uprising in China; on the other hand, they could have been part of a political tactic on the ambassador's part to send a message to policy circles at home that he intended to run for the presidency, and that he would have been more than willing to support democratic forces in China if he got the Republican nomination and won the elections.

Huntsman did run for the Republican nomination, but lost. Regardless, the incident most definitely complicated US–Chinese relations and added more tension to the situation. On Saturday 4 February 2012, Senator John McCain told Zhang Zhijun, the Chinese vice foreign minister who was on a panel with McCain and Kissinger in a security conference in Munich, that 'the Arab Spring is coming to China', pointing to the wave of Tibetans setting themselves on fire in China. Zhang termed the notion of an Arab Spring-style uprising in China as 'no more than fantasy.'[11] There were eighteen cases of self-immolation reported in Tibet and the western Chinese province of Sichuan.

Authoritarian solidarity

As much as democratic regimes do not fight each other, authoritarian regimes defend each other and support each other's agenda. China shares such an agenda with existing authoritarian regimes in the Middle East and Russia, all of whom feel that they have been under Western assault since 1989, with global advancements in democracy and the demise of communist regimes worldwide. If, on the one hand, the current Chinese process of development pursues its road to growth, reform and development at its own pace, and seems to be economically liberal but politically authoritarian, on the other hand, authoritarian regimes in the Middle East are developed neither economically nor politically. Even if some economic growth occurs, such as in Egypt, authoritarian structures benefit from such growth, not the deprived masses. Therefore, China sees defending itself and its allies in the region from the Western democratic offensive as a priority, at this point. This explains the unlimited support provided by other autocracies such as Russia, Iran, Venezuela and Algeria to the Syrian regime. It also explains China vetoing the UN resolution on 4 February 2012 in its efforts to show solidarity and 'support' for Russia's own veto. Authoritarian solidarity also explains Venezuela supplying Syria's Banias refinery with a load of two oil tankers over a period of 10 months.

Authoritarian interdependence

Solidarity implies interdependence. At least since the fall of the Soviet Union, authoritarian regimes owe their survival to dependence on each other in the areas of economic assistance and energy resources. Countries such as North Korea, Cuba and Burma would not have survived had it not been for the support of China, Russia and Venezuela in particular. China and Russia are clearly co-ordinating their policies towards the Arab Spring as if they depended on each other's support, especially in the UN. Taking the heat and sharing the blame for vetoing the UN resolutions softens the outrage towards both China and Russia.[12] Russian military support and Chinese trade, arms sales and oil are fundamental for Syria's regime to survive, and now even more so as both countries seem to have gone a long way in their support for Assad and against the setting up of any future democratic government, much less for the latter to forgive or forget. Russia and China are defending their own interests as well. Russian–Syrian bilateral trade is worth $20 thousand million annually, and Syria provides Russia with naval bases, assisting Russia in protecting its interests and maritime presence in the Mediterranean region.

Linkage politics

In international politics, linkage is a well-known mechanism used to enhance co-operation between allies and rivals. In Russia's and China's case, linking their energy collaboration to foreign policy decisions is seen as an instrument to improve bilateral relations. China's foreign policy decisions are designed to serve its domestic goals, namely to support economic growth. China needs Russian oil; the Sino–Russian oil pipeline began to function recently.

Therefore, China feels obliged to support Russia at the Security Council. If China finds itself in a similar situation, it will expect Russia to reciprocate.

Regime change vs. the Arab and Middle Eastern agenda

China clearly views the advancement of the cause of freedom and democracy in the Middle East as a policy of 'regime change', allegedly designed by American foreign policy circles and supported by Western allies and Qatar to rebuild a new Middle East that best suits Western interests. This narrative dictates support for authoritarian regimes in the region. China repeatedly stated that it opposes such a policy to the extent that even security issues involved with the Iranian nuclear project are viewed from a perspective of regime change. To China, the opposition to Iran's nuclear programme is more about regime change than a strict American or Western commitment to a non-proliferation regime. In fact, the Chinese government and the Chinese intellectual discourse on the Arab Spring subscribes to the assumption that transformations in the Middle East are an American–Western offensive seeking to undermine 'non-friendly' regimes such as Syria and Iran. In believing such a narrative on both formal and informal levels, the Chinese side ignores the fact that, even if transformations occurring in the region seem to be 'regime change' oriented, they are not primarily an American agenda; rather, they are an Arab and Middle Eastern agenda. They represent the hopes of the Arab people to live in freedom under the rule of law, in justice and in stable and economically developed societies. Therefore, the people of the region expect China to refrain from opposing the process of change, or at least to remain neutral.

Failure to capture the spirit of Arab Spring

China's foreign policy makers, the media and leaders are unable to understand the essence of the Arab Spring's spirit, hopes and aspirations. The causes of Arab anger and revolution are much deeper than Chinese officials believe. It is much more than unemployment or housing opportunities. It has to do with the collective Arab injured spirit and the systematic humiliation suffered at the hands of ruling elites that have traditionally been aligned more with external interests than with their own people's welfare. This process of humiliation began over 700 years ago and continues to the present day. The last time the Arabs were proud of their civilizational accomplishments was during the Abbasid period, just before the catastrophic Mongol invasion of 1257. China should relate and be sympathetic to this fact as it suffered from the same wave of Mongol destruction and dishonour. The accumulation of hundreds of years of humiliation, foreign rule, colonization and home-grown authoritarianism has brought the Arab mind to intolerable limits of acceptance: it is insane that the status quo should continue for Arabs; it is unsustainable and inconceivable. While the world is prospering, developing and enjoying freedom and human rights, Arabs are falling far behind in spite of the great wealth with which the region is endowed. Therefore, advocacy of and support for Arab dictatorial regimes to maintain the oppressive status quo is an unfair demand on the part of China and Russia, simply because they want to defend their own interests in the region.

The Arab people's quest for civilizational renewal is not something new. In the mid-nineteenth century, the Arab Reform Movement paralleled the European revolutions of the 1840s in calling for modernization, but it was sabotaged, ironically by the growing democracies in the West. Therefore, if China grasps the depth of Arab resentment, the humiliation, the hopes and aspirations and the desperate desire for change, then it would understand the willingness of Arabs to sacrifice themselves and fiercely defend their rights. With increased understanding of the major reasons at the root of the Arab Spring, perhaps China could find common ground with the legitimate demands of Arabs for equality, prosperity and social justice.

Sino–Western rivalry

China seems to be treating matters related to the Arab Spring as part of its resistance to Western hegemony. In vetoing UN resolutions that deal with the Syrian crisis, Chinese officials tend to highlight China's pride in pursuing an 'independent' foreign policy at the United Nations and downplaying the vitality of the Arab Spring. It perpetuates Sino–Western rivalry rather than articulating a systematic, goal-oriented foreign policy towards the Syrian crisis in particular. It is a power struggle between the US and the West, on one side, and China and Russia, on the other, but in the meantime the interests and fate of the Arab people are caught in between, and are compromised now just as much as they have been over the past 700 years. It is a Chinese and Russian expression of resistance to the international system at large. The two nations view the existing system as unfairly tipping the scale to the West despite declining Western economic contributions to the global economy. China wants to see a multipolar system, an equitable international economic order, with fair World Trade Organization rules and mechanisms of dispute resolution. However, China does not seem to understand its responsibilities towards international affairs. Amazingly, the West has the same complaints about China, accusing it of manipulating international economic rules to advance its trade polices, the value of its currency and complaining of its dumping policy. Over all, the 'challenging powers', i.e. China, Russia, Brazil, South Africa, etc., see the Arab Spring as an instrument to advance American and Western interests rather than a sincere commitment to democracy and human rights. Suffice it to say that China and Russia are undemocratic and, therefore unaccustomed to democratic political structures.

This trend of dealing with the Arab Spring as part of Sino–Western relations is expressed clearly in the Chinese media and in statements by foreign policy officials. For example, Zhai Jun, China's Special Envoy to Syria, stated that 'the Chinese government consistently pursues an independent foreign policy of peace and is committed to upholding regional and world peace and stability.'[13] However, dealing with the Syrian crisis as a Sino–Western power conflict reflects a clear Chinese detachment from the hardships of the Syrian people.

Misunderstanding Islamic and democratic forces in the region

Islam has a complicated relationship with China. At times, the religion was warmly received, whereas at others it was resented, fought and restricted. Clearly, the Islamic movement is the primary beneficiary of the Arab Spring, and China has no direct contact with it. There was no dialogue reported between China and the Islamic movement either, in comparison with direct dialogue initiated by the US or the Europeans. Chinese foreign policy makers seem to be unaware of the depth of Islam's role in the politics of the Middle East, especially within the Arab Spring paradigm. At the same time, China distrusts secular democratic forces that by default fall within the Western camp. China fears that such forces, mostly led by Islamists, would inspire a revolt in its Muslim Xinjiang province. It is true that Islamists have consistently condemned China's mistreatment of Muslims in Xinjiang, but it is wrong to assume that Islamists might be unwilling to deal with China or restrict its interests in the region should they gain power in the Middle East. If the West has taken drastic measures to accommodate Islamists in politics, it is also incumbent upon China to do so if it seeks to promote its economic interests and play a vital role in Middle Eastern politics. This applies to Russia as well. Mutual political accommodation would also require from China a process of reconciliation with its Muslim minority in Xinjiang and other parts of the country. China has repeatedly called on the different parties in the Syrian crisis to sit down and pursue dialogue and a peaceful resolution to their differences. Yet, when Islamists want China to do the same with Muslim minorities in its territory, they are being accused of promoting separatism and terrorism in China.

Shortsightedness or farsightedness towards the Arab Spring

The Libyan, Egyptian and Tunisian experiences, and those of many other nations before them, can be indicators of whether China's policy towards the Arab Spring is shortsighted or strategically farsighted and well positioned to advance China's national interests in the Middle East. China's shortsightedness became clear when it bid on the failure of the Arab Spring. Deficiency in grasping the depth of the Arabs' willingness to make sacrifices for their revolutions points to the fact that the region has not only been misunderstood by the West for so long, but also by China and the East. Therefore, bidding on the failure of the movement for change seems unwise, and all policy projections built around it are unwise as well. China needs to grasp the depth of Arab resentment, and the Arab people's anger over the mismanagement of their wealth, national resources and corruption. If that happens, China will be more confident to deal on an equal footing with a region with similar conditions to China's decline and reawakening. There are no indications that its interests in trade, oil and military co-operation will be threatened if elected governments take over. On the contrary, democratic governments diversify their network of co-operation much more than autocracies. Their business contacts will not be confined to the West.

If at times China's policy towards the region lacks consistency, at other times it is clearly confusing. In the cases of Egypt, Libya and Tunisia, China was exceptionally cautious and reactive, but finally accepted the change, although a little late and behind the West and many other developing countries. In fact, China waited until these regimes fell completely before it showed some support for the process of change. This convenient last-minute strategy might undermine China's interests with the new governments, in particular with Libya. China supported the Gadhafi regime militarily to the last minute even when Libya was under military sanctions after UN SC Resolution 1973. This procrastination makes it hard for Chinese corporations to resume their projects in Libya, whereas Western corporations are rapidly advancing their interests. At this point, China can only blame itself rather than shifting the fault on to Western corporations' assault or the animosity of revolutionary forces in the Arab world. The overall inconsistency and confusion in China's policy towards the Arab Spring could be eliminated if China made an effort to understand the depth of Arab resentment of the status quo. While defending self-interests and self-centredness is well grounded in the theory of international relations and practice, China's vehement defence of its own interests, unmoved by distressed calls for change, turns Arabs away from China and its model of development. Arabs tend to understand politics within moral perspectives whereas China understands politics in terms of Realpolitik, pure self-interest regardless of moral considerations. That, of course, does not mean that morality has no role to play in China's foreign policy; it means that China pursues a pragmatic business-like approach, whereas Arabs like to see at least a 'benign' and morally driven foreign policy towards the region. Arabs become angry when they connect the images of killings in Syria with China's and Russia's support. Even if ethics and morality have no room in foreign policy, China must ground its foreign policy in the region within 'moral' and ethical dimensions, rather than hide behind the principles of non-intervention in the internal affairs of other nations or a 'strict' commitment to the sovereignty of other nations. Such a position damages China's image and will definitely complicate the process of rebuilding its relations with the new governments across the region.

Alignment and realignment

The Arab Spring has clearly led to a process of alignment and realignment at international and regional levels. On the global scene, it has stretched the American–European and GCC alliance. It has led to an improvement in Saudi–American relations that suffered gravely after 9/11. It has also improved Saudi–Qatari relations, brought the Arab countries much closer and strengthened the role of the Arab League. The revolutions strengthened Chinese–Russian co-ordination. The double veto of the Syrian resolution at the UN Security Council on 4 February 2012 was intended to send a message that China and Russia are capable of establishing an alliance that can threaten Western interests. Regionally, with the exception of Algeria and Syria, the majority of Arab countries supported the revolution in Libya. While Syria rejected the outcome, Algeria had no option but to accept it, given their neighbourly relations, although bilateral Libyan–Algerian relations are very weak. In the Syrian revolution, with the exception of Algeria and to some extent the governments of Lebanon and Iraq, the Arab World is united in supporting the process of regime change. The overwhelming majority of people are with the Syrians, but the Lebanese and Iraqi governments, in particular the two prime ministers, Najib Mikati and Noru Al Maliki, are supportive of the Syrian regime. Al Maliki of Iraq is driven by sectarian solidity with Assad as he belongs to the same Shi'a sect; Mikati of Lebanon is under pressure from and the influence of Hezbollah, which also shares sectarian affiliation with the Syrian and Iraqi governments.

The Turkish case is unique. Turkey's views on Libya were a little cautious at the beginning, to the extent that at first it resisted the military campaign against Gadhafi's regime, but then closed ranks with the West and supported the process of change in Libya. Its opposition was based on the depth of Turkish–Libyan economic co-operation. It feared that the downfall of the regime would make Western corporations beneficiaries of such a change. In fact, after the fall of Tripoli and to protect their interests, the Turkish Prime Minister and the Foreign Affairs Minister visited Libya immediately after the British Prime Minister and the French President. On the other hand, Turkey was one of the very first countries to oppose the Syrian government in its crackdown on popular dissent. The Prime Minister and Minister of Foreign Affairs repeatedly visited the country and advised Assad to pursue a path of reform. Assad paid no attention to the advice, and Turkey cut off contacts with the Assad regime.

Iran strongly supports the Syrian regime by providing diplomatic and military support. It views its potential fall as weakening Iran's influence within the region and with its allies, for instance Hezbollah and the current pro-Hezbollah government in Lebanon. To prevent such a fall, it was reported that fighters from Iran's Quds Force and Hezbollah are fighting on the side of the Syrian government. The Arab Spring also strengthened co-ordination between Syria and Algeria to the extent that Algeria served as the voice of the Syrian regime in the absence of Syria's representation in the Arab League. Algeria supported Syrian views at the UN, while neighbouring Morocco presented the case for the Syrian people and the Arab League, given the fact that Morocco was a member of the Security Council in early winter 2012. Co-ordination on the Syrian and Libyan crises led to improved relations between Saudi Arabia and Qatar. In fact, draft resolutions for the Security Council and the General Assembly on Syria were drafted by these two countries and presented by Morocco and Egypt. The democratically elected governments of Morocco, Tunisia and Libya and the freely elected parliaments in Egypt and Kuwait have shown unprecedented support for the Syrian cause. The Prime Minister of Morocco, the Prime Minister of Tunisia and the Libyan leadership admonished the Syrian regime and declared their intention to recognize the Syrian National Council as the sole representative of the Syrian people. In Tripoli, Libya handed the Syrian embassy to the Syrian National Council, and Tunisia hosted the Friends of Syria International Conference in March 2012.

Other countries in the region, such as Jordan and Iraq, have had a confusing policy towards the Syrian crisis. Bordering Syria, Jordan offers support to refugees but refrains from angering the Syrian government. Iraq's Kurdish Foreign Minister manoeuvres his statements in support of the Arab League, and at the same time takes pressure from his boss, the sectarian Shi'ite ideologue and Prime Minister Al Maliki. The government openly supports the Assad regime as Al Maliki has repeatedly declared that his loyalty lies first and foremost with Shi'ism, then with Iraq, then with the Arab world. Arab Gulf countries are fully engaged in the regional crisis. Kuwait's parliament condemned the killings in Syria. It also called on the Kuwaiti government to hand the embassy over to the Syrian National Council. Saudi Arabia, the UAE, Oman, Libya, Egypt and Kuwait support the Syrian people in their efforts towards regime change. However, Bahrain has to deal with the internal revolt of its Shi'ite majority against the Sunni ruling minority, and Yemen has its own revolution to deal with, but Yemeni nationals have shown unprecedented support for the Syrian people.

The Israeli Government refrained from intervention in the course of the Arab Spring for many reasons. Some deal with fear that Israeli constituents may replicate the model; on several occasions, Israeli protesters have taken to the streets demanding justice and raising banners similar to those raised in Egypt and elsewhere. There is also a fear that the Arab Spring might bring about a Third Intifada in the occupied territories, especially among the Israeli-Arabs of 1948. As far as Syria is concerned, Israel shares with Arab countries its preference to see a rapid collapse of the Assad regime, not because the dictatorship ever represented a threat to Israel, but because it hopes to weaken Hezbollah, Hamas and Iran. The Golan Heights Front is the most stable border between Israel and any other neighbouring country. In spite of encouraging Palestinian resistance against Israel through Jordan and Lebanon, Assad's regime has guarded its Syrian–Israeli borders intensely since 1967, and never allowed resistance to infiltrate its territory or carry out attacks on Israeli targets. The US strongly shares Israeli views on weakening the Iran–Hezbollah, Hamas–Syrian alliance; so do the majority of Arab countries, although some believe that Hamas is based in Syria out of necessity and not by choice. In fact, Hamas was evicted from Jordan by King Abdullah, the Jordanian General Intelligence Department and Prime Minister Abdulraoof Rawabdeh. Over the past two years, Jordan and Hamas have been in a process of reconciliation initiated by Qatar. Although King Abdullah maintains his position of not allowing Hamas to reopen its offices in Jordan, he feels that he needs to show some improvement in this area as Hamas enjoys the full support of the Jordanian Islamic Movement, with whom the King needs peace. Moreover, because Hamas' heritage is deeply rooted in the Muslim Brotherhood, it refrained from supporting the Syrian regime's oppression of its own people. Hamas is currently searching for a home, most likely in Turkey, Egypt, Tunisia or Qatar. Qatar in particular provides unlimited 'good offices' for Hamas and facilitates indirect contact with Israel and the outside world, a role that Egypt shares with Qatar as well, whereas this role was exclusively reserved for Jordan, but under the wise leadership of late King Hussein. Finally, Israeli views on the Mubarak regime were benevolent given that Egypt served Israeli interests. Mubarak showed no sympathy for the Palestinians, and suffocated them by imposing tight control over the borders with Israel, sealing the Gaza blockade and boosting Israeli security.

China's policy towards the Syrian crisis

As stated earlier in the chapter, the Syrian crisis erupted in March 2011 as a minor protest in the southern city of Der'a, on the border with Jordan, calling for reforms in the country and demanding freedom from oppression. The response of state security agencies and the Syrian army was massive repression. The state also created the *Shabiha* paramilitary troopers, a strong and unrestrained force that attacks the opposition. The region and most of the world was shocked by the torture and murder of a 10-year-old boy named Hamazah Al Khatib, perpetrated by the Syrian secret police. The entire country erupted in solidarity with the city of Der'a and the boy's family, protesting against unprecedented levels of brutality against children, women and the protesters themselves. The Syrian people determined to rid themselves of a dictatorship similar to the Egyptian, Libyan and Tunisian model, but the reaction of the international community to their legitimate demands varied from support to total opposition. Although the United States, the European countries and the overwhelming majority of the Arab-Islamic countries supported the Syrians, some countries supported the regime, and some straddled the fence in a sort of wait-and-see state.

Over the past year (March 2011–present), China has reiterated its position on the Arab Spring issue in general and on the Syrian crisis in particular, stressing its commitment to a peaceful settlement of the crisis, condemning the use of violence by all parties and calling for a national unity government. However, China's use of the veto, along with Russia on 4 February 2012, angered the Arab people. Arab media and civil society institutions condemned the veto, protested in front of China's embassies and attacked some of its diplomatic missions in the region. For the first time, the Chinese and Russian flags were burnt by protesters: they replaced the traditional Israeli and American flags that used to be burnt in public protests. Furthermore, religious leaders such as Sheikh Yousf Al Qaradawi, a senior Muslim cleric, issued religious edicts demanding that Muslims boycott Chinese products. At this point, China found itself in a predicament, namely entanglement in Middle Eastern affairs, seemingly of defending dictatorial regimes in the Arab world and opposing popular demands for change. In order to untangle themselves and clear their views on the Syrian crisis, China's foreign policy circles have designed a massive counterattack at different levels.

At the Security Council and the General Assembly

After intensive meetings and months of negotiations within the structures of the Arab League on the Syrian crisis from March 2011 to February 2012, the League decided to take the case to the UN. Several Arab and non-Arab countries sponsored a UN resolution to condemn the violence in Syria and demand an immediate cessation of violence in the country. The UN Security Council Resolution 10536, which was vetoed by China and Russia on 4 February 2012, was designed to end violence in the country and called for a peaceful resolution of the crisis. However, at the General Assembly, Resolution GA/11206 was passed, although once again opposed by China and Russia. It called on the Syrian government to 'without delay, stop all violence and protect its people, release all those detained during the unrest, withdraw all armed forces from cities and towns, guarantee peaceful demonstrations and allow unhindered access for Arab League monitors and international media.'[14] The resolution expressed its full support for the Arab League's decision to facilitate a Syrian-led political transition to a democratic, pluralistic political system through a 'serious political dialogue between the Syrian Government and the whole spectrum of the Syrian opposition.'[15] Reaffirming its strong commitment to Syria's sovereignty, independence, unity and territorial integrity, it further reaffirmed that all member states 'should refrain in their international relations from the threat or use of force against the territorial integrity or political independence of any State.'[16] SC/10536 failed to pass, although thirteen out of fifteen members of the council supported it, because of a rare double veto exercised by China and Russia. The General Assembly Resolution 11206 passed, in spite of the opposing vote of both countries along with twelve others and the abstention of 37 others. The least China could have done was to abstain from voting rather than vetoing SC/10536 and let Russia alone bear the wrath of the international community, Arabs and Muslims in particular. But China did it in solidarity with Russia and in support of the Syrian regime, as stated above.

President Obama expressed his dismay at the insensitivity of China and Russia to the Syrians' pain, while the US Envoy to the UN held China and Russia responsible for any lives lost in Syria in the post-veto violence. King Abdullah of Saudi Arabia strongly criticized the Chinese and Russian vetoes. This is a grave rebuke and an admonishment to China and Russia from a respected monarch and statesman. To realize the weight of such criticism, we need to remember that, upon assuming the throne as monarch of Saudi Arabia in 2004, King Abdullah paid his first official visit to China, not to the US or any other European or even Arab or Islamic country. King Abdullah understands the depth of China's potential influence should China choose to assume a responsible role in the Middle East. Moreover, King Abdullah, in a telephone exchange with the Russian President on 22 February 2012, told Medvedev that Russia should have co-ordinated with Arab countries before it vetoed the UN's resolution. The king added that dialogue with the Syrian regime was 'futile.'[17]

At the General Assembly

Addressing the General Assembly on 17 February 2012, Wang Min, China's Deputy Permanent Representative to the UN, reiterated his Government's position on the Syrian crisis stating that China is 'deeply worried about the escalating crisis that has caused civilian casualties and affected peace and security in the Middle East.'[18] The envoy ignored the fact that violence escalated primarily in the days immediately following the fateful veto, viewed by the Syrian government as a licence to kill more innocent civilians and bring an end to the rebellion. Wang Min went on to state that 'China condemns all acts of violence against innocent civilians and urges the Syrian Government as well as all political factions to immediately and fully end all acts of violence and quickly restore order.'[19] The envoy seemed to not want to distinguish between the massive level of violence used by the state and the efforts of the opposition to defend itself. The government of Syria is not convinced of China's seriousness when it calls for an 'immediate and full' end to all acts of violence. Realizing the anger of the Arab people towards China, the envoy went on to say that 'as a friend of the Arab people, China has always followed the purposes and principles of the Charter and will continue to work with the international community to resolve the situation in Syria.'[20] The envoy went on to consolidate China's position: 'We do not approve of armed intervention or forcing a so-called regime change in Syria. … Neither did China believe that sanctions or the threat of such measures would be helpful in achieving an appropriate solution.'[21] It is astounding that the Chinese envoy still believes that the Syrian Government should not be under sanctions, and that the situation can be resolved peacefully in Syria after more than 8,000 people have been killed by the Syrian government, by the end of March 2012. Although the Arab League and envoys from Western countries reiterated that their intention was not to call for military intervention similar to the Libyan case, China continued to insist that it sees any condemnation of the Syrian government as an instrument of regime change and an authorization to use force against the Syrian Government. Regardless, the Arab people at this time do not believe or feel that China is truly a friend when China is acting irresponsibly towards a major event in the region.

The Ministry of Foreign Affairs

Repeatedly, since the eruption of Arab uprisings, Liu Weimin, spokesperson for the Ministry of Foreign Affairs, has been bombarded with enquires on China's views on the epic changes occurring in the Arab world and its veto of the Syrian resolution at the Security Council. Weimin reiterated that 'China is highly concerned about the developments in Syria and calls on all relevant parties in Syria, including the Syrian authorities to cease all violence, take concrete measures to ease the tension and avoid civilian casualties.'[22] He added that 'the Syrian people's reasonable aspiration for change and protection of their interests should be respected',[23] but he never specified how his Government intended to support such legitimate aspirations of the Syrian people when China refuses to apply any pressure on the Syrian regime pursuing a policy of oppression against the population. Weimin also reiterated that China called repeatedly on the Syrian government to 'honor its commitment of reform in real earnest, launch the inclusive political process with the extensive involvement of all parties as soon as possible, and remove differences through dialogue and consultation',[24] and encouraged dialogue between the Government and the opposition. However, it seems to be favouring groups with mild demands for reform, such as the Co-ordination Council, rather than those who demand radical change, such as the Syrian National Council.

Weimin rejected the accusation that China harbours animosity towards the Syrian people or seeks selfish interest in its opposition to the UN's efforts. He affirmed that 'China, as a friend of the entire Syrian people, seeks no selfish interests on the Syrian issue. … we bear in mind the fundamental interests of the Syrian people, peace and stability of the Middle East region and relevant norms governing international relations.'[25] Obviously, the overwhelming majority neither sees China as a friend nor feels its affection; Syrians feel that China is fully on the side of the government even though it claims that 'it neither shelters nor intentionally opposes anyone.'[26] These statements carry no credibility among the Arab people. At the same time that Weimin made his statements, Wang, the spokesperson for the Minister of Foreign Affairs, expressed his sympathy towards the Syrian regime, stating that 'China can feel Syria's pain as outside forces seek regime change in the country, since China never accepts interference by other countries in its internal affairs. … even if China might not stop further moves of the US and its followers, China has to make its intention clear.'[27] This statement clearly puts China on the side of the Syrian government. It also shows how China views the Syrian crisis as a power struggle against the US and the West rather than addressing the crisis as needing urgent attention.

Cui Tiankai, Deputy Minister of Foreign Affairs

On Thursday 16 February 2012, Cui Tiankai, Deputy Minister of Foreign Affairs, responded to world criticism of China's veto by stating that China opposes any measure that encourages intervention by force or regime change.[28] Once again, China fits the parameters of the crisis within the 'regime change' perspective, ignoring the humanitarian catastrophe. Tiankai downplayed the differences between the permanent members of the Security Council in response to incredible American criticism of China's veto: 'it is natural for the five permanent members of the United Nations Security Council to disagree ... [but] such differences do not rule out future cooperation and there's a tradition among the five countries to accommodate each other's major concerns.'[29] While it is true that there are disagreements, it seems that China goes far beyond the divergences to shelter the Syrian regime from any world criticism or real action to halt the violence in the country. Hope for co-operation came when Arab countries reintroduced the same vetoed resolution to the General Assembly. China opposed it on the same grounds it had used against the veto 13 days earlier. Tiankai also attempted to counter the French, British and American criticism that China's policy towards the crisis is amoral and a purely 'self-centred' policy that ignores the calamity occurring in Syria. He reiterated China's position in calling on all parties to end violence and enter into negotiations to put a peaceful end to the conflict. Tiankai also downplayed the use of the veto stating that China had used it only eight times since 1971, much less than other members.[30]

Wen Jiabao addressing the EU–China Summit

The Chinese veto also angered the EU. The European people, civil society institutions, human rights organizations and activists demanded that the EU express its condemnation in their upcoming meeting with China. In an attempt to ease European concerns over China's veto, Wen Jiabao defended it at the EU–China Summit on 14 February 2012: 'China supports all efforts consistent with the UN charter and principles, and is willing to strengthen communication with all parties in Syria and the international community ... China does not seek to protect any party, including the Syrian government.'[31] Jiabao's words brought no solace to EU officials or to the Syrian people who have been under intensive bombardment by their own government forces with considerable and unnecessary loss of life. However, as China is invested heavily in European markets, the EU cannot afford to sever ties over the Syrian crisis given its current economic hardship and its urgent need to lift itself out of recession.

Vice-President Xi Jinping

During his 3-day visit to the United States, on 14 February 2012, Vice-President Xi Jinping was confronted with criticism from the Obama Administration and members of the US Congress, who expressed their disappointment at China's veto. The objective of Jinping's visit was to introduce himself to US decision makers, given that he is expected to take on the presidency of China at the end of 2012. The visit was also designed to improve China's relations with the United States, and to quell some of the rising concerns among US Congressmen and the American public of the so called Chinese 'threat', in contrast to the economic downturn in the United States. However, Jinping's visit was overshadowed by the events in Syria. In answering the questions he received on China's veto, he either dodged the questions as he did in Congress or repeated the well-known Chinese views on the Syrian crisis, offering no concessions or any new perspective, which only added more frustration on the American side. At McCain's question on why China used the veto and supports the Syrian dictator, Jinping responded: 'Senator McCain, your candor is very well-known in China.'[32] Realizing the cold reception, Jinping tried to refocus his trip on bilateral relations, especially in his meetings with the business community in the US. The *People's Daily* reported that Jinping told US business leaders that the time was ripe for a 'new historical starting point for relations between the two sides.'[33] On the second day of his visit, he continued his attempt to confine discussions to US–Chinese relations and to calm the growing fear of China's economic growth and military spending. He assured his audience that the reduction in the trade imbalance between the two sides is a goal for China as well. Jinping was also more interested in discussing the American arms sales deal to Taiwan than the Syrian crisis. Commenting on the administration's decision on an arms sale to Taiwan worth $5.85 thousand million, he stated that the deal is 'another indication of Washington's nonchalance toward China's core interests … that the Taiwan question concerns China's sovereignty and territorial integrity, and remains, as always, the most important and most sensitive issue in Sino-US relations.'[34]

On his way back from the US, Jinping visited Ireland and Turkey. Once again, he showed more interest in discussing bilateral relations than discussing the Chinese veto or China's policy towards the Syrian crisis. However, in Turkey, he had no choice given that Turkey is a leading country in managing the crisis. Jinping also insisted on extracting unambiguous Turkish support for China's position on territorial integrity not only in the western province of Xinjiang, which has ethnic, historical, cultural and religious roots with Turkey, but also in Tibet and Taiwan. Jinping stated that 'mutual support on issues related with the other's core interests is the cornerstone of Sino-Turkish strategic ties.'[35] In response, the Turkish leadership reiterated its support for the One-China policy and the territorial integrity of China with reference to the rebellious Turkic East Turkistan, or Xinjiang.

Syria's Special Envoy, Zhai Jun

Chinese Deputy Foreign Minister Zhai Jun was appointed Special Envoy to Syria on 10 February 2012. Jun ruled out any serious external role in resolving the crisis when he met with a delegation from the Syrian Co-ordination Body for Democratic Change, an organization that opposes military intervention in Syria. The Syrian National Council, the umbrella for the Syrian opposition, criticized the visit calling it a reward to China for the veto 6 days earlier. The National Council accuses the Co-ordination Body of being an agent of the Syrian Government, given that it has been a major obstacle to co-ordination efforts against the government. The Chinese claimed that they have been meeting with all sides, including the Syrian National Council, the Syrian government and all 'concerned' parties. In the meeting, Jun reiterated the Chinese views on the crisis and proposed the formation of a national unity government, in which the Syrian National Co-ordination Body should also take part.

Before his scheduled departure for Syria, while the UN General Assembly was debating the Syrian crisis on 17 February 2012, Jun reiterated in a press conference that 'China has closely followed the developments of the situation and is deeply worried about the escalating crisis that has caused civilian casualties and affected peace and stability in the region.'[36] The deep worries have not motivated China enough to take drastic measures in dealing with the crisis. Jun added that 'China believes the international community should fully respect Syria's sovereignty, independence, unity and territorial integrity, the independent choice of the Syrian people, as well as the results of political dialogue among various parties of Syria.'[37] He seems to fully adopt the Syrian regime's claim that Syria is under an international conspiracy to divide its territory and infringe its sovereignty, but nowhere was Syria's territorial integrity threatened in any debate at the UN or in the Arab League. The opposite is true with the UN's draft resolutions. The Arab League initiated political dialogue with the Arab Solution supporting political answers to the crisis, but this was not accepted by the Syrian regime. Jun also added that, 'we don't believe that sanctions or the threat of sanctions are helpful to achieving an appropriate solution.'[38] In spite of China's views on sanctions, there are strong precedents that economic, diplomatic and political sanctions do make a difference in pressuring regimes to abide by international laws and protect the human rights of their population. Sanctions worked in Burma, Iraq and Libya and are currently placing tremendous pressure on Iran and Syria. Jun also added that the 'actions of the international community and the UN regarding Syria should be helpful to easing tensions, facilitating political dialogue and resolving differences instead of complicating the issue.'[39] This is a tacit condemnation of the role the UN has played, when in reality the double veto exercised by China and Russia is what escalated the conflict and complicated the situation in Syria. Prior to the veto, the daily average number of deaths was less than fifty people; in the post-veto phase of the conflict, the Syrian regime's violence against its people increased by 100 percent or more. Jun also added that 'the Chinese government consistently pursues an independent foreign policy of peace and is committed to upholding regional and world peace and stability.'[40]

The theme of dealing with the Syrian crisis as a Sino–Western power conflict repeats itself in the statements given by the Chinese leadership: 'China is a responsible country and a friend of the Arab people.'[41] Once again, it tacitly accuses Western countries in particular of being irresponsible in bringing the Syrian crisis to a vote at the Security Council, simultaneously responding to similar Western accusations that China is an irresponsible stakeholder in international affairs. Jun reiterated statements highlighted by other officials: 'We believe that the international community should fully respect Syria's sovereignty, independence, unity and territorial integrity … we do not approve of armed intervention or forcing a so-called "regime change" in Syria.'[42] During his visit and meetings with Assad and high-ranking officials in the Syrian Foreign Affairs Ministry, Jun highlighted the same themes: China opposes military intervention and regime change, but respects territorial integrity and the unity of Syria. 'We urge the Syrian government and all of its political parties to immediately and fully end all acts of violence and quickly restore stability and normal social order.'[43] Obviously, Jun holds the opposition responsible for instability, and equally responsible for the violence occurring in Syria. He ignores the defensive nature of the opposition and the level of force used by the government against unarmed civilians. He concluded that 'China condemns all acts of violence against innocent civilians and does not approve of armed intervention or forcing so-called regime change.'[44]

Li Huaxin, Envoy to the Arab League

On 13 February 2012, China sent Li Huaxin, the former Chinese Ambassador to Syria, as Envoy to the Arab League. The objective of his mission was to explain the rationale for the Chinese veto. During his meetings with high-ranking officials both at the Arab League and at the Egyptian Foreign Affairs Ministry, he reiterated China's well-known views on the crisis offering no concessions or new proposals. He proceeded to visit Qatar and Saudi Arabia. The latter in particular is outraged by the Chinese veto, and expressed its outrage loudly. Obviously, Huaxin's visit added nothing new to the debate, given the fact that China continued to oppose any serious pressure on the regime in Damascus.

China and the violence in Syria

After the Chinese–Russian veto, violence committed by the Syrian regime doubled against the Syrian people. One of the most troubling episodes was the deaths at Houla, in which the Syrian army shelled the town, and its military paratroopers went from house to house killing 108 people, 49 of whom were children. The UN's Human Rights Council examined the massacre on Friday 1 June 2012 and overwhelmingly condemned the Syrian government. Once again, China voted against the resolution along with Russia and Cuba, while Uganda and Ecuador abstained and the Philippines was absent. China condemned the killings and repeated its customary statement towards Syria, calling for an end to violence, but unwilling to substantiate its calls with actions.

In its resolution, the council condemned the violence against the civilian population in Houla, believing that such acts of violence committed by the Syrian regime may amount to crimes against humanity and other international crimes. The resolution called for an independent and transparent enquiry and a full report to be submitted to its next session on Syria, which was held between 18 June and 6 July 2012.[45] China and Russia are expected to continue to oppose any condemnation of the Syrian regime, and protect the Syrian dictatorial regime from international justice. While the Sino–Russian support for the Syrian regime angers Arabs, so far no mobilized systematic response has been articulated at the level of the Arab League and the GCC. This indicates that China and Russia do not take Arabs seriously, unless the Arab countries take strong action against both China and Russia. The Arab countries must restrict trade with China, withdraw their ambassadors, reduce their diplomatic representation in Beijing and threaten to expel China's diplomats unless China genuinely supports change in Syria. China must understand that the status quo in Syria is neither sustainable nor acceptable to the international community. China and Russia want to preserve the Assad regime, a step that is unacceptable to the majority of Arab governments, the Arab people and the international community. Therefore, if China insists on its support of the Syrian regime, it should be willing and ready to pay the price.

Conclusion

Clearly, Chinese foreign policy towards the Arab Spring and the ongoing developments in the region have been reactive rather than proactive. China has appointed a Special Envoy to the Middle East and Syria, and has created an Arab–Chinese and a GCC–Chinese Forum. While unpredictability has been a major feature of Middle Eastern politics, it is incumbent not only on China but also on all players in the region to develop proactive policies towards the region. Such a new paradigm should take into consideration the changing nature of the Middle East, the ongoing revolutions and the interest at heart of the Arab people. The Chinese Revolution was victorious only when its people made sacrifices and paid a heavy price to liberate themselves from corrupt ruling elites and foreign domination. The Arab people are willing to do the same. They have legitimate and reasonable demands and national aspirations similar to those that drove the Chinese Revolution and many other revolutions. They yearn for development, justice, employment, dignity, equality and a decent life; they want to live in peace and enjoy the wealth with which the region is endowed. History has taught us that Arabs are always triumphant in confrontations with dictatorial regimes. Therefore, opposing such a natural course of history will only complicate China's national interests in the region.

5 China and Israel

The Jewish presence in China

The presence of Jewish communities in China is reported as early as the mid-seventh century, along with Persian, Arab and Central Asian immigrants and traders. 'Foreign religions, including Islam, Judaism, Manichaeism, Zoroastrianism and Nestorian Christianity were practiced among the thousands of foreign merchant residents there, though none of these religions spread into the Chinese population the way Buddhism had centuries earlier.'[1] There were four major Jewish communities in China. Jewish merchants resided within the Hui community and were viewed as Hui. Historians recorded no violence carried out against them in comparison with major violent confrontations reported against the Hui Muslims by the Han majority since the ninth century. Historians, travellers and contemporary researchers have also reported 'the extraordinary story of the Jews of Kaifeng, long lost descendants of the Israelites who somehow found their way to Hunan in the twelfth century, or before.'[2]

Christian missionaries also reported the existence of these Jews of Kaifeng in the sixteenth century; they managed to survive marginally as they were cut off from the rest of the Jews, and not because of internal strife or majority pressure in China. The third citing of Jewish communities in China was the Harbin in northeast China. 'Harbin was home to one of the largest Jewish communities in the Far East.'[3] They migrated from Russia towards the end of the nineteenth century and established a viable and prosperous community. Russia had a concession from China to link its Siberian railway with the China Eastern Railway: this brought immigrants who established communities, villages and hamlets on the banks of the Songhua River. The Jewish community contributed to the business and cultural life of Harbin. After the Japanese invasion of eastern China in 1932, the majority of the Jewish community migrated to the US, Australia, New Zealand, Palestine and other countries. The fourth major citing of Jews in China comprised refugees and immigrants fleeing Nazi persecution and European violence. More than 20,000 European Jews escaped in the late 1930s and went to the Jewish quarter in Shanghai, a city that was open to immigrants and required no entry visa.[4] The majority of WWII immigrants were also relocated to the United States, Canada, Australia, New Zealand, Palestine and Israel, while a small percentage were repatriated to their European home countries.

The city of Shanghai welcomed the persecuted Jews and was sympathetic to their cause. Since the mid-1990s, some Shanghai Jews who left the city have come back to reminisce about their post-WWII Shanghai experience. Today, Shanghai is becoming a major destination and home for Jewish businesses. The city serves as a primary hub for Israeli corporations conducting business in China, and the Chinese people show tremendous pride in the fact that Jews were never persecuted in China in contrast to the extermination campaigns orchestrated against Jews in Europe and Russia.

The five pillars of Sino–Israeli relations

Over the past 60 years, Sino–Israeli ties have developed gradually into a strategic partnership that covers five main areas of co-operation: arms sales, trade, energy, political co-operation and deep cultural relations.

Arms sales

The core of the Sino–Israeli engagement is arms sales and defence, but the extraordinary success of the Israeli military industry has had a tremendous spillover effect on a wide range of bilateral interests; it is highly advanced and is in a constant search for markets. China represents a steady consumer. The Stockholm International Peace Research Institute (SIPRI) reported that there are over 200 arms-producing companies in Israel, some of which are large corporations owned by the Israeli government, such as Israel Aerospace Industries (IAI), Israel Military Industries and Rafel, a large, privately owned company such as Elbit, several medium-sized companies and a relatively substantial number of small private companies.[5] Israeli domestic consumption and its defence requirements do not justify this high number of companies. In fact, Israel exports 75 percent of its arms production. Sales for the largest four arms-producing companies in Israel ranged from a low of 62 percent (for IAI) to 94 percent (for both Elbit and IMI) and a high of 97 percent (for Rafael) from 2005 to 2009.[6]

Consumers of Israeli weapons include the US, China, India, Turkey and some African countries. Israel is in a continued quest to expand its arms sales markets. SIPRI reported that, 'over the past three decades, Israel has expanded its arms exports significantly, reaching a value of approximately $7.5 billion in export agreements in 2009.'[7] From 2005 to 2009, the largest recipients of weapons by volume from Israel were Turkey and India; the largest supplier to Israel by far was the US.[8] Although specific figures for Chinese imports of Israeli arms are not available, they are significant. The lack of accurate statistics on China's arms imports from Israel can be explained by the fact that both sides have learned the necessity of discreet co-operation, given the American opposition to the Israeli–Chinese military partnership. The military industry in Israel is considered the core of its industrial enterprise and economy. Defence technology has a direct impact on civilian industries and is also central to external trade relations. Israelis have accomplishments in the areas of agro-technology, space industry, water systems, cyber security and energy efficiency, and China aspires to a similar paradigm in which military technology complements the civilian sector, not only ensuring national security, but civilian prosperity as well.

SIPRI's list of the top 100 arms-producing companies in 2008 and 2009 (Table 5.1) includes three large Israeli corporations that have a combined arms sales of $6.3 thousand million. They produce and export different types of artillery, aircraft, electronics, engines, missiles, military vehicles, small arms, services, ships and space technology, and provide maintenance and servicing of military equipment.[9]

While some Chinese corporations qualify to get on the SIPRI list, the latter is unable to list them due to secrecy and for lack of data and verifiable mechanisms for their arms sales. Since the establishment of the PRC in 1949, China has followed the 'self-reliance' approach to meet its defence needs. However, self-reliance, autarchy and the inefficiency of the import substitution policy of military technology from the former Soviet Union and the Socialist bloc were insufficient for China to keep up with its growing security needs and the rapidly advancing defence technology. In view of its military confrontations in the 1950s, China realized that it was lagging far behind the US and the USSR during the Korean War, in its war with India in 1962 and in its catastrophic war with Vietnam in 1978. The Sino–Vietnamese War was disastrous by all standards.

Table 5.1 National shares of arms sales for the SIPRI top 100 arms-producing companies in 2008 and 2009, in dollars (000 million)

Number of companies	*Country*	*Arms sales in 2008*	*Arms sales in 2009*	*Share of total top 100 arms sales 2009*
45	USA	238	246.5	61.7
1	Canada	0.7	0.7	0.2
11	UK	49.7	50.3	12.5
6	France	22.4	23.0	5.7
4	Italy	15.2	15.5	3.9
5	Germany	8.0	7.6	1.9
2	Spain	2.9	2.9	0.7
1	Sweden	3.0	2.6	0.7
1	Norway	0.7	1.1	0.3
1	Switzerland	0.8	0.7	0.2
1	Finland	0.7	0.07	0.2
6	Russia	10.3	9.2	2.3
4	Japan	7.0	6.6	1.7
3	Israel	6.3	6.3	1.6
2	South Korea	1.8	1.9	0.5
1	Turkey	0.5	0.6	0.2
3	India	4.2	4.5	1.1
1	Kuwait	2.6	2.5	0.6
1	Singapore	1.3	1.5	0.4
100	Total	385.9	400.7	100

Source: SIPRI Yearbook 2011, p. 251.

While both China and Vietnam declared victory, it was obvious that China's army suffered major losses at the hands of an experienced Vietnamese army accustomed to successful wars against the French and Americans, which swiftly defeated the Khmer Rouge, China's allies in Cambodia. Although China initiated the war, Vietnam caused heavy casualties on the Chinese side as China fought with outdated weapons, lacked a clear strategy, a chain of command, secured routes for supply and had inefficient communication methods. It is estimated that China lost 60,000 soldiers and was finally forced to withdraw, although China's version was voluntary withdrawal. The outcome of the war made China realize the urgent need to modernize its armed forces. It was determined to end the gap between its armed forces and those of neighbouring countries, especially Vietnam, India and the USSR.

China's quest to modernize its armed forces has promoted close co-operation with Israel ever since the mid-1970s. Through its participation in international defence exhibitions, it began to notice the advanced Israeli defence industry, and determined to purchase arms and missile systems from Israel. Alterman and Graver report that 'in the 1980s, some analysts believed that Israel covertly sold China as much as $4 billion in weapons before diplomatic relations were established in 1992.'[10] The geostrategic environment since the early 1970s was conducive to close Sino–Israeli military co-operation, and the Sino–American rapprochement made such co-operation possible as the US, China and some Arab countries were engaged in the containment and prevention of Soviet advances in the Middle East. Therefore, the US made no objection to Israeli–Chinese arms co-operation. The Soviet Union itself was sinking in a decade-long war in Afghanistan in an epic encounter with the Islamic world. China was also reassessing its strategy of global engagement for the purpose of accelerating economic development and improving its image worldwide. However, the sudden collapse of the Soviet Union drastically altered international relations. The US began to view China as a competitor and potential adversary.

The intellectual discourse in the United States and the West was dominated by the clash of civilizations paradigm, which identified the Islamic world and China as potentially on a collision course with the West. On the Chinese political scene, the spillover of the Soviet collapse led to the civil strife that culminated with the Tiananmen Square student demonstrations in 1989. The situation between the US and China drastically worsened as China was condemned for its ruthless crackdown on demonstrators. The two countries took an entire decade to improve their relations, but the improvement did not prevent the US from being very critical of Israeli–Chinese military co-operation. The US clearly voiced its opposition to any Israeli military technology transfer to China: it viewed it as potentially threatening in any Sino–American confrontation over Taiwan, as the US have a defence commitment towards the island as set forth by the Taiwan Relations Act and the Six Assurances provided by the Reagan Administration, and honoured by subsequent administrations to this day.

Israeli–Chinese military co-operation grew steadily between 1992 and 1996, leading to signing the major Phalcon radar system arms deal in which Israel sold China four Phalcon radar systems worth $1,000 million. The advanced airborne radar system, developed by Israeli Aerospace Industries and Elta Electronics Industries of Israel, is capable of providing long-range simultaneous tracking of multiple air and surface targets. The deal sought to remedy a major deficiency in the Chinese defence system: the lack of an Airborne Early Warning (AEW) capability. China's goal was to purchase the Phalcon system from Israel, have it built in a Russian Il-76 aircraft (Ilyushin Il-76 military transport aircraft), thus providing an AEW system similar to the US airborne early warning and control system (AWACS) developed by Boeing, and fitted in Boeing E-3 Sentry. Both systems were designed for early warning, reconnaissance missions, regular air patrol and airborne control and command as well. The Phalcon system 'is built around an ELTA EL/M-2075 AESA L-band radar, then adds electronic and communications intelligence gathering (ELINT and COMINT) capabilities. The system can receive transmissions from other air and ground stations to round out its surveillance picture, and uses sensor fusion to provide a complete picture of the battle space out to several hundred kilometers.'[11] The US opposed the deal vehemently, and its opposition was governed by security concerns over the increasing influence of Taiwan in the US Congress. The US Department of Defense viewed it as disruptive to the fragile military balance in the Taiwan Strait as well. Interestingly, and without any US objection:

> in January 2004, India and Israel signed a $1.1 billion contract for three Phalcon AWACS aircraft as part of a $1.5 billion tripartite agreement with Russia. With the arrival of its first IL-76 Phalcon, India joined the global ranks of AWACS operators. The aircraft will monitor huge swathes of Indian airspace, intercept communications and log radar frequencies, add some ground surveillance, and help command IAF responses.[12]

Israel sold similar systems to Singapore, Chile and other countries discreetly.

Another related controversy deals with the Israeli Lavi fighter jet commissioned in the early 1980s by the Israeli government and produced by IAI. The project was a joint venture with the US who funded 40 percent of it. The IAI produced three Lavis at an estimated cost of $6.4 thousand million in 1983, before the US withdrew from the project as it was not interested in developing an Israeli jetfighter that competes with its F-16. In 1988 the Israeli Government decided to end production because of cost considerations. Some sources report that Israel sold the Lavi project to China, and this led to the production of the J-10 jetfighter, a multirole aircraft.[13] Interestingly, construction of the J-10 began in China in 1988, the year the project ended in Israel, and it was produced, tested and put into service in 2003. The aircraft took part in an air show in 2007. In addition to Israeli assistance, China imports engines for its J-10 fighters from Russia.[14] The J-10 has elevated China's stature as a growing supplier of advanced military technology. 'China, whose arms supply deals often involve small arms and light weapons for Asian, African, and Near Eastern states, concluded a contract to sell 36 J-10 fighter aircraft to Pakistan for $1.4 billion.'[15]

A third controversial arms deal between Israel and China was the Harpy drones. The Harpy unmanned aerial vehicle (UAV) was a 500-km-range drone also produced by the IAI, 100 of which were sold to China in the 1990s at a value between $55 million and 70 million. Although the United States had initially objected to the deal, it was not in a position to sack it, as supposedly there was no American technology involved in the manufacture of the drone. Hence, Israel was not in violation of agreements with the US not to transfer American military technology to China. The deal was concluded; the Harpy was delivered and became fully operational for China to monitor the Taiwan Strait, and it boosted its aerial reconnaissance capabilities. In 2003 China sent some of the Harpys to Israel for maintenance, according to the original purchase agreement. The US interpreted their return as a request for upgrading them with new detection capabilities that were developed after the initial Chinese–Israel agreement. The US strongly objected to the upgrade and accused Israel of deceptive practices; it demanded that the Israelis confiscate the Harpys and refrain from upgrading them. Israel conceded on the upgrading, but not on the confiscation aspect of the American demands. China's reaction to this episode of American intervention to prevent it from acquiring advanced drone technology was milder than its reaction to the cancellation of the Phalcon a few years earlier.[16] Both Israel and China have learned a great deal from the three experiences; therefore, China chose not to overreact towards Israel or jeopardize their bilateral relations. As a result, since 2003, their military co-operation has become discreet, making it difficult for any data mining to find reliable statistics on Israeli military transfer to China.

Trade relations

The earliest trade talks between China and Israel date back to 1955 in conjunction with the Bandung Conference in Indonesia. 'Trade diplomacy' was an instrument used by Israel and China at that time to explore diplomatic relations and political co-operation. However, because of missed opportunities, they were unable to move forward with diplomatic relations, although exploratory interaction never ceased, especially from the mid-1970s onward. While taking part in international exhibitions in the areas of defence, aerospace engineering and agricultural technology, China noticed the progress Israel was making in technology. China's frantic quest to accelerate co-operation and transfer of technology brought it closer to Israel as never before. It identified four major sectors as a priority for its development: agriculture, industry, science and technology. As Israel had made strides in all these areas since the early 1970s, it made sense that Sino–Israeli co-operation should expand in the early 1980s in the fields of defence and agro-technology, extending later to telecommunications, medical technology and software.

Chinese sources reported that bilateral trade in 1992 was estimated at $54 million,[17] grew drastically to over $8,000 million in 2011 and is expected to exceed $10 thousand million by the end of 2012 (Table 5.2). The scope of Israeli–Chinese trade relations is expanding gradually into an economic partnership that covers agricultural technology, defence, security, IT, investments, railways, shipping, construction, the motor industry, scientific research, jewelery and investing in the emerging Israeli energy sector, oil, gas and clean energy.

In order to enhance its trade relations with China, Israel designated China as an export target country. As such, all government-owned corporations and private sector-owned businesses were greatly encouraged to market and export their products to China. Israel also expanded its diplomatic presence in the country to include missions in Beijing, Shanghai, Hong Kong and Guangzhou. The Israeli Trade Representative Office expanded its presence to Guangzhou and Shenzhen in the south, Chengdu in the southwest, and soon another office will be opened in Dalian.[18] The purpose is to cover the entire country and provide business information and incentives to boost bilateral trade relations. In addition to government support, Israeli private businesses have made substantial strides in infiltrating China's market. Both government agencies and private businesses play a complementary role that maximizes co-operation and gains in Chinese markets, and boosts Sino–Israeli bilateral trade and strategic partnership.

Sino–Israeli IT co-operation

The Israeli IT industry has advanced significantly since the early 1990s, making Israel one of the most technologically oriented countries. IT revenue

Table 5.2 China–Israel: value of bilateral trade in US dollars (000 million)

2010	7,644.44
2009	5,178.07
2008	6,049.82
2007	5,309.94
2006	3875.72
2005	3,027.88
2004	2,484.85
2003	1,831.3
2002	1,417.09
2001	1,315.91
2000	1,050

Source: China Statistical Yearbook, 2010.

was estimated at $10,00 thousand million in 2000, soaring to $42.8 thousand million in 2005, to $46.5 thousand million in 2006 and $100.00 thousand million in 2010. Israel has a well-established 'Silicon Valley' that competes with major IT centres worldwide. 'At the core of Israeli cluster lies the information and communications technology (ICT) of software, data, communications, electro-optics, hardware design, and internet technologies. Related high technology industries include medical technology, biotechnology, agricultural technology, materials technology, and military technology.'[19] China and other countries such as India, Turkey, the US, UK, Belgium, Germany and Switzerland seek Israel's IT in all these sectors, and import some high-tech software and applied technology. China seeks Israel's agro-technology as the second most sought after area of expertise. In his visits to rural China, the Chinese President Hu Jintao 'urged party committees and governments at all levels to make issues related to agriculture, rural areas and farmers top priority of their agenda and called for increased investment in these areas … ' noting that '… Israel's miracle agriculture is of deep interest.'[20] Hu Jintao also called on the Israelis and Chinese to deepen their co-operation in agricultural technology transfer and rural development in China. Towards this goal, the Israel–Shandong Agriculture and Technology Forum was established in 2010; it is one of the leading co-ordination bodies in the area of agriculture based in Shandong Province, and the largest producer of agricultural products and related industries in the country. The forum is one of several entities that promote Sino–Israeli agricultural co-operation that began in the mid-1908s. Israel established prototype farms in China that have become models for Chinese farmers to emulate.

Business infrastructure

In order to respond to the designation of China as an export target country by Israel's Ministry of Industry, Trade and Labor, both the private and the public sector were mobilized to intensify exports of Israeli products and to expand trade relations with China. Towards that end, Chinese and Israeli enterprises built solid business infrastructure to promote bilateral trade co-operation. Their national and local chambers of commerce played a vital role in this respect. In addition to official economic, trade and business representative offices, both sides promoted the establishment of business associations. The following is an overview of some of these institutions and their goals and accomplishments.

Israel–China Institute (ICI)

The ICI was established in 2009. Its main goal is to 'cultivate and guide the Israel–China–Jewish relationship.'[21] The ICI is headquartered in Jerusalem and opened another branch in Jinan, Shandong Province. The institute is also considering opening other branches throughout China, 'with a mind for their effectiveness in providing multi-level opportunities for cooperation, cultural exchange, business and friendship, economic relations, trade, educational services, and other diverse opportunities between the two peoples.'[22] The ICI has been very active in promoting bilateral trade, matching Chinese and Israeli businesses, providing a network of businesses, facilitating bureaucratic procedures and producing an academic journal entitled *The Journal of Asian and Middle Eastern Studies*. The institute is also active in pairing twin cities and villages for the purpose of friendship agreements and business deals between communities in the two countries. Currently, the ICI is focusing on Shandong Province as it 'is the largest grower of crops, fruit, vegetables, fish, and cattle for China's domestic consumption as well a leading exporter. The surging needs of local farms, corporations, industries and leaders make cooperation with Israeli cities, towns and collective farms and organizations highly compatible.'[23] The ICI has also been negotiating what is called 'land for technology' agreements with provisional authorities in China. The purpose is to build Israeli scientific research institutions in China to foster research and development (R&D) efforts. Currently, ICI is in the process of co-establishing the Israel–Yellow River Delta Modern Science and Agriculture Research Institute in Binzhou. The goal is 'to attract Israeli scientists, farmers, and agriculture companies to cooperate with the region's agricultural sector via educational exchange and joint venture arrangements. Options exist to own land in the region; benefit from selling produce to the huge Chinese domestic market; build grass root Israel–Chinese relations.'[24]

Israel's trade mission to China

This unit, which is part of the Foreign Trade Administration in the Israeli Ministry of Industry, Trade and Labor, is attached to Israel's diplomatic missions to China. 'The Trade Mission is responsible for Trade policy issues, such as economic and trade agreements and trade barriers, and Trade promotion, such as business information, business seminars and delegations, exhibitions, meeting scheduling and other tailor-made services that are aimed to promote bilateral trade.'[25]

Israel Chamber of Commerce in China (IsCham)

IsCham was established in Beijing in 2008 to advance trade relations between the two sides. Although IsCham is a private association, it enjoys the support of Israel's diplomatic missions in China. It has been very active in providing services for the Israeli–Chinese business community, business information, networking, forums and workshops, conferences, lectures and exploring business opportunities for Israeli businesses in China. Recently, IsCham is paying significant attention to water and environmental technology, another area of expertise in Israel, but much needed in China. IsCham seeks to promote water treatment technology by building prototypes similar to the successful

Israeli farms previously established throughout China. IsCham provides business information, business opportunities in China and education in business etiquette to members and non-members through its website.[26]

The Israeli Chamber of Commerce in Shanghai

The Israeli Chamber of Commerce in Shanghai was established in 2007. Among other goals, the chamber's main mission is 'to strengthen Israel–China commercial ties and provide high quality information on businesses, and needed resources to enhance trade relations between Israel and China.'[27] The chamber established a popular website that provides valuable information to users in networking and advertising.

China–Israel Business Forum

Israel's Business Forums are organized around the world to promote Israeli businesses and trade ties with business partners. One of the most successful is the China and Asia–Israel Business Forum. China's main goal is technological co-operation with Israel, technology transfer and commercialization of Israeli high-tech innovations. The forum has been very successful in strengthening Sino–Israeli trade and technology co-operation.

China–Israel Joint Committee of Trade and Economy

This is a formal entity composed of the PRC's Ministry of Commerce and Israel's Ministry of Industry, Trade and Labor. They meet occasionally to assess and enhance trade relations. In its fifth session held in Jerusalem on 2 March 2011, both sides highlighted the success achieved since their last meeting in 2004, expressing their satisfaction over the level of co-operation between Israel and China in the areas of agro-technology, farming, water treatment, information technology and research and development.

China–Israel Ltd

The main goal of The China–Israel Ltd is to 'accelerate the penetration of Israeli companies into the China market.'[28] It also matches Chinese corporations with Israeli business partners, conducts workshops and provides consultations in business development, marketing and management.

Energy: oil, gas and clean energy

As part of its global survey of energy resources, the US Geological Survey (USGS) estimated that the Levant Basin, 32,000 square miles in the eastern Mediterranean region consisting of the territorial waters and economic zones of Israel, the Palestinian Authority (Gaza), Syria, Lebanon, Cyprus, Turkish

Republic of Northern Cyprus and, by default, Turkey, encompasses large natural gas and substantial oil reserves. The USGS estimated 122 trillion cubic feet (tcf) of natural gas and 1.7 thousand million barrels of oil undiscovered and technically recoverable using currently available technology. The USGS maintains that 'The Levant Basin Province is comparable to some of the other large provinces around the world and its gas resources are bigger than anything we have assessed in the United States.'[29] Israel has been exploring with Cyprus joint ventures to exploit the reserves. Lebanon is in constant dispute with Israel over territorial waters, while Turkey expressed its concerns over the Israel–Cyprus co-operation for fear of compromising the interests of the Turkish Republic of Northern Cyprus.

Syria's internal strife over the past year and the Gaza Strip (PNA) in a power struggle with ruling Hamas since 2006 marginalized their respective roles in offshore exploration. The PNA is not in a position to take part in offshore joint ventures as it is totally under Israeli control. When the joint Israel–Cyprus venture announced the discovery of new reserves, China expressed its interest in becoming part of the project, and talks are under way with Israel and Cyprus to exploit the oil and natural gas reserves in the eastern Mediterranean region. In this regard, China and Israel discussed the potential of building a railway that connects Israel's gas and oil reserves from the port of Haifa on its Mediterranean coast, through the Negev Desert to Israel's port of Eilat on the Red Sea. This would allow delivery of oil and gas to China bypassing the tensions in the Gulf region. China has extensive expertise in deep offshore drilling and is willing to take part in the project. China can also play the role of peacemaker between Israel and Lebanon, Israel and Turkey and in any potential disputes between Syria and Israel. Exploitation of the East Mediterranean region is expected to earn Israel \$2,000 million to \$3,000 million a year, and provide it with oil and natural gas needs estimated at 238,000 bd,[30] while its annual gas consumption is estimated at 3.25 thousand million cubic metres annually.[31] Sino–Israeli oil co-operation will certainly boost bilateral economic ties and enhance strategic partnerships.

The increase in oil and gas infrastructure in the Red Sea area will also highlight its importance in global oil markets. In fact, China and Saudi Arabia have recently signed a deal in which 'the China Petroleum and Chemical Corp. will build an \$8.5 billion export refinery to handle 400,000 bd at Yanbu, on the kingdom's Red Sea coast, thereby also bypassing Hormuz.'[32] In fact, bypassing the Strait of Hormuz is not new in the world's quest for energy security. Iraq explored it seriously with Jordan in the 1980s. While Iraq was enthusiastic about an alternative route for its oil exports, Jordan defaulted on the talks on account of 'political' considerations when it could have been its economic saviour. The Iraqi government explored two pipelines: an oil pipeline from Iraq's oil fields through Jordanian territory to the port of Aqaba on the Red Sea and a water supply pipeline. The goal of the latter was to provide fresh drinking water from the Tigris and Euphrates rivers to meet

Jordan's water needs. Jordan rethought the project and decided not to continue with it on the grounds that both the water and the oil pipeline would make the kingdom dependent on Iraq. This issue proved that Jordan took an irrational decision as its dependence on oil imports continues to escalate and create major energy crises in the country, while water shortages continue to choke the country's lifeline. Jordan purchases water from Israel as well.

Political relations

After the declaration of the state of Israel in 1948 and the establishment of the PRC in 1949, both countries were in desperate need of diplomatic recognition and the support of the international community to ensure their survival. For its part, farsighted Israel began to build long-term strategic relations with existing powers, and with newly emerging nations in Asia and Africa in particular. It recognized the PRC on 9 January 1950, becoming the first Middle Eastern government to do so. The Arab world had its own share of struggles for independence, state formation, liberation and development; therefore, recognition of China was not a priority. The region's views on the Soviet Union and communist nations in general also tinged China's reputation as an emerging communist country. In comparison with neighbouring Arab and non-Arab Middle Eastern countries such as Iran and Turkey who were unsure of China's identity and its foreign policy direction, Israel's recognition of China was an impressive political step. For the period between 1950 and 1978, China itself was also in desperate need of diplomatic support to ensure its legitimate representation to the Chinese people. The PRC was in a fierce struggle with the Republic of China (ROC) located on Formosa Island. The ROC enjoyed the support of the US and Europe, as well as the majority of the world, while friends of the PRC were few.

Both Israel and China contemplated establishing diplomatic relations in the early 1950s, but missed several opportunities. As Shichor states, the implicit and sometimes explicit messages sent by the Chinese expressing a desire to establish diplomatic relations between the two sides went unnoticed in Israel.[33] To some extent, China's close relation with the Palestinians complicated the prospect of diplomatic relations, but this was by no means sufficient grounds to prevent the establishment of diplomatic relations between Israel and China. In the Chinese media, Israel was viewed as an aggressor, part of the reactionary Middle Eastern alliance and a home base for neoimperialism. On the Israeli side, China was viewed as backward, violent and a supporter of their enemies, the Palestinians. While stereotyping was reported in media exchanges, in reality, Chou En-lai, the Premier of China (1949–76) had been conducting 'trade' talks with Israeli delegations in conjunction with the Bandung Conference and Israel's diplomatic mission to Burma since 1955. China also had contact with the Israeli diplomatic mission to Moscow, given that, in Israel's early years, the bulk of its international support came from Moscow and the Socialist bloc. In fact, China never called for the elimination of the state of Israel or questioned its legitimacy. On the contrary, Chinese officials held Israel in high esteem 'as a country which had succeeded in gaining independence from Western colonial rule after a bitter national liberation war.'[34] Shichor maintains that China's interest in Israel stems from the latter's active role in the United Nations.[35]

During this time, particularly through international forums, Nasser's rise in the Non-Aligned Movement and Africa and the Arab world at large highlighted the diplomatic potential of the Arab countries, as well as possible Arab support for China at the UN and affiliated organizations. In addition, the Soviet-Sino discord that intensified in the 1960s made it compulsory for China to solidify its support for the Middle East and contribute to Soviet containment. The alignment also put Israel completely on the side of the free world; in fact, the diplomatic recognition of China was governed to some extent by Israel's relations with the United States. When the US and China engaged in fierce fighting in Korea, Israel voted to condemn China at the United Nations for its aggression, but Israel's support for the American resolution did not prevent the conflict from continuing. Several wars also occurred between the Arab countries and Israel: 1956, 1967, the War of Attrition from 1967 to 1973, 1973 and the 1982 Israeli invasion of Lebanon. China maintained its views on the conflicts calling on combatants to opt for peace to resolve their differences. It maintained that the US and the USSR were responsible for the longevity of the Arab–Israeli conflict as they fuelled it, escalated it and prevented the combatants from a genuine compromise to end the conflict. The Arabs also exaggerated China's support for the Palestinian and Arab cause. In essence, neither Soviet nor Chinese support was significant in altering the imbalance of power in the Middle East that tilted towards Israel in 1967. China continued its diplomatic support for the Arab side, simultaneously advocating a peaceful settlement and, as such, it emerged from the conflict with a better image than the USSR and the US. The Soviet Union was held partially responsible for Nasser's defeat as it supplied Egypt with low quality weaponry against the high-tech armaments that the US, France, Britain and other Western countries provided for Israel.

The devastating Cultural Revolution and the power struggle within the CCP were very disruptive to China's developmental process in politics, economics and social expansion. China came out of it devastated and bankrupt. Millions of people perished and valuable human talent was sacrificed to settle power struggles among the CCP's leadership, thus damaging China's image worldwide, but Mao's death opened the way for a new era. The leadership change and Deng Xiaoping's policy of reform made it incumbent on China to pursue global engagement aimed at reviving its economy and improving its regional and international relations. The scope of such engagement brought China to the Middle East in search of energy resources, raw materials and technology. Changes in Chinese domestic and foreign policy made an improvement in Chinese–Israeli relations imperative, among which were Israel's support of China's membership to the UN, the Sino–American rapprochement, the Soviet predicament in Afghanistan and the Egyptian–Israeli peace accords. China's permanent seat on the UN Security Council provided endless opportunities and challenges in managing international crises. Moreover, the era of openness made China more aware of its economic and technical backwardness compared with its neighbour, Japan, the rising Korea and Western countries. In order to accelerate the process of economic development, China began to appreciate Israel's comparative advantage in the technology sector. It realized that the 'arms quality gap' it had with the West and with Russia could only be bridged by close co-operation with Israel so, in the 1980s, China embarked upon an ambitious process of normalization and strategic partnership. At the beginning, America's tacit support of the China–Western engagement solidified this approach, and China's pragmatic foreign policy and economic orientation, in addition to showing support for the peace process in the Middle East, eliminated any reservations as to the scope of Sino–Israeli relations. Sutter sums up China's engagement with Israel and with the region's affairs:

> continuing past Chinese efforts to build productive ties with all Middle Eastern countries, Beijing's relations with Israel flourished in trade, political exchanges, and defense ties. Chinese officials continued to lean toward the Arab and Palestinians positions on the Middle East peace issues but duly acknowledge the legitimacy of Israeli concerns.[36]

Cultural relations

Both China and Israel have official Cultural Attaché offices devoted to promoting cultural exchanges and cultural relations. Towards this effort, in 2009 Israel built its pavilion at the Shanghai Expo to showcase its development. The structure resembles a seashell with themes built around Jewish history, and recalls a connection to nature and innovation.[37] To reciprocate, China began its 'Experience China in Israel' mobile festival in 2009, which was well received in Israel. It highlights China's culture, music and economic miracles. Chinese universities began to teach Hebrew in the mid-1980s, in addition to offering courses on the culture, history and politics of Israel; Israel offers scholarships for Chinese students to pursue their higher education in the country. For example, the Weizmann Institute of Science and the Israel Institute of Technology, two of the top 25 engineering schools worldwide, are a main destination for Chinese students pursuing degrees in this field, and Jewish Studies have been established in several universities in China.

The Confucius Centre in Israel promotes Chinese culture, language and China's business interests, and Einstein Centres have been opened in China to promote Israeli culture and business, trade and technology. The Israeli–Chinese academic co-operation that began in the 1980s is deepening to the extent that most, if not all, Israeli universities and higher educational institutions co-operate with Chinese universities. Their scope includes joint programmes, joint research, admission, conference and technical advancements. A growing Asian community is present in Israel, so much so that elements of an emerging Chinatown can be detected in Tel Aviv. Simultaneously, an Israeli community currently estimated at 10,000 people is growing in China. They are mostly diplomats and entrepreneurs, but they augment the previously existing Jewish communities in Kaifeng and Shanghai. Their community centres, synagogues, schools and clinics are taking shape to serve the community. Both China and Israel have also taken all necessary steps to facilitate tourist and business visas for their nationals. Chinese tourists are flocking to Jerusalem and to Israel's Mediterranean and Red Sea resorts. Chinese and Israeli airlines have direct flights from the main Chinese cities to Tel Aviv and Eilat, facilitating travel between the two countries. The Israeli Pavilion at the Shanghai Expo with its unique architectural design not only became a major destination for visitors to the Expo, but has been marketing Israeli tourism, business and industry since 2010, and leaving a positive impression on millions of Chinese visitors.

Conclusion

The Jewish presence in China goes back to the days of the Tang Dynasty, a multicultural civilization. Jews have lived among the Hui community since the seventh century and have managed to survive up to modern-day China. While Jewish communities were persecuted in many parts of the world, China prides itself on being one of the very few countries in which Jews lived peacefully and prospered side by side with the Han majority. The city of Shanghai was a primary destination for persecuted Jews fleeing Nazi extermination in Europe. Upon the establishment of the PRC, Israel was the first Middle Eastern country to recognize China in January 1950, even though diplomatic relations were established four decades later. During this period of time, China and Israel maintained direct and indirect contact. China held its views on the Arab–Israeli conflict advocating a peaceful solution. In the era of openness, China and Israel developed their bilateral relations into a mutually beneficial partnership. Israel has become a major source of military technology transfer to China and a primary source of modern technology. The scope of Sino–Israeli relations is expanding. It includes arms sales, agro-technology, research and development, science, water systems technology, clean energy, cultural ties and political co-ordination. This trend is expected to be enhanced, solidified and intensified as both countries aim to triple their bilateral trade, estimated currently at $10,000 million annually. Such a goal is attainable given the increasing involvement of Israeli entrepreneurs in Chinese markets, and the increase in Chinese investments and joint ventures in Israel.

6 China and Saudi Arabia

The earliest contact between Saudi Arabia and China goes deep into the history of the Silk Road, of Islam–Chinese relations and back to the famous voyages of the Chinese Muslim Admiral Zheng He to the shores of Arabia. His voyage to the holy city of Mecca in 1421 is celebrated as the starting point of modern contacts between China and Saudi Arabia. When King Abdelaziz Ibn Saud launched his campaign to re-establish the Saudi Third Kingdom and unite the Arabian Peninsula under the Al Saud family in 1902, he established friendly relations with the newly declared Republic of China (ROC) and, in 1949, extended diplomatic relations that continued until 1990. Saudi relations were strategic and pivotal to the ROC, given that the bulk of its energy imports came from Saudi Arabia. The latter maintained its distinguished relations with the ROC even when the majority of the world abandoned Taiwan diplomatically and defected to the PRC in 1971. By the summer of 1989, Saudi Arabia was the only Arab country that did not recognize the PRC, much less had established diplomatic relations with it. It was also the second Middle Eastern country after Israel that had no diplomatic relations with China, a step both countries took in 1990 and 1992 respectively. The loss of diplomatic relations between Taiwan and Saudi Arabia was one of the fundamental diplomacy setbacks for the ROC since WWII, but the two sides still maintain economic representative offices and trade relations. Taiwanese construction companies carried out major construction projects in Saudi Arabia between the 1970s and 1990s, a role currently taken over by China's corporations. Over the past four decades, whether interactions were direct or indirect, Saudi-Sino bilateral relations have developed rapidly, shifted from animosity and discord to pragmatism and friendship and grown into a strategic partnership.

The five pillars of Saudi–Chinese relations

Saudi–Chinese relations

King Abdelaziz Ibn Saud, referred to in the literature as Ibn Saud, the modern founder of Saudi Arabia, was in desperate need of diplomatic recognition to legitimize his conquest of the Arabian Peninsula. He was in political struggles with his rivals on all sides, western, eastern, northern and southern Arabia, and each of these regions had its own political structures. Establishing diplomatic relations with foreign powers such as Britain, France, the United States, China and the USSR was of paramount importance at this stage of power consolidation. By the mid-1930s, Ibn Saud had accomplished his goals, although he later declined Soviet diplomatic relations. At the same time, he continued diplomatic relations with the ROC, not the PRC, as the sole representative of the Chinese people. Saudi Arabia did not intervene in the Chinese civil war, the raging conflict between communist and republican forces, although it favoured a triumph of the republicans. Several hundred Chinese Muslims fled to Mecca because of the civil war and the mistreatment of Muslims in China, and established communities in the two holy cities of Mecca and Medina. Other Muslims fled to Taiwan, whereas East Turkistan Muslims coming from Xinjiang resided in Turkey and have continued their resistance to China's rule since the communist takeover in 1949.

Ideological discord between 1949 and 1978

Saudi Arabia and China found themselves on a natural path of discord following the communist triumph and the birth of the PRC in 1949. This was normal, given the contending ideological differences between communism and Islam, and between Islam as a religion and communism as an anti-religious creed. While China viewed Saudi Arabia as a 'reactionary' kingdom, the cradle of British and later American imperialism, Saudi Arabia viewed China as a 'godless' and lawless country. As the self-declared protector of Islam and Muslims around the world, Saudi Arabia was infuriated by some reports that Muslim minorities were being mistreated under the rule of the PRC. Such reports also discouraged any potential diplomatic relations between the two sides and complicated contacts, especially in international forums. In order to calm Muslim fears, the PRC launched a diplomatic offensive in Third World forums to convince Islamic countries that Muslims in China enjoyed their freedoms and privileges, and that the majority and minorities in China co-exist peacefully. Chou En-lai met the Saudi Foreign Minister, then Prince Faisal, later King of Saudi Arabia from 1964 to 1975, in conjunction with the Bandung Conference in 1955. Price Faisal encouraged China to improve its treatment of Muslims and allow Muslims to perform Hajj, a request the premier honoured and Hajj pilgrimage continued until 1966, with an average of 2,000 pilgrims annually. Because of the Cultural Revolution, Hajj was totally cut off in 1966, then resumed in 1979.

However, China continued to highlight the way in which Muslims were being integrated normally into a multi-ethnic and multicultural country. Shichor maintains that 'the Chinese made extensive use of Islam; they invited Muslims, and appointed Chinese Muslims as leaders and members of cultural delegations sent to the Middle East. These delegations and pilgrimages often remained in the Middle East for several months, visiting most of the countries in the area and meeting not only religious personalities but also high-ranking political leaders.'[1] Shichor points to Burhan Shahidi (his Chinese name is Pao Erhan), the chairman of China's Islamic Association, as one of the influential figures who met King Saud of Saudi Arabia, King Hussein of Jordan and Prince Al Bader of Yemen. Shahidi secured Yemen's diplomatic recognition of the PRC and enhanced bilateral cultural relations with the region.[2] Despite Pao Erhan's eloquence, the Saudi monarch was not convinced of the legitimacy of the PRC's claims for freedom of worship for Muslims in China. The King and his sons after him, Saud, Faisal and Khalid, continued their recognition of and co-operation with the Republic of China as sole representative of the Chinese people. It was not until 21 July 1990 that King Fahd – aided by his pragmatic nephew, Bander bin Sultan, the Saudi ambassador to the United States – decided to recognize the PRC and exchange diplomatic missions with China.

During the 1950s, Saudi–Chinese relations were viewed as 'unfriendly' at times, and characterized by animosity at other times. Aside from the conditions of Muslim minorities in China, the PRC's support of leftist and Maoist forces in the Arabian Gulf region, particularly the United Arab Emirates and Oman, aggravated Saudi Arabia. The Sultanate of Oman was embroiled in a civil war with the Dhofar Liberation Movement, which received substantial military support from China through South Yemen. Furthermore, China was a major supporter of Nasser who intervened in the Yemeni civil war in favour of the republican forces at the expense of the Imamat (kingdom) in Yemen. Saudi Arabia came to the rescue of Imam Al-Bader; therefore, Egypt and Saudi Arabia collided militarily in Yemen. Only Nasser's defeat in the 1967 War at the hands of Israel reduced tensions between Egypt and Saudi Arabia; King Al-Bader of Yemen lost the war and northern Yemen republican forces established the Arab Republic of Yemen.

At a later stage, Saudi Arabia reconciled with Yemen, and the latter compromised on its borders with Saudi Arabia, giving up control over major territorial areas. In exchange, Saudi Arabia provided economic assistance to Yemen, and opened up its cities to a Yemeni labour force in search of employment. This arrangement continued until Yemen sided with Saddam Hussein in his invasion of Kuwait in 1990. At that point, Saudi Arabia and other Gulf countries imposed sanctions on Yemen that lasted for an entire decade. Yemen never fully recovered, and still suffers from their catastrophic effects on its economy. Undoubtedly, the deportation of hundreds of thousands of Yemeni labourers and their families from the Gulf region represented the greatest economic loss to Yemen over the past half century as the country used to count on their remittances to sustain its economy.

Socio-cultural, political and economic developments in China from the mid-1960s to the mid-1970s also complicated China's foreign policy. Internally, China was tangled in unending revolutionary conditions and, externally, ensnared in an ideological war with the two superpowers: the US and the former Soviet Union. Fighting at home and abroad proved to be draining and costly. The systematic persecution of Muslims in China ruined its image across the Islamic world. Its Cultural Revolution was understood as a revolution against its tradition, religion and culture, especially in Saudi Arabia. Communist leaders were aware of Saudi and Muslim resentment towards the revolution and its impact on Muslims in China. They were also fully aware of the growing stature of Saudi Arabia after King Faisal imposed an oil embargo on the West in 1973, increased oil prices and established the Organization of Islamic Conference (OIC) in 1969. The charismatic leadership of King Faisal made China re-evaluate its views on the independence of the so called 'reactionary' kingdoms from their imperial masters, i.e. the US. Furthermore, China needed all the support it could secure in its battle with the Soviet Union, and Saudi Arabia fitted perfectly within the containment paradigm. In fact, Saudi Arabia contributed tremendously to curbing the expansion of the Soviets in the Middle East. It was also instrumental in curbing the USSR's expansion in the Far East.

China has been closely following the 'American containment' paradigm against the Soviet Union since 1963. This impetus served as a prelude for American–Chinese rapprochements in 1968. Realizing the importance of the Saudi role, China reduced its criticism of 'reactionary kingdoms', but this mellowing of terms did not lead to the securing of Saudi support when China's membership of the United Nations came up for a vote in 1971. Saudi Arabia voted no on the resolution, whereas some other Arab countries such as Algeria co-sponsored it, and others such as Kuwait lobbied for it and mobilized support in its favour.

Triple containment

Saudi Arabia, China and the United States resented the Soviet Union's attempts to penetrate the Middle East and the Islamic world via Southern Yemen, Egypt, Syria and Algeria in the 1960s. Therefore, a tacit and sometimes explicit alliance developed, even though the three participants were not on good terms or even in direct contact with each other. However, by the end of the 1960s, the US and China closely co-ordinated their efforts to contain the Soviets. In the post-Mao era, their co-operation was open and significant in halting the so called 'Soviet advances in every corner of the globe.'[3] Their goals were identical, but their means differed. Both the US and China promoted and implemented containment of the Soviet threat in the Middle East, and so did Saudi Arabia. In 1964 Crown Prince Faisal deposed his brother, King Saud, in a family–clergy orchestrated coup. King Saud was charged with mismanagement of the treasury, with jeopardizing the prestige of the monarchy and being vulnerable to the influence of Arab nationalists and leftists. King Faisal restored the prestige of the monarchy and redrew its foreign policy path. He strengthened the alliance of Saudi Arabia with the West, even though at times he collided with its closest ally, the United States, on major issues, such as the Arab–Israeli conflict. The king also excluded from government posts the so called 'red princes', members of the royal family with leftist and Arab nationalist leanings. These wanted to align Saudi Arabia with Egypt, with Arab nationalism, with the left and therefore with the Soviet Union.

To highlight the kingdom's Islamic legitimacy, King Faisal underlined Saudi guardianship of the holy shrines and of Muslim minorities around the world with an ambitious expansion in Mecca and Medina, this being the cradle and seat of Islam. The guardianship of the holy shrines provided Saudi Arabia with the privilege to examine the conditions of all Muslims, including those in China, and at the same time to support the cause of Arabs and Muslims around the world. Such claims were used as grounds to confront the Soviets in Afghanistan between 1979 and 1985. King Faisal was a farsighted leader. His goal was to solidify the Islamic front and provide it with enduring institutions in all fields, politics, economics, education, etc. Among his greatest accomplishments were the OIC and the Islamic Development Bank in 1969. The OIC is an umbrella organization for Islamic countries to rival the growing threat of the left and of nationalism across the Islamic world. Its goals, among others, were to co-ordinate foreign policies among Islamic states and to defend the rights of Muslim minorities around the world. Nationalism vs. Islam became the subject of the intellectual discourse in the post-1967 War defeat. By establishing the OIC, King Faisal added a primary component to Saudi political legitimacy that rests on a pan-Islamic perspective: Saudi Arabia made pan-Islamism the centre of its foreign policy, which earned it the respect of the international community. King Faisal's pan-Islamism was heightened by the tragic defeat of Arab nationalism in the 1967 War but, as he was a staunch supporter of the rights of the Palestinian people, he never celebrated its demise. Nationalist and leftist forces were fatally debilitated and held responsible for the humiliation of the Arab people, albeit the defeat made Islam a dominant political force in the region. It had also augmented the leadership role of Saudi Arabia in regional and international affairs.

In addition to the triple containment of the Soviet threat, China admired King Faisal's support for the Palestinians and their rights all along and developed an appreciation for his independent foreign policy, especially his imposition of an oil embargo on the US and the West in 1973, protesting against their continued support for Israel. For the first time, oil became an instrument in support of the Palestinian cause and the Arab people in their struggle against Israel. Even though European countries were negatively affected by the embargo, they, along with the entire world, admired and respected King Faisal's move. Even Egypt, Saudi Arabia's traditional foe from 1954 to 1970, admired it and greatly benefited from it. In fact, after Nasser's sudden death in 1970, Anwar Sadat determined to pursue a path of peace and was open to the idea of realigning with the United States, a step that materialized through the shuttle diplomacy conducted by Kissinger between 1971 and 1977 in his capacities as Secretary of State and National Security Adviser to Nixon and Ford; this was also done through the efforts of Cyrus Vance, Carter's Secretary of State from 1977 to 1980.

The growing importance of Saudi Arabia in regional and international relations prompted China to explore diplomatic ties once again from 1964 to 1982, even soliciting Kuwait's assistance, but diplomatic relations did not materialize. Chinese media began favourable coverage of issues related to the kingdom, especially its rising stature in the Gulf and the Middle East region. Behbehani affirms that, despite evidence that China desired to establish relations with Saudi Arabia as an emerging power, and despite 'its acceptance of Saudi policies, Saudi Arabia remained adamant in its refusal to recognize China.'[4] Saudi Arabia insisted on the normal development of relations between the two sides, which finally occurred on 21 July 1990, 12 days before the Iraqi invasion of Kuwait.

In hindsight, Saudi rejection of diplomatic relations with China can be viewed as a poor foreign policy decision. In this period of time (1971–90), the US–Chinese rapprochement was well under way, and the US would have not objected to it, but the US would have supported a Saudi decision to establish diplomatic relations with China. The American goal was to speed up China's realignment with the West, and deepen the wedge between China and the Soviet Union. China itself was very supportive of the US role in the Middle East, as Kissinger claimed, although its media campaign against 'American imperialism' in the Middle East never stopped; but this was something the US understood and was more than willing to live with. Whereas the Arabs continued to believe in China's media attacks, the Israelis and Americans were more concerned about the substance of China's policy than what its propaganda machines broadcast.[5] China also supported Saudi views on 'Gulf security' and Prince (later King) Fahd's talks with the Shah of Iran in May 1975 and the subsequent visit of the Iranian prime minister to Saudi Arabia.[6] Saudi Arabia, the US and China were also engaged in a triple containment of the Soviet Union in Afghanistan.

In other words, Saudi Arabia had no substantial grounds to reject diplomatic relations with China except for ideological differences: Islam vs. communism. Saudi Arabia's fear of its own clergy was another related element, as the religious establishment would have vehemently opposed seeing the flag of a communist country flying in Riyadh or in Jeddah, the home of some diplomatic missions and only 70 miles from the holy shrines of Mecca. Furthermore, it could have antagonized Saudis who continuously condemned the mistreatment of Muslim minorities in China. Undaunted, China continued its attempts to establish diplomatic relations with Saudi Arabia and other Gulf countries, and to infiltrate Gulf markets through Kuwait and later via the Omani route.

Since the mid-1970s, political developments on the world scene have contributed to the improvement in Saudi–Chinese relations. The course of events fell in the right places to improve the relationship between the two sides that eventually led to full diplomatic recognition in the summer of 1990. As stated previously, the Soviet invasion of Afghanistan in 1978 served as an impetus for co-ordination between the foes of the USSR. It had provided the United

States, China, Saudi Arabia and the Islamic world with the needed opportunity to put an end to Soviet expansionism in the region. In invading Afghanistan, the Soviet Union was acting under the premise that the Vietnam War weakened the US beyond its ability to respond to any Soviet expansionist scheme in the Middle East and Indian Ocean. All along, the Soviets had the dream of reaching the warm waters of the Indian Ocean and the rich oil fields of the Middle East. The Soviets reasoned that the US needed a decade or two to recover from its catastrophic defeat in Vietnam and recuperate from the three decades of civil strife caused by the civil rights movement.

The seeming deterioration of American prestige in Latin America, in the Far East and in Africa convinced the Soviets that it was time to pursue its expansionist dreams. The developments on the Iranian scene, the fall of the Shah's regime, marked another notch in America's diminishing influence. When Iranian revolutionaries took American diplomats hostage for 444 days, Jimmy Carter was tagged as a weak president who was unable to free American diplomats taken as hostages, much less halt Soviet advances worldwide. The Carter Administration was reinforcing globally and domestically the same impression of an incompetent America. It seemed as if an opportunity was present for the Soviets to expand and encircle the American presence in the Middle East, and to pursue its goals in the Indian Ocean and the Far East as well. Suddenly, the USSR's popularity was rising in the 1970s, and socialism was surging and thriving in Latin America and Africa, but the scenarios drawn by Soviet planners proved to be fatal miscalculations.

When Reagan was elected in 1980, he determined to make the Soviets in Afghanistan suffer the same fate the US had had in Vietnam, just as a decade earlier the Soviet Union had made the US presence in Vietnam costly. In its mobilization of Muslims against the Soviets in Afghanistan, the US enjoyed the unconditional support of Saudi Arabia, the Gulf countries, Jordan and Egypt. Added to this coalition were the majority of Muslim countries, the West and China. To evict the Soviets from Afghanistan, these allies funded what has come to be known as the modern Jihad movement at the grassroots level. The sense of defeatism in the Middle East conflict was utilized by Jihadists as a motivational instrument to resist the Soviet invasion of Afghanistan. Suddenly, thousands of young Muslims began to drop out of schools, colleges and universities and moved to training camps in Pakistan and on the borders of Afghanistan to fight the Soviets. Arab Jihadists in particular looked at the opportunity to fight the Soviets as a sort of compensation for their failure to come to the assistance of Palestinians in their time of need. Muslim youth prided themselves in taking on the challenge of confronting a superpower.

The US spent over $28,000 million in training and armaments to fund the movement.[7] Saudi Arabia served as the core for the mobilization process, while Pakistan served as the military staging point. Such developments served China's interests on a platter. China assisted Pakistan militarily, and their relations were fortified. The abundance of weapons in Afghanistan, American generosity in providing anti-aircraft missiles, especially Stinger missiles, anti-tank missiles and the quality of the resources made available to the Mujahideen made the Soviet presence in Afghanistan exceptionally costly. In 1982, four years after the initial invasion, the Soviets turned on the defensive. The Reagan and Thatcher Administrations, King Fahd and General Zia Ul-Haq of Pakistan made it impossible for the Soviets to stay in Afghanistan and, as Reagan was elected on a tough foreign policy platform, he delivered beyond expectations. When Mikhail Gorbachev was elected as General Secretary of the Communist Party of the Soviet Union in 1985, he realized the limitations of Soviet power and the futility of the occupation of Afghanistan. Therefore, he decided to withdraw in 1988. The Soviet Union came out of the war economically bankrupt, morally devastated and politically demoralized. Gorbachev's attempts to revive the USSR were insufficient to extend its life; it finally collapsed in the autumn of 1989, and was officially dissolved on 25 December 1991. The Soviet invasion of Afghanistan also proved to be costly to the entire world. The current War on Terror and the clash of civilizations that ensued after the demise of the Soviet Union, along with Afghanistan's perpetual instability, are some of the enduring repercussions of that invasion.

Deng Xiaoping and Saudi–Chinese relations

Since Deng Xiaoping consolidated his power in 1978, he determined to alter China's domestic and foreign policy entirely.[8] Xiaoping's main goal was to accelerate economic reforms. He understood well and more than any other contemporary Chinese leader the vitality of economic reform, growth, productivity and efficiency in the overall scheme of rebuilding China. Therefore, China became one of most rapidly growing economies. Sutter affirmed that 'from 1979 to 2007, the average annual growth rate of China's gross domestic product (GDP) was over 9.8 percent. The Chinese economy in 2007 was nearly fourteen times larger than it was in 1979, and per capita GDP was more than ten times larger.'[9] To fuel this gigantic economic growth, China turned to the Middle East and to Saudi Arabia in particular. Oman was the first Arab Gulf country to sell oil to China in 1983 even though China's domestic oil production was still sufficient to meet its needs. Under Deng Xiaoping's tenure, conditions were ripe for the establishment of diplomatic relations between China and Saudi Arabia, but the Saudis, as well as Muslims around the world, were entrenched in their resistance to the communist invasion of Afghanistan. Muslims made no distinction between China and the Soviet Union: all communists were a monolith, and anti-communist attitudes were tinged with the resentment caused by the invasion. Muslims in general were also influenced by the emerging Jihadi political discourse that dominated the Islamic awakening and the Islamic resurgence since 1967. The Saudi government did not dare to establish diplomatic relations with communist China between 1976 and 1988 for this very reason. The step would have provoked unnecessary confrontation with the clergy, with the public and with

Muslims outraged by communist repression of fellow Muslims in Afghanistan, in the USSR and China.

The golden age

Saudi–Chinese partnership has grown smoothly since the late 1980s, prospered in the 1990s and peaked in 2006. Their bilateral relations were strengthened as China tacitly positioned itself with the triumphant coalition in the war against Iraq. Their first successful arms sales deal in 1988 had a spillover effect on their bilateral relations. On its part, China highlighted its objection to the sanctions imposed on Iraq throughout the 1990s, but did not object to the international efforts of dislodging Saddam Hussein from Kuwait in 1991. China's opposition to the sanctions stems from the fact that it had built strong military, trade and energy ties with Iraq since the late 1970s. Under sanctions, Iraqis suffered greatly, and hundreds of thousands, especially children, women and the elderly, died between 1991 and 2003. The sanctions also crippled Iraq's health sector, agriculture, electricity and aviation, and food shortages were reported everywhere. Iraq's infrastructure deteriorated to the brink of collapse. In the late 1990s, the world realized the devastating impact of these sanctions and approved the Food-for-oil programme. China benefited enormously from the programme.

In his 3-day state visit to Saudi Arabia on 1 November 1999, President Jiang Zemin signed lucrative deals with Saudi Arabia. China agreed to open up its refinery sector to Saudi investments, and Saudi Arabia agreed to joint oil exploration and development ventures, natural gas exploration and co-operation in the petrochemicals sector. The increase in trade volume and Chinese reliance on Saudi oil intensified the exchange of high-ranking officials. Upon assuming the throne in the summer of 2005, King Abdullah Ibn Abdelaziz made his first official visit to China in January 2006, not to the United States, Saudi Arabia's traditional ally. It was a clear indication of the importance of the Sino–Saudi strategic partnership. Hu Jintao returned the visit 2 months later. The partnership continues to grow unhindered in spite of King Abdullah's criticism of China's veto of the UN's Security Council Resolution 77 condemning Syria on 4 February 2012. China itself rushed to calm Saudi anger, sending its Middle East Envoy, its Special Envoy to Syria and other senior officials to Riyadh to explain its views on the Syrian revolution.

Security threats and opportunities

The 11 September terrorist attacks drastically altered international relations. The US was shocked that fifteen of the nineteen terrorists were from its closest ally in the Middle East, Saudi Arabia, and the latter was no less shocked to learn that its nationals were involved in such horrific attacks of this magnitude against civilians in the United States.[10] Suddenly, calls for nuclear attacks and annihilation of the holy shrines of Mecca and Medina, dividing Saudi Arabia, eliminating the 'Wahhabi threat' and occupying the country were regular material discussed by the American media and think tanks, on university campuses, in political circles and congressional committees. It was dreadful for US and Saudi Arabia to realize that, after seven decades of close partnership, they knew little about each other, or for them to comprehend the level of resentment and sometimes open animosity they harboured towards each other. For the first time since the 1930s, Saudi Arabia realized that its territorial integrity and sovereignty might be threatened by its closest ally. Frantically searching for security guarantees, it wholeheartedly pursued the Sino–Russian option. In return, Russia and China were delighted to secure some grounds in the Middle East, but careful not to antagonize a wounded hegemonic power such as the United States in its traditional sphere of influence. Therefore, Saudi Arabia, China and Russia understood and supported America's need to eradicate Al-Qaeda and the Taliban regime in Afghanistan; after all, it was a major security threat to them as well.

Saudi Arabia had already been the victim of terrorist attacks carried out by Al-Qaeda, while China was eager to eliminate its Taliban neighbours who pledged to support the East Turkistan Islamic Movement in Xinjiang. As for Russia, the influence of the Jihadi movement was paramount in its Muslim breakaway republics, especially Chechnya. In the aftermath of the terrorist attacks, global support was overwhelming. American allies and foes alike felt the pain. Even countries such as Iran hurried to condemn the attacks and offer support in US efforts to combat terrorism. Iran supported the US occupation of Afghanistan through its allies, the Northern Alliance of Ahmed Shah Massoud. The Shi'a government in Iran was happier than China to see its 'fundamentalist' Sunni-Taliban neighbours toppled, and expedited their defeat and departure. Saudi Arabia was accused of being supportive of terrorism, and the US placed a wide range of demands that included cracking down on Islamists in the country, reforming the education system, moderating its 'Wahhabi' doctrine, liberalizing its socio-political system and showing whole-hearted support for the peace process. Feeling guilty, weak and shaken, the Saudis submitted fully to all American demands, without exception.

Towards the end of 2001, the world rallied behind the US in its war against Al-Qaeda and the Taliban regime, and soon after that the US occupied Afghanistan; the Taliban and their Al-Qaeda allies were on the run. In early 2002, the Bush Administration began to publicly discuss the elimination of Saddam Hussein's regime and the invasion of Iraq. However, the intention to do so was circulated even during the 2000 election campaign and the early days of the administration, but the terrorist attacks hastened the decision. The Bush Administration began to build a case for the invasion: it accused Saddam Hussein of possessing nuclear weapons of mass destruction (WMD), and of supporting Al-Qaeda. Both accusations proved to be unfounded. Saudi Minister of Foreign Affairs, Prince Saud Al Faisal, objected to the invasion of Iraq and explained the potential consequences: Iranian dominance in the region, the surge of Shi'ism in Iraq and the Middle East, a civil war in Iraq, a bloody invasion and severe American casualties. Bush gave no heed to such advice as, clearly, he did not comprehend the ramifications of war efforts against Iraq. Surprisingly, when the US introduced Resolution 1441 on 8 November 2002, China cast its second vote in favour of 'Chapter 7' since 1971, tacitly authorizing the use of force against Iraq to compel Saddam Hussein to comply with Iraq's previous commitment towards inspection of WMD. While China and Saudi Arabia knew that Saddam had no such weapons, and that the goal of the Bush Administration was regime change, Chinese–American relations were much more important than defending Saddam Hussein's regime. The sincere Saudi advice given to Bush on the consequences of the war proved to be fully accurate, and Saudi fears of a Shi'a fundamentalist takeover and a potential alliance with Iran materialized. In the beginning, the invasion accomplished its immediate goal: occupy Iraq and topple the Saddam government. The US and its allies occupied Iraq without major resistance, but they had no postwar plans, and this led to eight devastating years of war. However, in exchange for China's vote in favour of the military option against Iraq, the US allowed the Iraqi government to honour oil agreements signed between the Saddam government and China. Therefore, China's oil and trade interests were not hindered, while Saudi Arabia was left to deal with security against the Iranian threat and a surge of Shi'ism in the Middle East.

Current political co-operation

High-ranking Saudi and Chinese officials have been exchanging visits since the mid-1990s. Chinese Presidents Jiang Zemin and Hu Jintao, along with State Council Premier Wen Jiabao, exchanged numerous visits with King Abdullah, Minister of Defence Prince Sultan and Minister of Foreign Affairs Prince Saud to work on bilateral and multilateral issues pertaining to the region. The current political co-operation between China and Saudi Arabia encompasses a wide range of issues. Chinese leaders seek to further the One-China policy by limiting Taiwan's ability to manoeuvre in the Gulf region, combating terrorism and separatism, and curbing East Turkistan's ability to secure Saudi support for its cause. The Saudis are interested in increasing Chinese involvement in the Middle East and international affairs at large, and believe that China should be involved in issues such as the Palestinian peace process, the UN peacekeeping missions and peace building in Afghanistan and Iraq. Saudi Arabia wants to see China play a 'constructive role' in the international response to the 'Arab Spring', especially regarding Syria, where both China and Russia have extended the life of Bashar al-Assad's oppressive, dictatorial regime. Saudi Arabia also wants China to press Iran to abandon its nuclear project and refrain from jeopardizing the security of the Gulf region.

Energy co-operation

Saudi Arabia is one of China's primary sources for oil imports, and is soon projected to be its main source of oil and natural gas. Energy is at the centre of Saudi–Chinese co-operation. Chinese Vice Premier Li Keqiang's statement accurately summed up Saudi–Chinese relations: '(I)t conforms to the fundamental interests of the two states to progress all-round cooperation in energy exploration, technology service, business and policy exchange so as to realize win-win and common development.'[11] Saudi–Chinese energy co-operation is multifaceted in nature; it includes oil imports, upstreaming, downstreaming, building oil reserve tanks, refining and petrochemical industries. Over the last 4 years, Saudi Arabia has provided 17 percent of China's total oil imports. China is in the process of displacing the US as Saudi Arabia's number one oil importer. 'Last year, Saudi exports to the United States fell to 989,000 barrels a day, the lowest level in 22 years, from 1.5 million barrels a day the previous year, according to the Energy Information Administration. Meanwhile, Saudi sales to China surged above a million barrels a day last year, nearly doubling from the previous year. The kingdom now accounts for a quarter of Chinese oil imports.'[12] Given the volatility of the global oil market and the ongoing standoff between Iran and the rest of the world, these numbers are only expected to increase. Saudi Arabia will continue to play its main role of being a 'balancer' by assuring global markets of its ability to make up for any shortages resulting from the decline in Iran's oil exports. The International Energy Agency has estimated that the sanctions imposed on Iran would carve out between 800,000 and 1 mbd. However, Saudi Arabia is capable of producing double that figure, even at short notice. Saudi oil production currently stands at 9.9 mbd, but its production capacity can exceed 12 mbd without stressing its oil infrastructure. The ability to increase its oil production so easily allows Saudi Arabia not only to marginalize Iran, but also to calm world markets and boost economic growth at a critical stage when the American and European economies are showing some signs of recovery. Figure 6.1 illustrates China's major oil exporters.

Saudi–Chinese energy co-operation also extends to building China's strategic oil reserves. Currently, China maintains a 30-day oil reserve, which falls well below the 90-day reserve level of the average developed country and the 150-day reserve of the US. China's main goal is to increase its reserve capacity to 90 days in 5–10 years. Saudi Arabia is assisting China in building the Dalian oil reserve base, one of four strategic oil reserves in China. The others are being built in Qingdao, Ningbo and Zhoushan. According to Chinese sources, 'construction on another eight bases will be completed by the end of 2012.'[13] A third aspect of the co-operation between the two sides is building refineries in both markets. In early 2012 Sinopec signed an agreement with Saudi Armco to build the Yanbu refinery on the Saudi Red Sea coast. Originally, the project began in 2006 as a joint venture between Aramco and ConocoPhillips. Sinopec will own a 37.5 percent stake in the refinery,

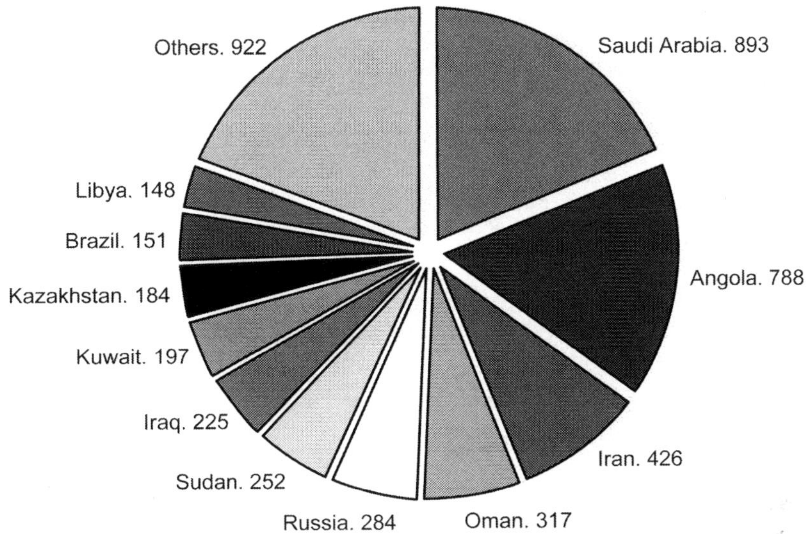

Figure 6.1 China's crude oil imports in 2010 (000 bpd)
Source: Energy Information Administration at: http://www.eia.gov/cabs/china/Full.html

boosting Chinese presence in Saudi domestic markets. The construction of the refinery will boost the ability of Aramco and Sinopec to export refined oil to Asian and world markets given the fact that the city of Yanbu is strategically located on the western shore of the Arabian Peninsula.[14] Use of the Yanbu refinery would also bypass the Strait of Hormuz, thereby reducing China's vulnerability to security developments in the Gulf region. Talks are also under way between Sinopec and Aramco to build a refinery in the Chinese province of Fujian. A related aspect of the Saudi–Chinese energy co-operation is the petrochemicals industry. Saudi Arabia has made significant strides in the industry in recent years. Saudi Arabia Basic Industries Corporation (SABIC), a leading world petrochemicals company, exports petrochemical products to China worth over $2.00 thousand million annually.

Trade relations

Indirect trade relations between China and Saudi Arabia began in the late 1970s through Kuwait and Oman. However, the first successful arms sale to Saudi Arabia in 1988 and the subsequent mutual diplomatic recognition two years later accelerated bilateral trade between the two sides. Their trade relations cover a wide range of sectors, including petrochemicals, construction, aluminium, iron ore, phosphate, cement, consumer commodities, railway construction, motor production and various high-tech products. The last two decades have witnessed a drastic increase in trade between the two sides. During the 2003–8 period, China–Saudi Arabia trade registered annual growth rates of 30 to

50 percent. In 2008, bilateral trade surged by 64.7 percent to $41.8 billion, two years ahead of the goal set in 2006.'[15] Table 6.1 illustrates their bilateral trade in millions of dollars for the period from 2001 to 2010.

The two countries set a goal of $100 thousand million in trade relations by the end of 2015. Given China's heavy investment and presence not only in the oil and gas sectors but also in petrochemicals and minerals in Saudi Arabia, this goal appears very realistic. 'It (the goal) is a conservative estimate. There is high possibility that the China–Saudi Arabia trade would far exceed the target by 2015, as bilateral relations are getting stronger and the two nations' industries are highly complementary.'[16] Direct investment in Sino–Saudi markets is also contributing to the enhancement of their bilateral partnership and is considered to be a major step towards the 2015 goal.

Cultural relations

Sino–Saudi partnership in the energy and trade sectors has had positive spillover effects on cultural exchanges between the two sides. Saudi public opinion concerning China has changed drastically from regarding the country as a communist enemy to seeing it as both a friendly nation and a strategic partner. For its part, China has taken major steps towards improving its image among the Saudi public. By some distance, the construction of the Holy Shrines Metro by the China Railway Construction Corporation Limited is the high point of China's cultural construction projects in Saudi Arabia so far. In the Hajj season of 2011, Saudi and international media broadcast live images of the metro transporting hundreds of thousands of pilgrims to the Hajj sites in and outside the holy city of Mecca. It was a captivating scene and a triumph of engineering and technology in terms of the safety and speed of moving pilgrims to and out of the Grand Mosque in Mecca. The task of managing the movement of three million pilgrims performing identical Hajj rituals has been challenging for the Saudi authorities in terms of speed, efficiency and safety over the past five decades. The 2011 season was one of the

Table 6.1 Saudi–Chinese volume of trade in millions of dollars from 2001 to 2010

Year	*Volume of trade in millions of dollars*
2010	43,195.49
2009	32,548.39
2008	41,846.17
2007	25,366.97
2006	20,140.37
2005	16,070.14
2004	10,298.10
2003	7,319.12
2002	5,106.89
2001	4,075.19

Source: China Statistical Year Book, 2010.

most successful in recent memory in terms of the number of pilgrims and overall safety, and China contributed greatly towards that end. It was also a successful season for Chinese Muslims; their numbers exceeded 15,000 pilgrims for the first time, a 10 percent increase over the previous year.

Another aspect of the noticeable increase in cultural relations between the two countries is the fact that Saudi Arabia is sending students to study in China, a step that was inconceivable three decades ago. Saudi Arabia is no longer worried about communist indoctrination, atheism or 'red decadence', a reference to comradeship between genders in China schools. Currently, the Saudi Ministry of Higher Education is sponsoring 1,500 students studying in Chinese universities across the country.[17] Saudi Arabia has also made its universities available to Chinese students seeking to learn Arabic and pursue education in its higher education institutions. China also sends Muslim students to Saudi Arabia to specialize in Islamic studies so that they can serve as Imams (religious leaders) when they return to China.

China has also become a tourist destination. Saudis have nearly unlimited access to China, and the process of obtaining visas has been simplified and made more convenient to encourage intercultural relations. Many Saudis visit China in search of healthcare services. Youth exchange programmes are another important aspect of cultural exchange. In commemoration of the twentieth anniversary of the establishment of Saudi–Chinese diplomatic relations, a Saudi youth delegation held the first Sino–Saudi Youth Forum in Beijing on 21 July 2011. Three decades ago, this cultural exchange would have been far beyond the comprehension of the wildest Saudi-Sino dreams. Saudi Arabia would never have exposed its youth to 'communist' indoctrination, infiltration or interaction. However, in the new China, such exchange is termed 'cultural' and serves as an instrument of interpersonal relations. It is also a means of enhancing mutual understanding and friendship between the two sides.

Another aspect of the bilateral relations is the active participation of Saudi Arabia in the Shanghai World Expo since 2010. Saudi Arabia spent $150 million on its pavilion, making it one of the most visited and most attractive in the Expo. The design of the Saudi pavilion was a joint collaboration between Saudi and Chinese architectural engineers. Their final product was a captivating pavilion in the shape of a half-moon silk treasure boat, surrounded by deserts, seas and fifty palm trees. It symbolizes Saudi Arabia, a land of the generous, endlessly giving 'mother desert', with access to world seas and endowed with blessed date palm trees. It was estimated that over four million people visited the pavilion at the 2010 Expo.[18] The pavilion remains open and serves to promote Saudi culture and bilateral Sino–Saudi relations.

In Saudi Arabia, there are over 100 Chinese corporations operating in the domestic market, most of which are construction firms carrying out major building projects throughout the kingdom. These corporations employ a Chinese community of about 20,000 that resides in Saudi Arabia. Sino–Saudi communal relations are described as friendly. There have been no incidents of violence reported as in the case of Algeria.

Arms sales

Saudi Arabia is a major arms importer from the US, Britain, France, Germany, China, Russia and Italy (Table 6.2). Saudi Arabia spends 10 percent of its annual gross domestic product (GDP) on armaments.[19] Although Saudi–Chinese military co-operation is shrouded in extreme secrecy, arms sales are a substantial component of Saudi–Chinese relations. Alterman and Garver maintain that 'Saudi Arabia has become the third largest buyer of Chinese arms in the Middle East, lagging only behind Egypt and Iran.'[20] Saudi–Chinese co-operation in this area goes back to the 1980s. Having been turned down by the Reagan Administration because of Congressional objections to selling Saudi Arabia medium- and long-range missiles, Saudi Arabia turned to China. The Congressional objections came from the Israeli lobby that feared the missiles might undermine Israeli military superiority in the Middle East. Saudi Arabia began talks about the purchase of the DF (Dongfeng, or East Wind) CSS-2 in the mid-1980s and successfully concluded the deal in 1988. Saudi Arabia purchased fifty CSS-2 intermediate missiles 'which are capable of carrying a nuclear payload',[21] in addition to nine missile launchers. The United States objected strongly to the deal, protested against it and demanded that the Saudis open up the missile sites for inspection, a demand dismissed by the Saudis. Ironically, the leading negotiator was the Saudi ambassador to the United States, Bander bin Sultan.

In 2007 acting on an advice from Kuwait, Saudi Arabia ordered 54 Chinese PLZ-45 155/45 mm self-propelled howitzers, sufficient to equip two artillery battalions, from China North Industries Group Corporation (CNGC). The company 'developed the PLZ45 155 mm self-propelled gun-howitzer system in the early 1990s for the export market. The artillery system is armed with a 155 mm main gun derived from the Type 89 (PLL01) 155 mm/45-calibre towed gun-howitzer, mounted on a newly-developed tracked chassis. China obtained the 155 mm/45-calibre howitzer technologies from Austria in the 1980s, and developed its own 155 mm/45-calibre howitzer.'[22] In addition to

Table 6.2 Saudi Arabia's military expenditures from 2001 to 2010 in dollars (000 million)

Year	*Dollars (000 million)*
2010	42,917
2009	41,273
2008	40,159
2007	40,919
2006	35,522
2005	31,183
2004	25,879
2003	23,279
2002	23,109
2001	26,322

Source: SIPRI Yearbook 2011, p. 211

Kuwait and Saudi Arabia, Pakistan has shown interest in the howitzers, and will probably acquire them soon.

Chinese arms sales to the Middle East peaked in the 1980s, reaching 87 percent of China's overall arms sales. During the 1990s, however, sales declined to nearly 32 percent, and the average share of the Middle East in China's arms sales stood at 34 percent between 2000 and 2008. However, these figures are less impressive from the Saudi perspective. Only about 3.5 percent of the Middle East's overall arms are purchased from China.[23] Although China continues to aim high in Middle East markets, the US, Britain, France and Russia remain Saudi Arabia's primary arms suppliers. Table 6.3 illustrates arms transfer agreements by supplier for the period between 2003 and 2010.

Obviously, the US, Britain and Russia remain the primary suppliers of arms to the Middle East. Although other European countries such as France, Italy and Germany maintain their role of supplying allies in the region with arms, China's contributions remain modest. Saudi Arabia also remains a major importer of American weapons, followed by the UAE. Israel also remains a destination for state-of-the-art American military technology, which has allowed it to maintain its military superiority in the Middle East. Among the developing nations, Saudi Arabia ranked third in 2010, purchasing $2.2 thousand million worth of arms. It was preceded by Taiwan, with $2.7 thousand million, and India, which led the developing world with $5.8 thousand million in arms agreements. The latest figures for the period from 2007 to 2010 place the total value of Saudi Arabia's arms agreements at $28.9 thousand million, most of which are supplied by Western arms suppliers. The neighbouring UAE, which has nearly identical security threats to Saudi Arabia, also placed substantial orders, estimated at $15.1 thousand million, during the same period.[24] Chinese advancements in the manufacture of modern jet-fighters such as the J-10 and J-17 could bolster its presence in the high-tech arms sales markets. The J-10 and J-17 have already attracted the attention of countries such as Pakistan, which concluded a deal worth $140 million to purchase 100 J-10s. This development will probably influence the Saudi

Table 6.3 Regional arms transfer agreements, by supplier, 2003–10 in millions of current US dollars

Supplier	*2003–2006*	*2007–2010*
United States	16,059	51,865
Russia	12,100	8,300
France	2,100	5,000
United Kingdom	10,100	10,700
China	2,100	2,000
Germany	2,000	3,200
Italy	800	4,000

Source: Data provided by Grimmett, Richard. Congressional Research Service, *Annual Report on Conventional Arms Transfers to Developing Nations, 2003–2010*

result of the traditional Pakistani–Saudi military co-operation asing Sino–Saudi partnership. Saudi Arabia continues to diver- imports given the fact that it still has no direct access to the ican arms technology. Whereas Saudi Arabia continues to pur- -15 series, for example, Israel is well ahead in purchasing the F-32. The ntinues to provide more advanced arms to Israel, most of which are grants or part of the $2.1 thousand million annual military assistance it gives to its primary ally in the Middle East.

Conclusion

Sino–Saudi relations have developed rapidly over the past three decades. An arms deal in 1988 has had a lasting impact on the growth of the Sino–Saudi partnership in the areas of energy, trade and cultural exchange. Saudi Arabia and China continue to build a strong partnership based on mutual interests. Saudi Arabia provides oil while China provides consumer goods, services and markets. Politically speaking, China and Saudi Arabia are manoeuvring their interests among contending forces in the Middle East, namely the US, Iran, Israel and Turkey. For the most part, they are succeeding, even though Saudi Arabia has been unable to end the Iranian nuclear project and China has proved unwilling to sever contacts with Iran. As for the Arab–Israeli conflict, China and Saudi Arabia support the peace process and the peaceful settlement of the conflict. Simultaneously, Saudi Arabia seeks to ensure its security in a Middle East characterized by Israeli military superiority.

As for the latest development in the Arab world, the 'Arab Spring', Saudi Arabia was frustrated by the Chinese UN Security Council veto on 4 February 2012 that blocked international efforts to condemn the Syrian government for its opposition to civilian protesters. The Saudi monarch King Abdullah criticized both China and Russia for their double veto. While China reacted swiftly to calm the Saudis, Russia's reaction was defensive and accused Saudi Arabia of supporting 'terrorism' in Syria. In the wake of this irrational accusation, the Russian foreign minister met the Saudi foreign affairs minister in Cairo to present Russia's views on the Syrian uprising. As for bilateral trade relations, oil co-operation, cultural ties and arms sales, Saudi–Chinese relations are consolidating a comprehensive partnership that is viewed as mutually beneficial and vital to their national interests.

7 China and Iran

An overview of Sino–Iranian relations

Sino–Iranian relations are as ancient as the Persian and Chinese civilizations. Their origins extend far back into the era of the Silk Road. The Parthians, the Sassanids of Persia, and the Han and Tang Chinese dynasties had built strong commercial and cultural ties. The Hans signed a commercial treaty with Persia in 100 BCE to organize their trade and customs relations, while the Tangs enhanced trade and strengthened their cultural ties with Persia. Since then, trade flourished between the two sides when Silk Road caravans travelled from China across the plains, mountains and valleys of Central Asia towards Persia and through Turkey to Europe's ports. Silk Road merchandise of silk, species, textiles, horses and camels strengthened relations among world nations at that time and continued its role in promoting trade and cultural exchange well into the thirteenth century.

The Arab conquest ended the Persian Empire in the year 651 after 17 years of skirmishes and major wars between the two sides. In the first round of confrontation between Persia and the rising Arab power, Persia held its position and then began retreating. When Persia realized its imminent fall, it solicited the assistance of the Tang Dynasty. China was not in a position to prevent the demise of Persia, given the geographic distance between the two sides. Chinese armies would need six months to one year to assemble, crossing China westward towards Central Asia, then through northern Afghanistan, towards southern Persia and down to Iraq. Therefore the Persians, although militarily superior to Arab armies, were defeated because of the tenacity of the Muslim armies. Muslim Caliphs adopted the Persian style of administration, trade arrangements and irrigation systems. Persia was far more advanced than Arabia and other contemporary civilizations. The Umayyad and the Abbasids benefited significantly from Persian knowledge in civil engineering, urban planning and administration. Therefore, the administrative substance of the Islamic Empire was essentially Persian.

The Islamic Empire also built upon the accomplishments of the conquered peoples rather than the elimination of their civilizational accomplishments. Khurasan or Persia (which includes possessions from Iraq, Iran, Afghanistan and Central Asia down to Xinjiang) was incorporated within the Islamic Empire, a previous possession of Persia. Islam stood at the borders of China and, with one exception, the Talas Battle, relations between the two sides remained peaceful. Chinese emperors welcomed Persians, Arabs and Muslims who resided throughout China, especially in the city of Xian. Pirooz, the last Persian Crown Prince, resided in China along with his son Prince Narsieh and the royal family. They were granted high honours and adopted Chinese names. Pirooz and Narsieh became military commanders in the Tang Dynasty's armies. The Persian community, along with the Arab and Muslim communities, prospered in China until 878 when they were victimized by the Han majority who were jealous of their prosperity. Some of the survivors left for East Asia. China and the Islamic Empire also fell prey first to the devastating Mongol campaigns, then to Western colonialism which lasted through the mid-twentieth century.

The five pillars of Sino–Iranian relations

Political co-operation

Persia recognized the Republic of China (ROC) in 1911, signed a friendship agreement with the ROC in 1922 and withdrew its recognition of China in 1949. However, Iran re-established its diplomatic relations with the ROC in 1956 and maintained close political, economic, trade and diplomatic relations. These relations continued until 1971 when Iran decided to recognize the PRC, whose leadership showed major interest in developments in Iran throughout the Long March period. Communist leaders were concerned about the consequences of political developments in the Middle East, as well as WWII efforts and their potential impact on China. Developments in Iran were also of primary concern to Mao and to Chou En-lai. These were a clear indication of the direction of Middle Eastern politics in the foreseeable future at that time. Iran, a centre for British colonialism, was embroiled in a power struggle in the early 1950s between the Shah and the nationalists. The Shah, Mohammad Rezā Shāh Pahlavī, who took over in 1941 in the aftermath of a joint Anglo-Soviet invasion that deposed his father, aligned himself with British and rising American interests and security arrangements in the region, whereas the nationalists were seeking an independent Iran with its own independent foreign and domestic policy. The nationalist Prime Minister, Mohammad Mossadegh, carried out a peaceful coup that led to the expulsion of the Shah. Mossadegh nationalized the Anglo-Iranian Oil Company, and China praised the rising spirit of independence in Iran and the anti-imperialist policies of Mossadegh.

China criticized the neoimperial security pacts designed by the US such as the Baghdad Pact (known as the Middle East Treaty Organization, an anti-communism security arrangement) and any attempt to link Iran to such organizations. However, in a coup orchestrated by the US Central Intelligence Agency and Britain in 1953, the Shah was brought back and Mossadegh was removed from office, arrested and subjected to humiliation and house arrest.

He was also denied medication and died at his home in 1967. China continued its attack on the Shah's policies and his association with 'imperialist' security pacts (especially with Iran joining the Baghdad Pact), along with the reactionary hosts of imperialism in the Middle East such as Iraq, Jordan, Israel and Saudi Arabia. China and Iran collided in Oman as China was the main supporter of the Dhofar Liberation Front (DLF) and Iran supported the Popular Front for the Liberation of the Occupied Arabia Gulf (PFLOAG), a Maoist-leftist organization that began in the Dhofar region of Oman. The DLF's and PFLOAG's main goal was liberating Oman from the rule of the British-controlled Sultanate and liberating the Gulf region from Western control.[1]

China also supported the Iranian Communist Party, Tudeh. However, in this period, the Shah of Iran consolidated his power domestically and became a major regional and international figure. Iran under the Shah also become one of the two main pillars of the US presence in the Middle East, the other being Israel. When China realized its limited success in the region, it opted for a more pragmatic foreign policy and began reducing its rhetorical attacks on the Shah and other Middle Eastern monarchies. This trend became a fundamental component in China's global engagement towards the end of the decade. So, in 1971, Iran and China exchanged diplomatic recognition, and China completely ended its criticism of the Shah's regime. Both countries resumed trade relations and political co-ordination, and they nurtured a nascent partnership with the tacit approval of the United States, which was in the process of rapprochement and realignment with China as well. Sino–American relations improved drastically and as a result were reflected positively in China's relations with the Middle East. Senior Iranian officials such as Prime Minister Amir Abbas Hoveida (1965–77), Empress Farah Pahlavi and other members of the royal family and senior government officials visited China repeatedly. Ji Peng-fei, China's foreign affairs minister, visited Iran in June 1973. He recognized Iran's deep civilizational roots that date back thousands of years and reaffirmed China's long-standing views on Iran's regional and international status and its impressive role and stature in international relations.[2]

Relations continued to improve until the Iranian Revolution from 1978 to 1979. China had called for peaceful negotiations between the Government and the opposition all along, a process that failed and led to the demise of the Shah's regime. China recognized the revolution and attempted to continue normal relations with Iran, but the new regime received China's gestures poorly. The revolutionaries sought to punish countries that had aided the Shah or had diplomatic or strategic relations with him. Although China did establish diplomatic relations with Iran, its relations with that country could not be classified at that time as strategic or distinguished. Regardless, regional developments limited the revolutionary forces' ability to manoeuvre with China in particular. A year after the revolution, Iraq declared war against Iran over territorial claims leading to an 8-year war that devastated both combatants. Iran–Iraq border disputes had been going on for many centuries before finally resulting in the 1937 border treaty drafted by Britain (the colonial mandating power at that time), marking the borders at the Shat Al Arab waterway.

In its reaction to the first devastating Iraqi advance into Iranian territory, Iran's goals were altered from punishment of previous collaborators with the Shah to soliciting their assistance to absorb Iraqi advancements, contain them and turn the direction of the war around. Therefore, reconciliation with China resumed, and China became Iran's primary supplier of arms. China welcomed Iran's arms orders, and at times sold weapons to both Iran and Iraq. The Gulf War ended after an agonizing 8 years with no victor, but both Iran and Iraq emerged as economically devastated. Both sought Chinese assistance with the rebuilding of their countries. In addition, the US and its allies had also supplied weapons to both sides. The goal was to prevent either combatant from emerging triumphant in the war. The world was in an agreement on 'double containment' of the Iranian and Iraqi threat. Realizing their inability to break up world consensus in the direction or the outcome of the war, in 1988, Iran and Iraq accepted the UN Security Council's Resolution 598 (passed a year earlier) calling for an immediate ceasefire. China was delighted that the war had ended, as it was eager for lucrative deals in the postwar reconstruction period and had an interest in the energy sectors in both Iran and Iraq. Iran went to China wholeheartedly, and trade grew rapidly between the two sides. Iraq did so as well, although Iraq's conditions were totally different on account of Saddam's invasion of Kuwait on 2 August 1990 and the stringent sanctions subsequently imposed on Iraq. In the war with Iran, Iraq became the centre of both American and world attention as it had emerged from the war with substantial military strength that was viewed as threatening to Gulf security, to Israel and to Kuwait in particular.

Iraq did not fail the pessimistic observers who predicted that it would soon flex its muscles against Kuwait and Saudi Arabia, its closest allies in the war against Iran. While Kuwait made unrealistic demands for immediate debt repayment at the end of the war with Iran, Saudi Arabia was mainly concerned about Iraq's security threat to its territorial integrity and sovereignty and the security of the GCC countries. Saddam Hussein's miscalculation in invading Kuwait refocused US attention towards Iraq and the Middle East at the most critical time in the twentieth century: the disintegration of the Soviet Union and the Eastern bloc. While the US managed to assemble an international coalition to evict Saddam Hussein from Kuwait, Iran tacitly (and sometimes explicitly) supported this eviction. Iran finally realized that the US and Saudi Arabia would take steps against Saddam Hussein that would relieve Iran from his threat, thus providing Iran with relative 'space' necessary to rebuild itself after the war. Iran, for the first time since 1979, was offered the 'breathing room' it needed. It benefited from the collapse of the Soviet Union and turned inwardly on its domestic postwar reconstruction. Iran saw great opportunities in dealing with former USSR republics, especially Ukraine and Belarus, in the areas of arms sales and nuclear technology. The Iranian government took advantage of the regional and international atmosphere that was conducive to 'relative peace' with Iran and then embarked upon an ambitious process of building strong relations worldwide.

Iran approached European countries and succeeded in securing markets for its crude oil. It also established a strong partnership with China that at times reached a 'strategic level.' It also strengthened its relations with post-Soviet Russia, Ukraine and the emerging former Soviet Republics in Central Asia. Strong relations were also established with Eastern Europe, Central Europe, Africa and Latin American countries. The 1990s were the greatest decade for post-Revolution Iran, whereas that decade was one of the most devastating times in the recent history of its rival, Iraq. The constant American pressure on Iraq, the obsession of the Bush Administration with the removal of Saddam Hussein, the stringent sanctions imposed on Iraq since 1990, the continuous pressure of the International Atomic Energy Agency, the alleged ties of Saddam Hussein with the terrorist attacks on 9/11 2001 escalated the situation between Iraq and the US beyond the scope of crisis management into an all-out war in 2003. The demise of Saddam Hussein was long overdue, although it brought the American threat to its doorstep. Iran assisted in the invasion, but its reward was George W. Bush designating Iran as part of the 'axis of evil', with the other two being Syria and North Korea. Iran's fears of its traditional menace, the United States, began to materialize when the Bush Administration began exploring the idea of regime change in Iran and making the case for an invasion of Iran in the summer and autumn of 2003. Iran was in fact supposed to be the country that bore the wrath of America in the post-9/11 era, not Iraq.

In preparing for the imminent showdown with the US in Iraq, and the strong likelihood of a war on Iranian territory, the Iranian Revolutionary Guard, the military, intelligence services and militia decided to make the American presence in Iraq costly so as to prevent the US from any thought of expanding the scope of the invasion to Iran, and potentially to Syria, and eliminating Hezbollah in Lebanon. As a result, Iran embarked upon a process of empowering the emerging Shi'a militia in Iraq, such as the Mahdi Army, which waged a war against the US, making its occupation of Iraq painful, costly and unbearable. Instead of invading Iran, the US began secretly communicating with it to secure stability in Iraq and an eventual American withdrawal. Iran did just that, although the American, Israeli and IAEA's pressure on Iran's nuclear programme never eased. On the contrary, it escalated. China welcomed the American withdrawal from Iraq and insisted all along that the Iranian nuclear standoff should also be resolved peacefully; it took a leading role in the P 5+1 (permanent members) and Germany's negotiations with Iran over its nuclear programme.

Arms sales

China's arms sales to Iran began in the early 1980s, associated with the Iran–Iraq War, 1980–88. China's weapon shipments sustained Iran and boosted its ability to counter Iraqi advancements in the war, and eventually turn the tide of the war two years later, in 1982. China became the main arms supplier as Iran had no access to American or Soviet arms sales, so its only option was China in the 1980s. Dittmer and Yu maintain that, during that decade, Chinese arms exports to the Middle East 'had reached an annual average of nearly 87 percent of China's total arms exports and over 74 percent of the total arms agreements, declined in the 1990s to nearly 32 and 26.5 percent, respectively. [From] 2000 [to] 2008, the average share of the Middle East in China's arms sales stood at about 34 percent, with most of the weapons going to Iran (some 18 percent), Egypt, and Sudan.'[3] China provided Iran with conventional weapons such as ammunition, tanks, missiles, landmines and non-conventional weapons as well. In 1987 the US was outraged when China provided Iran with anti-ship missiles known as Silkworm (Hy-2), CS-801 and CS-802, which fatally threatened the American navy in the Gulf, in addition to threatening the safe passage of oil cargo ships in the Hormuz Strait. Alterman and Garver added that China was 'also suspected of having produced several classes of tactical guided missiles "specifically for Iran", including JJ/TL-6bs and 10As, KJ/TL-10Bs, and a new variant of the C-107 anti ship missile.'[4] Alterman and Garver also identified the three top arms importers from China in the 1980s as Iran, Egypt and Saudi Arabia.[5] China's arms sales to the Middle East declined in the 1990s. It 'had reached an annual average of around 8 percent of deliveries and nearly 7 percent of agreements in the 1980s, deteriorated to 1.6 and 1.8 percent, respectively, in the 1990s.'[6]

The decline in arms sales was also attributed to the growing sanctions towards Iraq and Iran, as well as the opening up of alternative arms markets for China especially in Africa, Latin America and East Asia. Alterman and Garver also reported that, in spite of this, China continued to export arms to the region, as 'from 1995 to 2002, China supplied more than $1.2 billion dollars in military equipment to Iran, Algeria, Kuwait and Libya.'[7] Iran maintained its interest in military co-operation with China, whereas Algeria was in need of China's conventional weapons to combat the raging insurgency in the country and, while Kuwait was rebuilding its military in the post-Saddam invasion period, Libya continued to be a major arms importer as it had been since 1969. Kemp maintains that 'Tehran has become the largest market for Chinese arms exports, valued at $200 million over the 2001–4 period.'[8] Shichor also reports that 'from 2000 to 2008, the share of Chinese arms sales to the Middle East reached an average of around 3.5 percent (compared to 48 percent for the United States, 21 for Russia, 17 percent for France, and 3.6 percent for the UK.'[9] SIPRI reports that China's arms sales to Iran for the period from 1987 to 2011 are estimated at $3.225 thousand million (see Table 7.1). While China decreased its arms sales to the region, its trade grew steadily.

Richard Grimmett maintains that 'North Korea and Iran have also reportedly received Chinese missile technology, which may have increased their capabilities to threaten other countries in their respective neighborhoods.'[10]

Table 7.1 Iranian arms imports from China in millions of dollars from 1987 to 2011

Year	*Value in $ million*	*Year*	*Value in $ million*
1987	612	2001	82
1988	225	2002	83
1989	68	2003	86
1990	94	2004	89
1991	103	2005	52
1992	98	2006	71
1993	304	2007	64
1994	274	2008	64
1995	58	2009	64
1996	320	2010	79
1997	54	2011	79
1998	70		
1999	63		
2000	71		
Total			3,225

Source: SIPRI. For more information, see www.sipri.org/databases/armstransfers/background.

This highlights concerns about China's commitment to its obligations on restricting missile transfers as clearly set forth by the Missile Technology Control Regime (MTCR), especially refraining from assisting other countries in building missiles with nuclear weapons capability. Iran has developed a series of missiles known as Shahab series (1–6) missiles with a range between 1,200 and 2,000 km. Development of Shahab 6 with a range estimated at 6,000 km is under way.

The Iranian nuclear energy programme

The alleged Chinese–Iranian cooperation in the nuclear arena is one of the most scrutinized aspects of Sino–Iranian relations. Although China continues to deny any involvement in assisting Iran with developing its nuclear programme, China is taking a leading role in the ongoing negotiations between Iran and the P 5+1. On principle, China supports Iran's right to develop a peaceful nuclear programme, as do India, South Africa and Brazil, the coalition of the emerging powers. However, there is a general worldwide consensus of opposition to Iran's nuclear programme, given that the international community has no confidence that Iran will confine development of nuclear energy to peaceful use rather than towards developing a nuclear weapon. Israel and the US vowed to prevent it by all means, including surgical attacks to take out Iran's nuclear facilities. China continues to oppose any potential US or Israeli attack on Iran's nuclear installations. China also opposes the sanctions imposed on Iran and continues to advocate a peaceful resolution to the current standoff. In the spring of 2012, negotiations, threats and discussions over the Iranian nuclear programme intensified. China continues its active participation in the negotiations process, while the US has continued to take the lead in the global pressure on Iran. Israel maintains its threat of an attack on Iran's nuclear installations, although the domestic momentum for the attack appears shaky at times.

On 30 and 31 March 2012 the US met the GCC under the umbrella of the Strategic Cooperation Forum (SCF), a forum that includes the US and GCC foreign ministers and security leadership from both sides. The SCF seeks to reaffirm US commitment to the security of the GCC countries. The US Secretary of State, Hillary Clinton, affirmed that, 'In today's inaugural session of the Strategic Cooperation Forum, I underscore the rock-solid commitment of the United States to the people and nations of the Gulf.'[11] The forum, which the Secretary hopes to be a permanent addition to US–Gulf co-operation entities, has considered the potential deployment of a ballistic missile system to protect the GCC from Iranian threats. She also highlighted the fact that some aspects of the defence system have already been deployed, and what is needed is to work out details of the 'interoperability' of the system. She also stated clearly that US policy towards Iran is 'one of prevention, not containment.' The US seeks to prevent Iranian threats rather than to contain Iran.

The secretary added that 'the window for a peaceful solution to Iran's nuclear program won't remain open.'[12] She reiterated the 'time is running out' theme on several occasions in the hope of getting Iran to the negotiations table, which materialized in the Iran–P 5+1 Istanbul talks from 13 to 14 April 2012 and the Baghdad talks from 23 to 24 May. Another round of talks is scheduled for June 2012 in Moscow. The next round might be held in Beijing. The negotiations were termed 'fruitful', although no specific developments were reported. The ongoing negotiations, talks and discussions are a continuation of several previous rounds of negotiations with Iran over the past 10 years that created no concrete results. However, the IAE, the UN, the EU, the US and the P 5+1 Group seem to be determined to get solid results at the end of the current process; otherwise, the window for seeking a peaceful resolution to the standoff will not remain 'open forever.'

Oil and energy co-operation

Chinese–Iranian co-operation in the 1980s was dominated primarily by arms sales, then by commodities and service trade and co-operation in carrying out major construction projects in Iran such as the Tehran Subway System, then by co-operation in the field of arms sales again in the 1990s, followed by a major concentration on oil and energy. China's early oil importing from Iran goes back to the 1960s, although both countries had no diplomatic relations until 1971. 'During the first phases of Sino–Iran relations, even though China had oil reserves of its own during the 1960s, it imported 1,393,000 tons of crude oil (100,000 tons per annum), in 1976 it imported 200,000 tons, and in 1977 it imported 300,000 tons from Iran.'[13] After the Iranian Revolution, for the period from 1979 to 2000, China assisted Iran in rehabilitating its oil and gas fields. China exported oil technology to Iran that allowed Iran to increase its production capacity. China had also assisted Iran in the maintenance and upgrading of three of its oil refineries as early as 2000, tapping into oil reserves in the Caspian Sea Basin and developing gas fields in the Persian Gulf.

The essence of Sino–Iranian relations is the abundance of Iranian oil and gas reserves, associated with Western withdrawal from Iranian markets due to continued sanctions and renewed sanctions on Iran since the Iran–Iraq War in the 1980s. In 1999 Sinopec imported 7.35 million metric tons of crude oil from the National Iranian Oil Company (NIOC). In January 2001, Sinopec and the NIOC signed an agreement to exploit the Zavareh–Kashan oil block, an area 4,670 square kilometres in size, in which Sinopec was in charge of the operation. Simultaneously, the two companies also signed another agreement worth $150 million to upgrade two NIOC refineries. The project was described by both sides as the largest, although no official price tag was disclosed.[14] Another aspect of their energy co-operation is that the National Iranian Tanker Company ordered five giant oil tankers from the China Shipbuilding Industry Corporation in 2000. The first of these oil tankers was 330 metres long and 58 metres wide, and it was delivered to Iran in April 2002. China is the third country after Japan and South Korea worldwide with the capacity to build giant ships that can hold 300,000 tons.[15]

Alterman and Garver maintain that 'bilateral trade between China and Iran, heavily weighted in favor of oil exports, rose from $4 billion to $7 billion between 2003 and 2004 alone, and by 2005 topped $10 billion.'[16] The Chinese reliance on Iranian oil and the growth of oil imports as a percentage of China's overall worldwide energy imports continues to grow. By 2009 Iran provided 11 percent of China's oil imports, ranking third after Saudi Arabia and Angola, according to Chinese customs data.[17] Kemp reported that, 'in March 2004, China's state-owned oil company, Zhuhi Zhenrong Cooperation, signed a 25-year deal to import 110 million tons of liquefied natural gas (LNG) from Iran.'[18]

In addition to existing oil deals, on 9 December 2007, Sinopec signed an agreement with the Iranian Ministry of Oil to develop the Yadavaran oil field in southwestern Iran, which turned out to be one of the most significant deals that China has signed with Iran so far. Discussions between the two sides began in October 2004, resulting in the signing of a memorandum of understanding, and discussions continued until it materialized into a major contract for Sinopec three years later. Sinopec holds a 51 percent equity share of the field, while the India Oil and Natural Gas Company and the Iranian Government hold the remaining 49 percent of the joint venture. The Yadavaran oil field is also considered to be the most untapped field worldwide, with an estimated oil reserve of over 30,000 million barrels of crude oil. The initial cost of the project was estimated at $2,000 million, and the project is to be carried out in two phases. The first phase to produce 85,000 bd was concluded in 2011, while the second phase to produce another 100,000 bd is under way, to be concluded in 2015. According to Iranian estimates, the Yadavaran field has in-place oil reserves of 18.3 thousand million barrels and gas reserves amounting to 12.5 trillion cubic feet, of which 3.2 thousand million barrels and 2.7 trillion cubic feet are recoverable respectively.[19] On 28 May 2012 Fars Press Agency announced that the Yadavaran began its first phase of production, producing 16,000 bd.[20]

In early January 2006, China's Oilfield Services, a subsidiary of the China National Offshore Oil Corporation (CNOOC), signed a $35 million deal with Iran's North Drilling Company (NDC). The agreement 'includes the repair, management, and maintenance of the Alborz semi-floating platform in the Caspian Seas.'[21] The agreement boosts Iran's capacity to tap into deeper oil reserves in the Caspian basin, although the field lies in a disputed area between Iran and Azerbaijan. The project added a daily crude oil production of 60,000 bd. In 2008, Iran's Pars Oil and Gas Company reached a deal with CNOOC to exploit the North Pars gas field. The pact was signed after oil giant Royal Dutch Shell and Spanish oil company Respol withdrew from Iran; French energy firm Total had also announced plans to abandon its investment in a gas project in Iran.[22] The General Administration of Customs (GAC) reported the top three countries supplying oil to China, accounting for 47.7 percent of China's oil imports in 2009: 'Saudi Arabia, the largest oil supplier to China, accounted for 20.5 percent of China's total imports in 2009. Angola supplied 15.8 percent while Iran contributed 11.3 percent.'[23] Also, 'GAC figures showed that China's oil imports from the three nations last year stood at 41.86 million tonnes, 32.17 million tonnes and 23.15 million tonnes, respectively. They represented a year-on-year increase of 15.1 percent, 7.6 percent and 8.6 percent, respectively.'[24]

Iran's NDC, a state-owned oil exploration company, signed an agreement in March 2010 to import an oil rig (one of three that the NDC intends to import) from China Petroleum Technology & Development Corporation, a subsidiary of China National Petroleum Corporation (CNPC), for $143 million.[25] It will be deployed in the Persian Gulf for the exploration of oil and natural gas. CNPC also signed an agreement in 2009 with Iran's Petroleum Engineering and Development Company to develop the North Azadegan oil field (part of the giant Azadegan oil field) in Iran's western province of Khuzestan. It is located on the Iran–Iraq border in southwest Iran. The deal is a buyback contract worth $1.76 thousand million. The project is being carried out in two phases over a 29-year period; the first phase would produce 75,000 bd of crude oil and 39.08 million cubic feet of natural gas, with the second producing 75,000 bd and 39.08 million cubic feet of natural gas. At the end of the two phases, the North Azadegan oil field will produce 150,000 bd, boosting Iran's oil production capacity and deepening Sino–Iranian energy co-operation for decades to come.[26] In early June 2009 Iran stripped Total of its role in the development of Iran's South Pars Gas Project, accusing Total of delaying tactics in its commitment to the project. Iran replaced Total with China's CNPC partnering with Malaysia's Petronas. The deal is estimated at $4.7 thousand million. CNPC's responsibility is to develop phase 11 of South

Pars, a major natural gas project in Iran.[27] Iran's estimated investment in the South Pars project by the end of March 2010 was $18 thousand million.[28]

In 2011 Chinese crude oil imports from Iran were 17 percent of its total crude oil imports. Towards the end of 2011, China's oil imports from Iran averaged 557,000 bd, up 30 percent from 2010. However, due to a price dispute between the two sides, China's imports plunged in the first quarter of 2012 to 220,000 bd in January and continued to decline, but negotiations are under way between the two sides to remedy the price dispute. Although the decline in China's oil imports from Iran is attributed to this dispute, China prefers to diversify its oil imports and show some kind of support for the sanctions regime imposed on Iran. China could be using the contractual dispute to reduce its oil imports from Iran, seemingly abiding by American sanctions, although for different reasons. China is increasing its oil orders from Saudi Arabia, pitting the traditional Gulf rivals against each other. Saudi Arabia is more than delighted to increase its oil exports and production capacity from 9.9 million bd to 12.5 million bd. In fact, it has announced its willingness, ability and desire to increase production capacity to meet any demand caused by the decline in Iranian oil exports.

While Iran resents that, and some of its officials announced their intention to punish any Gulf that substitutes for Iranian oil, Iran seems to be unable to take any substantial steps to prevent it. The US provides full security guarantees to the Gulf region, and China had warned Iran not to attempt to close the Hormuz Strait. For its part, the US increased its naval presence in the Gulf, and Iran's threats of attacking 'enemy' naval presence dematerialized. As for the latest outlook for Iran's oil sector, on 4 April 2012, Iran's oil minister stated that 'at least 30 billion dollars will be invested in Iran's oil industry this year and the lion's share of it will be allocated to South Pars gas field projects.'[29] China is the beneficiary of resource allocation and contracts in the oil field as well. It is also projected that Chinese and Indian oil corporations will continue their co-operation with Iran undeterred by US sanctions. For strategic reasons that have to do with China's trade interests with the US and India's strategic partnership with the US, both are expected to manipulate the sanctions regime and empty it of its substance. In the end, American, Japanese, South Korean and European oil companies will be affected by the sanctions more than anyone else.

Trade and the political economy of Sino–Iranian relations

Although Sino–Iranian trade relations were weak and at times non-existent between 1949 and 1971, their bilateral trade relations have grown steadily since the early 1980s, and have greatly intensified since the early 2000s. Kemp reported that 'total trade between the two countries rose from $3.1 billion in 2001 to $6.1 billion in 2004, to $9.2 billion in 2005, and to a staggering $27 billion in 2008.'[30] Table 7.2 illustrates bilateral trade volume in millions of dollars for the period from 2001 to 2010.

Table 7.2 Bilateral trade relations in millions of dollars for the period from 2001 to 2010

Year	*Value in $ million*
2010	29,391.08
2009	21,219.09
2008	27,757.62
2007	20,589.65
2006	11,444.3
2005	10,083.27
2004	7,045.46
2003	5,622.52
2002	3,739.57
2001	3,312.89

Source: China Statistical Yearbook, 2010.

The *South China Morning Post* reported similar figures stating that 'the volume of bilateral trade has increased more than tenfold over the past decade, from US $2.5 billion in 2000 to US$29.3 billion last year'[31] in 2011. Iranian–Chinese trade is mainly concentrated in the oil and gas sector as Western, Korean and Japanese companies have been withdrawing from investing or engaging in business with Iran on account of the sanctions regime imposed on the country. Chinese corporations are the beneficiaries of such withdrawal, making China Iran's primary trading partner. In addition to the oil sector, China exports consumer goods and services to Iran, and its construction corporations continue to carry out major infrastructure projects in Iran. Other areas of co-operation include the petrochemical sector as well as the motor, cement and mineral industries.

Cultural exchange

Sino-Persian cultural relations are deeply rooted and embedded within the Silk Road paradigm. Persian culture, musical instruments (lute), religious doctrines (Zoroastrianism, Manichaeism), costumes and traditional folklore were highly celebrated in China, especially during the Tang Dynasty. Familial relationships of marriage and kinship between the two sides were common throughout history as well. These cultural relations also thrived under the Abbasid–Tang co-operation but began to decline with the Mongol near total destruction of both Islamic and Chinese civilizations. This trend continued through the era of Chinese isolationism and the century of humiliation (1848–1949). Concomitantly with the decline of the Silk Road, cultural exchanges suffered a major blow as the Chinese people developed mistrust of Persians, Arabs and Muslims who co-operated with the Mongol invaders. The image of Persians, Arabs and Muslims as enlightened peoples who were well disciplined and industrious was tarnished and, gradually, cultural barriers began rising between the Chinese and their neighbours to the west. Kemp states that 'the cultural barriers between the Islamic people of Persia and the Buddhists of China, as well as natural barriers such as the mountains and deserts Central Asia, discouraged trade. Meanwhile, nations encouraged isolationism, which led to xenophobia among their populations, and trade and communications led to the Silk Road dwindled.'[32]

Contrary to Kemp's assumption that the incompatibility of the Islamic and Buddhist values contributed to isolationism, Islam was well received in China and celebrated. However, isolationism comes from the feeling of being betrayed by Persian and Arab communities who co-operated with the Mongol invaders and served as 'abusive' tax collectors, administrators, soldiers and heads of the Mongol armies. The Persian and Arab merchants and communities provided the Mongol invaders with the necessary cadres to establish and then run the Yuan Dynasty for over a century, from 1271 to 1368, given the fact that the Mongols ruled northern China for several decades before they estabilished the Yuan Dynasty. For that tragic mistake, the two communities paid a heavy price. Mistrust continues among the Han and the Hui communities in China. However, gradually since WWII, confidence, trust and friendly relationships have grown steadily until they were nearly restored in the mid-1990s. Post-WWII contacts between the two sides were associated with the Bandung Conference and the non-aligned movement and China's quest to reintroduce itself to the people of the Middle East. China sent Muslim delegations to Islamic countries, especially Iran and Saudi Arabia, to assure Muslims of the well-being of Chinese Muslims. Usually, Hajj delegations from China toured the region and attempted to secure diplomatic recognition and establish cultural ties with China. For the period between 1949 and 1971, however, cultural contacts as well as trade were weak as ideological rigidities on both sides limited their cultural interaction.

Relaxing ideological tensions and improving trade relations led to a significant volume of cultural contacts not only between China and Iran but also between China and the people of the Middle East during the Deng Xiaoping era and afterwards. Cultural exchange is viewed as an instrument to further ties between two sides. In 1983, both parties signed the agreement on Sino–Iranian cultural, scientific, and technical co-operation in Beijing. In his visit to Iran in April 2002, Jiang Zemin made sure to visit Iran's cultural capital, Shiraz, where he signed a cultural agreement to translate and publish some Iranian masterpieces into Chinese; the project was successfully carried out. Both countries celebrate an 'Iranian' and a Chinese week, a sort of annual cultural festival to highlight culture, cuisine, folklore, traditions and bilateral co-operation. The Iranian film industry also holds the Iranian film week in China. In August 2008 the first Confucius Centre in Iran was opened at the University of Tehran. Similar to other Confucius centres around the world, its mission is to promote Chinese culture and language. The Confucius centres 'have become a platform for cultural exchanges between China and the world as well as a bridge reinforcing friendship and cooperation between China and the rest of the world and are much welcomed across the globe.'[33] The centres also seek to promote China's economy.

anghai International Expo, Iran opened the doors of its pavilion isitors. 'The pavilion fully embodies the traditional Islamic eveals its glorious ancient art and colorful contemporary lives.'[34] three parts: Iran's past, present and future. It reflects Iranian ıth, its current developmental accomplishments and its future ese people also have a tremendous interest in learning Persian. Chinese entrepreneurs are educating themselves in Iranian language, culture and history. Their goal is to equip themselves with the necessary tools to conduct successful business deals with their Iranian counterparts. The Chinese New Year and the Nowruz (Iranian New Year) festivals are frequently celebrated in both countries. They are a testament to the cultural depth between China and Iran. Other aspects of the cultural exchange include but are not limited to student exchange programmes and scholarships for students to study in Iran and China. Earlier in 2012, Iran and China established the China–Iran Joint Cultural Committee. Its goal is to review existing cultural agreements, ensure their implementation, expand cultural exchanges and establish cultural centres in the two countries this year. 'The cultural centers will be used to promote cooperation between the two nations in the areas of tourism, media, and publishing.'[35] There is also an increase in tourism between the two sides, as Iran is becoming one of the destinations for Chinese tourists.

Conclusion

Iranian–Chinese relations are deeply rooted in history and have been enhanced recently with bilateral co-operation in the areas of energy, arms sales, trade, political co-operation and cultural ties. In the critical moments of Iran's modern history, China has always come to Iran's rescue. China assisted Iran to resist Iraqi advances, achieve parity with Iraq and turn the tide of war at times against Iraq. Upon the ending of the war, China assisted Iran in the rebuilding process. Its construction corporations carried out major highway projects, the subway system in Tehran, bridge building and dam construction. China assisted Iran in developing its oil sector and provided Iran with the needed technical skills, material and equipment to triple its oil production. China provided Iran with oil rigs, refineries, pipelines and expertise for exploration for oil and natural gas in Iran.

When Iran requested China's assistance to develop a nuclear programme in the early 1990s, China never hesitated. Their co-operation brought world scrutiny, which led to more secrecy and discreet co-operation. China is also playing a major role in ending the current standoff between Iran and the world over Iran's nuclear programme. China is Iran's major trade partner and a major exporter of goods and services. China and Iran's cultural relations are also boosted by a host of mechanisms such as the opening of a Confucius Centre, Iran's pavilion at the Shanghai Expo and the organization of film weeks and New Year celebrations. Relations between these two countries are expected to continue to prosper.

8 China and the United Arab Emirates

On 3 December 1971, Sheikh Zayed bin Sultan, the founder and the first President of the newly independent United Arab Emirates (UAE), sent a diplomatic cable to both the Republic of China (ROC) and the People's Republic of China (PRC) to inform their governments of the independence of the UAE. This is a customary procedure in international relations; it has been used as an informative step and as an instrument to secure diplomatic recognition. Chou En-lai, PRC's premier, sent a letter back in 5 days recognizing the UAE. To China's dismay, the UAE's government 'did not reciprocate'[1] the recognition because of Saudi pressure. The UAE had no grounds for rejection; if anything, it had many reasons to recognize China and expand its diplomatic recognition base, unlike Kuwait in 1961 or later Oman. In fact, China sent military aid to the Dhofar Liberation Front (DLF), lengthening the civil war in Oman for the period from 1962 to 1976. The DLF was a leftist-Maoist organization that fought against the Sultan of Oman, while Kuwait and China had normal relations despite Saudi opposition since 1962. Saudi Arabia was the only Gulf country to oppose China's membership of the United Nations in 1971, whereas Kuwait advocated it, supported it and lobbied for it. By the end of 1978, four Gulf countries had denied PRC recognition: the UAE, Bahrain, Qatar and Saudi Arabia. Other regional monarchies such as Oman, Jordan and Iran realized early on the pragmatic nature of China's foreign policy (a trend that began at the end of the 1960s), and began to establish diplomatic relations with China as early as 1971. Instead, it took Saudi Arabia two more decades to comprehend the changes in China's foreign policy and establish diplomatic relations (21 July 1990). Since 1984, when the UAE finally recognized the PRC, Sino–Emirati relations have developed dramatically, to the extent that, currently, the UAE is serving as an economic hub for China, but also for the Gulf and Middle East region, Africa and the world.

The five pillars of Sino–Emirati relations

Trade relations

The centre of Sino–Emirati relations is trade, but the extraordinarily successful partnership has also influenced energy, military, political and cultural ties. Bilateral trade relations began in the mid-1980s and grew to a strategic conglomerate in three decades. Both countries were transformed in an unprecedented record in modern history: while the UAE was extremely poor and its land was mostly desert with vast uninhabited areas, China had hundreds of millions of people in poverty. Over the past three decades, their trade ties have accelerated their bilateral agreements in a wide range of sectors, and economic growth and development has averaged over 8 percent annually. China and the UAE's first agreement for economic, trade and scientific research was signed in 1986, followed in 1990 by an air cargo agreement. Both sides signed a protocol for the prevention of double taxation and trade promotion in 1993. Between 1993 and 2004, both sides signed a framework for economic co-operation, investment and technical support, and several rounds of talks have occurred since then to establish the China–GCC free trade zone (FTZ) in Riyadh in 2009, and most recently in Abu Dhabi in January 2012. The agreement is expected to materialize in the span of three years. The FTZ will revolutionize trade between member states. During the China premier's visit to the Gulf in January 2012, both sides highlighted the importance of bringing the FTZ to fruition.

In July 2011, the UAE's Central Bank signed a framework with China for financial co-operation in the areas of financial supervision, monitoring and information exchange. Wen Jiabao, senior Chinese business leaders, energy entrepreneurs and senior political officials signed a host of agreements, among which are the CNPC–ADNOC (Abu Dhabi National Oil Company) oil agreement, the energy co-operation protocol, a currency exchange swap worth $5.54 thousand million for three years to enhance bilateral trade, a sports protocol and exemption from obtaining entry visas for holders of diplomatic passports. The peak of their co-operation was the signing of a joint communiqué early in 2012 that provides a comprehensive framework of strategic partnership in the areas of trade, political co-operation, energy, construction and culture and tourism. Bilateral co-operation continues, and the Sharjah International Commercial Arbitration Centre recently signed a framework with the Chinese in the area of commercial arbitration.

Bilateral trade and trade volume

There are 3,900 Chinese corporations in the United Arab Emirates: 3,000 of them are registered companies, and 900 corporations operate in the free trade zones around the country. Their main goal is to promote Sino–Emirati bilateral trade, and they serve as China's business hub for the GCC, the Middle East,

Central Asia, Africa and the world. Bilateral trade volume has grown steadily since early 1990, then deepened around 2007 and continues its steady progress towards reaching its goal of $100 thousand million by 2015. The UAE has become China's second trade partner in the Arab world, slightly trailing Saudi Arabia, but catching up with it swiftly. In 2007, bilateral trade was estimated at over $20 thousand million, an increase of over 40 percent from the previous year. The same trend continued for the period from 2007 to 2012. Table 8.1 illustrates bilateral trade value between China and the UAE since 2001.

In its special report on Sino–Emirati bilateral trade from 2008 to 2010, the Ministry of International Trade of the United Arab Emirates presented a detailed table for exports, imports and re-exports, as shown in Table 8.2.

Sino–Emirati trade is comprehensive in scope. China exports textiles, electronics, motor parts, chemicals, foodstuffs, high-tech equipment, machinery, solar energy, clean energy, solar panels, etc. In return, the UAE exports oil, natural gas, merchandise and services. UAE corporations such as Dubai Port World are making headway in China, particularly in managing property

Table 8.1 Value of bilateral trade between China and the UAE in millions of dollars

2012	25,600.00
2011	35,100.00
2010	25,686.89
2009	21,226.88
2008	28,256.94
2007	20,035.65
2006	14,201.53
2005	10,775.44
2004	8,145.61
2003	5,810.46
2002	3,896.26
2001	2,824.99

Source: China Statistical Yearbook, 2010.
Figures for 2010, 2011 and 2012 from the UAE Ministry of Foreign Trade
The figure for 2012 is an estimate for the first 4 months of 2012.

Table 8.2 Bilateral Trade in $ millions for the years 2008–2010

Data	*Growth Rate in 2009 and 2010*	*2010*	*2009*	*2008*
Export	18.5	269.7	227.5	266.9
Re-Export	83.7	349.4	190.2	876.4
Total Export	48.2	619.1	417.7	1143.2
Import	4.3	13586.1	13019.9	17367.9
Total Exchange Trade	5.7	14205.3	13438	18511
Trade Balance	2.9	-12967	-12602.2	-16225

Source: UAE's Ministry of Foreign Trade, 2012.

construction projects, hotels and ports. Historically speaking, between the eighth and tenth centuries, ports management was entrusted to Arab immigrants in China. Dubai Port World is no different: it wants to infiltrate Chinese markets just as in India's ports where the company handles 70 percent of container movements. While penetrating Chinese ports might not be an easy task on account of national sovereignty concerns, it is conceivable that DP World, with its established credibility, will manage China's ports in the near future. In the UAE, Chinese corporations have managed to establish a strong foothold in the construction sector. The China State Construction Engineering Corp. Ltd. (CSCE-Middle East) has provided engineering, construction and services in the UAE for the past three decades. The CSCE's headquarters in the country are located in Dubai, with branches in Abu Dhabi, Sharjah and Ras Al Khaimah (RAK). CSCE 'has undertaken various projects in UAE, for instance, Palm Jumeirah Garden Villa Projects, Lake B2, Global View A2, Lake D2, Mirdif Villas & Apartment, Mudon free-standing Villas, Skycourts Apartment Complex, Bayswater & Gemini office towers, Ned Al Sheba Racehorse, Wafi Bridge, Parallel Road, Emirates Road Extension, City of Lights in Abu Dhabi, and Sheikh Khalifa Specialist Hospital in RAK and etc..'[2] The company has also expanded the scope of its services to oil pipelines, roads and bridges so that it has become a prominent contractor with comprehensive capabilities to undertake building works, as well as the construction of infrastructure facilities.[3] Sino–Emirati trade relations are only expected to increase at an even faster pace.

A trade triangle: China, India and the United Arab Emirates

China, India and the UAE inadvertently form a trade triangle. China and India emerged as the UAE's two major trade partners in 2010, gradually replacing the UAE's traditional trade partners, the US, Europe and Japan. India exported goods and services to the UAE worth $13 thousand million in 2009, equivalent to 24.5 percent of the UAE's total trade, while China accounted for $13.00 thousand million, equivalent to 10.7 percent of UAE total trade, estimated at $121.8 thousand million in 2009. Therefore, India and China account for nearly a quarter of the UAE's total trade, 24.5 percent. The trend only increases and China aims to be the UAE's top business partner. India surpasses China with labour exports to the UAE, but China's labour tends to be specialized; it concentrates on running Chinese business and carrying out contracts and construction projects. In 2010 China ranked second as the UAE's trade partner, with an estimated bilateral trade worth $14 thousand million, while the bilateral trade in 2011 rose to $25.6 thousand million. This increase makes the UAE China's second regional trading partner to Saudi Arabia, with an estimated bilateral trade of $43.1 thousand million in 2011. The triangle affects UAE–Iran's trade relations. Although Iran has been under a different set of economic and financial sanctions over the past decade, Indian and Chinese products find their way to Iran via

Dubai, making this city a primary destination for UAE trade. In 2009 Dubai alone traded an estimated $7.05 thousand million with Iran, or 17.6 percent of the UAE's total non-oil external trade. Although the UAE continues to have trade interests with Iran, the latest escalation of tensions with reference to Iran's occupation of three UAE islands has significantly jeopardized their relationship.

The Dragon Mart

The largest property developer in Dubai is Nakheel. The company is well known for its mammoth structures such as Jumeirah Islands, which are visible from the moon. It built Palm Jumeirah, the World, Jumeirah Village, Jumeirah Park, Jumeirah Heights, Ibn Batoutta Mall, Discovery Gardens, International City, The Gardens, Al Furjan and the Dragon Mart, located in Nakheel's International City.[4] The mart is described as the largest trading hub for Chinese products outside mainland China. It is in the shape of a dragon, and spreads over an area of 150,000 square metres, in addition to 30,000 square metres of warehouses. The mart hosts Chinese businesses and businesses associated with products and services from China, including joint venture companies and companies operating from China through the Chinamex Middle East Investment and Trade Promotion Centre.[5] It includes showrooms, offices, a Chinese-themed residential district and negotiation rooms. Major Chinese corporations offer a variety of Chinese merchandise including textiles, food products, electronics, high-tech goods, etc. The Dragon Mart also serves as a cultural monument for China, not only in the UAE, but in the entire Middle East. The mart receives millions of tourists and shoppers annually who are captivated by its structure, its services and its cultural expression.

Financial co-operation

China and the UAE signed a currency swap agreement on 17 January 2012. The purpose is to strengthen bilateral trade, boost the international status of the yuan and make it a competitive worldwide currency. 'China has signed a series of currency swap agreements in recent years with key trading partners in a bid to boost the use of the Yuan for the direct settlement of international trade. Other countries that have signed such deals recently include Thailand and South Korea.'[6] The increasing exchange of the yuan will also motivate the International Monetary Fund (IMF) to include it in its basket of international currencies. It will also reflect China's real weight and increasing stature as a dominant, top exporting country.

In 2011 the UAE's Mashreq Bank signed an agreement with the Bank of China to establish the China Desk at Mashreq's headquarters in Abu Dhabi, to be managed jointly. 'The primary objective of the partnership is to assist Chinese companies in expanding their footprint overseas as well as local investors looking to make their mark in China.'[7] The agreement will facilitate bilateral trade, financial transactions for corporations and assist in doing business in both markets and regional markets. The Desk will also assist the Bank of China in serving the Chinese national community estimated at 200,000 and the 3,900 Chinese corporations operating in the Emirates. In addition, in 2008 the Industrial and Commercial Bank of China (ICBC) – the largest in assets held in China – and the Best International Transaction Bank in Asia opened their first branch in Dubai. The ICBC-Middle East seeks to 'provide a full range of financial services, including accepting deposits, providing credits, trade financing, dealing in investments as principal and as agent, arranging credit or deals in investments, managing assets, advising on financial products or credit, arranging custody, etc..'[8] The ICBC is a major pillar of the Chinese presence in the UAE and the Middle East. Since its establishment, it has contributed significantly to Chinese commercial ties with the region, assisting Chinese businesses, individuals and corporations. The bank also provides full-scale financial services for UAE and other Middle Eastern businesses engaging in trade in China and East Asia. The year 2012 seems to be promising for the future outlook of Sino–Emirati co-operation. It began with Wen Jiabao's visit and the signing of several major agreements in the areas of trade, energy, culture and political co-operation. Several Chinese business delegations have visited the UAE, among which was the Ningxia Hui Autonomous Region's delegation. Ningxia will be hosting the International Fair for Investment and Trade from 12 to 16 September 2012. Ningxia Hui are interested in exporting *Halal* (certified Muslim food) products to the UAE, and establishing production and distribution centres in Abu Dhabi. Their bilateral trade volume is expected to reach $100 thousand million by 2015. The goal seems to be reachable because Chinese businesses grasp the opportunities the UAE can provide, and the UAE's highly advanced infrastructure can be utilized to advance China's business interests in the Middle East.

Business infrastructure

Both the UAE and China have built strong forums and friendship associations to promote their bilateral trade. Here are a few: the Chinese Embassy and consulates in the UAE, the UAE embassy in Beijing, its consulates in Hong Kong and Shanghai, the Abu Dhabi Chamber of Commerce, the China–UAE Economic Forum, the UAE's Ministry of International Trade, Emirates Investment Authority, Dubai Chamber of Commerce and Industry, Dubai Investment Authority, Abu Dhabi Investment Authority, Abu Dhabi Chamber of Commerce and Industry, Fujairah Chamber of Commerce, Mashreq Bank, the Bank of China, Industrial and Commercial Bank of China and many other entities promoting and managing their bilateral interests. Sino–Emirati trade relations are also served by Sino–Arab and Sino–GCC trade organizations, associations and forums.

Oil and energy co-operation

The UAE's oil exports to China are modest in comparison with neighbouring countries such as Saudi Arabia or Iran. However, it is determined to increase oil exports to China to meet the growing demand and to replace Iran's decreased exports. PetroChina, the second largest oil and gas company in the world and a subsidiary of CNPC, has incorporated nearly twenty companies in the UAE in less than five years. Its goal is to expand UAE–China energy co-operation. The Abu Dhabi National Oil Company (ADNOC) announced recently that it will begin shipping 200,000 bd to CNPC beginning in 2014 as a result of ongoing negotiations over the past 2 years.[9] In 2009, Baoji Oilfield Machinery, a subsidiary of CNPC, won a bid to supply Abu Dhabi with oil rigs for onshore drilling. The Emirate of Fujairah (UAE) on the Gulf of Oman makes an attractive home for oil storage facilities and a strategic port for oil and gas exports. The advantage of the Port of Fujairah is that it bypasses the contentious Strait of Hormuz. PetroChina has been negotiating with the Emirate of Fujairah as well: 'The port, which has established itself as a major bunkering hub along with Singapore and Rotterdam, is now aiming to do the same for oil storage by more than doubling its capacity to over 7 million cubic meters by 2012 from the current 3 million cubic meters.'[10] The concentration of Chinese businesses has traditionally been in the Dubai–Abu Dhabi area, while Fujairah and other northern Emirates are underutilized, so Fujairah is making every effort to attract other Chinese companies.

The CNPC built an alliance with the UAE's Gulf Oil & Gas and two other South Korean corporations in 2009 and won a $9.7 thousand million gas contract in Turkmenistan. 'The Yolotan field is considered to be one of the biggest five natural gas deposits in the world and may hold around 6 trillion cu m of gas.'[11] Accordingly, Turkmenistan will also export 30 thousand million cubic metres of natural gas to China annually. China's growing role in producing talented geoscientists and environmental engineers is another changing aspect of co-operation between China, the UAE and oil-producing countries. The role of China University of Petroleum (CUP), established in Beijing in 1953, has become fundamental as a top tier 'national university in China and its mission is to prepare qualified engineers and technical service for the global oil industry through its quality education and research.'[12] The university offers degrees in engineering at all levels, with 32 distinguished PhD programmes. Other universities and colleges in China such as the Beijing Institute of Technology founded in 1940, China University of Science and Technology founded in 1967, North China University of Science and Technology, North China University of Technology, South China University of Technology, Huazhong University of Science & Technology and many other higher educational institutions are producing tomorrow's leading engineers, unlike Western universities which are undergoing budgetary restraint. CUP, in particular, has state-of-the-art petroleum centres and research facilities. About 80 percent of university research projects are sponsored by CNPC, China

Petroleum and Chemical Corporation (Sinopec) and China National Offshore Oil Corporation (CNOOC). The university has set up co-operative relations with eighty-nine overseas universities, research institutions and oil companies, and most of the relations are very active and productive.[13]

On 15 January 2008, France and the UAE signed nuclear and military co-operation agreements. This is significant given the UAE's interest in securing as many resources as possible to counter the possible Iranian threat. The April 2012 joint military excises held in Abu Dhabi were the most recent result of such agreements. To ensure support and to eliminate any potential misunderstanding of its intentions, the United States and the UAE signed a nuclear co-operation agreement on 15 January 2009. The agreement came into effect the end of 2009, making the UAE the first Arab country to openly seek nuclear energy for peaceful use. Other Arab countries such as Jordan, Saudi Arabia and Egypt are following suit. The UAE has also been co-ordinating with Germany, France, Russia, China, Britain, Japan and the Republic of Korea for direct consultation with the International Atomic Energy Agency (IAEA) to mobilize international support for its programme, establishing frameworks of co-operation, safety mechanisms and building a strong management team to run the UAE's nuclear facilities. The UAE's purpose is to produce enough electricity to meet its growing needs, especially in powering the 16 current desalination stations around the city of Abu Dhabi and the many more that are being built around the country, in addition to meeting the energy needs of Plan Abu Dhabi 2030, the most ambitious development project so far in the history of the UAE.[14] The UAE has already begun consulting and using design services from leading American nuclear energy corporations, and plans to have its first reactor functional in 2017.

Nuclear energy co-operation is also an area of interest between China and the UAE. Chinese corporations are eager, like their counterparts, to compete on contracts, construction sites and providing nuclear equipment, consulting services and expertise. Since 2008, Abu Dhabi has been hosting the World's Future Energy Summit, another aspect of UAE–China and world energy co-operation. The summit attracts world leaders and leading corporations in the area of renewable energy. For the past two years, Chinese energy companies such as Suntech Power, Yingli Green Energy Holding and China Sunergy have participated in the expo.

Arms sales

Given regional threats to national security, the UAE has been modernizing its armed forces by providing them with the most advanced and sophisticated weapons. SIPRI reported that China sold the UAE arms worth $14 million in 1993 and 1994.[15] Since then, no arms sales have been reported between the two countries. The US, France and Britain are the UAE's main source of weapons. It is estimated that, between 2006 and 2010, the UAE accounted for 8 per cent of US arms exports to the Middle East, followed by Israel with 7 percent and Egypt with 4 percent. For the period between 2007 and 2010, the UAE signed arms contracts worth $15.1 thousand million. Richard Grimmett ranked the UAE as the third country in arms imports (Table 8.3).[16]

In efforts to boost the UAE's military capabilities, on 31 December 2011, the US and the UAE signed an arms deal worth $3.5 thousand million on an advanced anti-missile interception system.[17] It is part of a military build-up in the region to counter Iranian threats that prompted the US to station some of its most advanced F-22 fighters at the Dhafra airbase.

Senior Chinese and UAE officials have been highlighting the forging of a strategic partnership in military co-operation. A major portion of the UAE's arms deals is conducted at the International Defence Exhibition, a biennial defence show organized in the UAE since 1993, where hundreds of defence manufacturers display and market their state-of-the-art weapons and defence equipment. The 2011 exhibition organized in Dubai attracted major producers from the US, Europe, Russia, India, China, Pakistan, Turkey and other countries. Products worth thousands of millions of dollars are sold at the exhibition annually. At Dubai's International Air Show of 2009, China presented its L-15 Falcon training aircraft. Interest was also generated in some countries for the J-10 and J-17. The Gulf and the Middle East are great markets for Chinese fighter jets and training aircraft. Similar to previous figures provided by Grimmett, SIPRI reported a substantial increase in the UAE's military spending, estimated in 2010 at $16.062 thousand million.[18] Table 8.4 illustrates UAE's increasing defence spending since 2001.

The UAE and China signed a defence and co-operation pact in 2008. Repeated visits by chiefs of staff, senior naval, air force and army officials from the two countries are the primary aspect of this bilateral co-operation. The UAE sought to purchase Chinese military products and weapons systems. Although there are no specific statistics on recent UAE arms imports from

Table 8.3 Arms transfer agreements with developing nations, 2003–10: agreements by the leading recipients in current US dollars (000 million)

Rank	*Country*	*Value in dollars (000 million)*
1	Saudi Arabia	44,300
2	India	38,100
3	UAE	18,700
4	Egypt	14,400
5	Pakistan	13,000
6	Venezuela	12,700
7	South Korea	10,000
8	Brazil	9,800
9	Algeria	8,700
10	Iraq	8,600

Source: American Government
Grimmett, Richard F., 2011. *Conventional Arms Transfers to Developing Countries*, Congressional Research Service, Washington, DC, p. 45

Table 8.4 UAE's military spending and armaments from 2001 to 2011 in millions of current US dollars

Year	*Dollars (millions)*
2011	16,062
2010	15,749
2009	15,774
2008	13,585
2007	11,275
2006	10,504
2005	10,380
2004	11,153
2003	10,329
2002	9,844
2001	10,703

Source: SIPRI, 2011, p. 211.

China, the latter's presence in the UAE's defence sector is noticeable even if the UAE's dominant defence partners remain the United States, Britain and France. Since the spring of 2010, Chinese naval ships have been patrolling the Gulf of Aden, the Horn of Africa and the Indian Ocean to protect freight from the threat of Somali pirates, and have been making frequent stops in UAE ports.

Political co-operation

The new Chinese foreign policy approach motivated the UAE, Saudi Arabia and other Gulf countries to recognize the PRC. Since the 1970s, a key issue between the Gulf and China was its support of leftist organizations operating in the region. Gulf countries demanded an end to such support, and China agreed. From that point on, China's goal was the stability of the existing status quo instead of supporting the stability of monarchies in the Gulf region. Changes that have occurred on the international scene since the early 1970s, such as the American–Chinese rapprochement and the reduction in tension between the two countries, and the defeat of the Soviet Union in Afghanistan also motivated China to radically alter its foreign policy.

China, the UAE, Saudi Arabia, the US, Jordan, Egypt, Pakistan and many other countries supported the freedom fighters of Afghanistan in evicting the Soviets from the country and, as a result of this support, the UAE recognized China in 1984. Since then, the two countries have steadily nurtured their ties in the political, economic and energy spheres, in addition to relations in culture and tourism. China and the UAE also advocated an immediate ceasefire between Iran and Iraq during the eight years of devastating war, although the Emirates was influenced by the Iranian revolutionary rhetoric, making it incumbent on the UAE's Government to support Iraq to put an end to the Iranian threat. Both countries condemned Iraq for the invasion of Kuwait on

2 August 1990. Although the UAE supported the Saudi leadership in calling for a military solution and took part in military efforts to evict Saddam Hussein from Kuwait, China abstained at the UN Security Council, continued to oppose sanctions imposed on Iraq between 1990 and 2003 and called for lifting of the embargo. The UAE and China encouraged Arabs and Palestinians to reach a peaceful settlement in the Arab–Israeli conflict, and supported the Clinton Administration and European efforts in the 1990s. They continued to call for the revival of the peace process and supported the Saudi, Egyptian, Jordanian and the Quartet's efforts, although these yielded no substantial results.

China and the UAE condemned the terrorist attacks on the United States on 11 September 2001. Both supported the US in its efforts to eradicate terrorism, and China seized this opportunity to eradicate resistance in Xinjiang, or East Turkistan. Although the UAE and China weathered the American invasion of Iraq, other crises dominated regional and international relations, such as the Iranian nuclear programme. While the UAE does not object to the use of nuclear energy for civilian purposes, it strongly opposes the nuclearization of the Gulf region for aggressive purposes. China provided some technology necessary to develop Iran's ambitious nuclear programme but, under US, European and Arab pressure, it seems to have halted that support. China is taking an active role in the current negotiations between the P 5+1 (five permanent members and Germany) and Iran to find a peaceful solution to the Iran–Western standoff. China opposes Israeli use of force to strike Iran's nuclear facilities, and continues to advocate a peaceful resolution to the crisis. The UAE supports China's territorial integrity with reference to Taiwan, Tibet and Xingjian.

The foremost issue for the UAE is its national security juxtaposed to repeated and unwarranted Iranian threats. In fact, diplomatic support is needed to resolve the conflict over three UAE islands occupied by Iran since 1971. The UAE has been mobilizing its foreign policy apparatuses to generate international support. China clearly confirmed the UAE's territorial integrity and sovereignty, although the latest communiqué signed between the UAE's Vice president and the Chinese premier in January 2012 did not mention the three islands by name. Wen Jiabo highlighted how a 'peaceful and stable gulf region is of great significance to world peace. … China is willing to strengthen communication and coordination with the UAE on important issues.'[19] Wen also signed a joint statement to establish strategic partnership with the UAE. In fact, the joint communiqué is comprehensive in nature. It consists of 12 points, among which 'China supports the policies and moves taken by the UAE in respect to national sovereignty and territorial integrity, while the UAE backs the One-China policy. Both countries uphold the principles of sovereignty, non-interference in other countries' internal affairs and solving problems by peaceful means.'[20] Wen's objective was to send a message to Iran to reduce unnecessary tension in the region, to which Iran did not respond positively. In fact, it escalated its differences with the UAE as never before over the three islands to make military threats. In this and every case, China always advocates a peaceful settlement and opposes military confrontation.

Cultural relations

UAE and Chinese officials have highlighted the importance of cultural co-operation between the two countries. A major step was relaxing the process of obtaining visas to encourage nationals to visit and do business. Tourism increased. It is estimated that, of the 8 million tourists who flocked to the UAE, '150,000 Chinese people visited the Emirates in 2010, up 41 percent from 2009.'[21] Chinese tourists created a demand for luxury goods similar to Russian, European, Central Asian and other East Asian elites, such as jewelery, gold, diamond, cigars, perfumes, clothing, watches, wines, etc. They are also enjoying luxury hotels in Dubai, Abu Dhabi and Fujairah. It is expected that, by 2020, there will be 100 million outbound Chinese travellers; it is already quite close to 50 million outbound tourists,[22] and the UAE intends to be a major destination for such a wave of tourists. Its luxury 7-star Jumeirah Hotel and Burj Al Arab attract substantial numbers of Chinese tourists. The Jumeirah Group opened its first hotel in Shanghai, and is in the process of building and managing five more hotels in China. In 2009 China granted the UAE the approved destination status (ADS), a unilateral agreement that organizes tourism between China and other countries. Its purpose is to ensure the safety and quality of services provided to Chinese tourists by travel agencies organizing group trips to the UAE. The Abu Dhabi Tourism Authority (ADTA) opened an office in Beijing to promote tourism in the UAE, and teamed up with the Hong Kong University Polytechnic to organize courses and workshops in the Abu Dhabi hospitality sector, educating students on Chinese culture and the needs of Chinese tourists.[23] The UAE's pavilion at the Shanghai Expo opened its doors to millions of visitors in 2010. It is a unique piece of architectural design equipped with top technology that reflects the eternal beauty of the UAE's desert landscape: the shape of a sand dune. The pavilion appears rough and textured on one side; it bears the full force of the wind, but is smooth on the other side. The northern elevation is more porous to admit natural light, whereas the southern elevation has a solid façade to minimize solar gain. A stainless steel skin, treated to appear golden, encloses the jewel-like shell.[24] The pavilion represents a permanent aesthetic piece of architecture that serves to educate the Chinese people and guests at the Expo about the UAE and the resilience of its people.

Chinese and UAE universities have begun co-operation in the areas of research, scholarships and student and faculty exchange programmes. The Foreign Studies University in China and Zayed University are leading in this area. Their co-operation has led to the establishment of a Confucius Institute on Zayed University's Abu Dhabi campus. The institute's goal is to disseminate Chinese culture, teach the Chinese language and promote China's trade interests in the UAE, similar to other Confucius Institutes around the world. Dubai serves as a global hub for travellers. In order to between the two countries, Abu Dhabi-based Etihad Airway based Emirates have increased their flights to major Chinese procity, Chinese airlines have also added more direct flight increasing demands of travellers to both destinations. Dubai is a transiting city to Chinese business people and entrepreneurs travelling across the Middle East, Africa and Europe.

Conclusion

Three decades ago, the UAE and China shared a major factor in common: both were underdeveloped and impoverished. However, despite the disparity in demographics, both have managed to accomplish unprecedented levels of economic growth and development. China has lifted millions of people from poverty to prosperity, while the UAE has transformed desert to oil fields, factories, shopping malls, ski slopes and ever-rising cities. China and the UAE have established a strong economic partnership since the establishment of diplomatic relations, which grew steadily during the 1980s and 1990s and intensified around 2007. Their current bilateral trade is estimated at $35 thousand million dollars and is marching towards its goal of $100 thousand million by 2015. China is the UAE's second trading partner after India, competing strongly for first place. It is a matter of time before China becomes the UAE's first and most valuable trading partner. To this end, both countries have built the necessary infrastructure: bilateral agreements, forums, councils, frameworks, friendship and business associations and major corporations functioning in both markets. The Dragon Mart in Dubai is the largest Chinese business complex outside mainland China. Sino–Emirati co-operation extends to energy, nuclear technology, natural gas, consumer goods and services, the motor industry, textiles and all aspects of trade. The UAE recognizes the One-China policy and has gradually reduced its economic relations with Taiwan to the satisfaction of the PRC. In return, China acknowledges the sovereignty and territorial integrity of the UAE, and supports its quest to build a force capable of defending its interests and borders. Huge UAE corporations, such as Nakheel and Dubai Port World, lead in their respective fields; Nakheel manages some of the world's most popular resorts and is interested in building the Jumeirah Hotel brand in China, whereas Dubai Port World is interested in managing some of China's ports in the same way that it is currently doing in India.

9 China–Algeria relations

Algeria is the largest African country, the centre of Arab presence in North Africa, and a country endowed with a strategic location and remarkable national wealth. It has a GDP purchasing power estimated in 2011 at $264.1 thousand million and an accumulated foreign reserve of $173 thousand million (Table 9.1).[1] Algeria's economy is classified as less performing, with low growth and high unemployment rates, in spite of the country being endowed with plenty of national wealth that includes oil, natural gas, phosphates, iron, uranium, zinc, agriculture, small industries, a skilled labour force and an educated population. Decades of economic mismanagement, inefficient public and private sectors, corruption, civil war and continued domestic instability have wrecked Algeria's economy.

Algeria is China's most loyal friend, and China is Algeria's second trading partner (10.6 percent), second only to France (18 percent), but steadily catching up and expected to surpass it by 2015. Since the 1950s, China has rendered the Algerian people profound sympathy and admiration in their struggle for liberation, and provided political, economic and military support for its independence movement. When in December 1958 the National Liberation Front (FLN) declared the Algerian provisional government, China recognized it within five days and established full diplomatic ties on 20 December 1958, thus becoming the first non-Arab country to recognize Algeria. In 1971 together with Albania, Algeria co-sponsored the motion to restore China's membership of the United Nations and played a pivotal role in mobilizing international support. Sino–Algerian relations have grown steadily since and withstood six decades of internal upheavals and regional and international crises. China admired Algeria's fierce war of independence as an example for Third World nations to seek national liberation from Western colonialism.

Algeria's revolution became the core of modern literature on revolutionary wars, and an example for revolutionaries around the world seeking national liberation. Leading world revolutionary Frantz Fanon joined the FLN, documented the revolution and wrote the most popular literature on national liberation and anti-colonialism, especially in Africa. Fanon reflected on the depth of the Algerian liberation experience and the unwavering determination

Table 9.1 Algeria's real GDP and unemployment rates

Year	*Real GDP growth rate*	*Unemployment rate*	*GDP purchasing power*
2011	2.5	10.0	$264.1 thousand million
2012	3.1	9.7	NA
2013	3.4	9.3	NA

Source: constructed from data provided by the International Monetary Fund, *World Economic Outlook*, April 2012, p. 72.
Figures for 2012 and 2013 are also estimates provided by the IMF, at www.imf.org/external/pubs/ft/weo/2012/01/pdf/text.pdf (accessed 14 May 2012).

of the people to earn their independence by force.[2] Such experience captured the hearts and minds of Chinese leaders. Mao, Chou En-lai and China's foreign affairs ministers Chen Yi, Ji Pengfei and Qiao Guanhua closely followed developments in the Algerian arena.

Post WWII, China's understanding of developments in the Middle East and North Africa and its understanding of the Algeria War of Independence was inspired by Mao's intermediate zone theory, in which the Middle East and North Africa represent a middle point where Western powers determined to establish an eternal strong foothold. Their goal is to subjugate Africa and the Middle East on their march towards the Far East. Mao condemned French brutality in Algeria and the American–Western security alliances in the Middle East as instruments of perpetual imperialism in the region. He saw that the West had failed to undermine the socialist world, and understood the Western offensive in the region in terms of an attack on nationalism: 'as we see it now, their attack is directed against nationalism, that is … against Egypt, Lebanon, and other weak Middle Eastern countries … they want to overthrow Nasser, destroy Iraq, subjugate Algeria, and so on.'[3]

Although Shichor maintains that China's support for the Arab world was rhetorical in nature, nowhere did it materialize so much as in the Algerian Revolution. Behbehani maintains that 'until 1967, when China's militant stand was exemplified by support for national liberation movements, Sino–Arab relations were of minor importance to internal developments in the Arab world, except Algeria, where China played a significant role in both military and political aid to the Front de Libération Nationale (FLN).'[4] Algeria's struggle resonated with the Chinese people's struggle for liberation from foreign dominance in mainland China, in Hong Kong, Macao and Taiwan. Chou En-lai visited Algeria in 1962 and 1965. During his visits, he and senior Chinese officials signed several political, trade and cultural agreements. By offering military assistance and diplomatic and political support, China laid the foundation for a long-lasting friendship with Algeria. Chou En-lai set the precedent for co-ordination of senior-to-senior government officials, party–party and people-to-people relations. Algeria and China signed twenty agreements between 1963 and 1975. They cover a wide range of issues such as cultural co-operation, economic and technical co-operation, friendship, communication, trade, trade payment agreements, scientific co-operation, medical co-operation, maritime co-operation, shipping, insurance, etc.[5]

Algeria and China exchanged delegations in all fields to enhance their bilateral co-operation. China hosted an Algerian student delegation in September 1958 when the Algerian Revolution was reaching its zenith. China also received a military delegation in April 1959 that sought Chinese military assistance and to which Chou En-lai responded generously. The Algerian Communist Party also sent a delegation to China in the same year, while the Algerian provisional government sent its first delegation in September 1959 and a second a year later, led by Premier Belkacem. Algerian Youth and Trade Union delegations visited China in April 1960 and in September it was Premier Abbas's turn, followed by Algeria's official diplomatic mission in May 1961 in Beijing. Algerian writers, intellectuals and intelligentsia also sent a delegation to China in March 1962, followed a year later by Algeria's trade union, Algerian women's and journalist delegations, Algerian militia, cultural, scientific and trade delegations. The peak of this flurry of relations culminated with the visit of Algeria's first President, Ahmed ben Bella, who visited China in August 1964. His visit sought to show gratitude for China's assistance during the War of Independence, and to strengthen the Sino–Algerian partnership. Subsequent Algerian governments such as Boumediene's and Ben Jaded's administrations also exchanged delegations.[6] Algerian–Chinese relations were special in their endurance, unlike other Middle Eastern countries' volatile agreements, as in Egypt. These accords flourished under Mao, Xiaoping, Zemin and Hu Jintao and are expected to continue under the upcoming Jinping's administration, the fifth generation of Chinese leadership.

The five pillars of Sino–Algerian relations

Political co-ordination

Sino–Algerian relations are multifaceted in nature and span over six decades of close ties. The core revolves around political co-ordination, and has then spilled over to trade, health education, science research and development, defence and energy co-ordination. They are characterized by the visits of senior state officials who continue to keep the tradition established by Chou En-lai in 1962. Jiang Zemin visited Algeria in 1991, followed by Hu Jintao in 2004. During this visit, he signed a joint declaration with President Abdelaziz Bouteflika in which both sides reaffirmed their strategic partnership. Bouteflika visited China in 2002, paid another state visit for three days in 2006 and attended the opening ceremony of the 2008 Olympic Games hosted by China. His attendance was a show of support as China was under tremendous pressure from human rights organizations with reference to its policy in Africa, and especially in its dealings with the Sudan over the Darfur genocide.

China and Algeria closely co-ordinated anti-imperialist effor and 1970s. They condemned colonial policies in the Middle Ea Asia and Latin America. Both supported national liberatic especially in Africa, and assisted the Palestinian cause. Their South African National Congress, Angola's national liberati especially UNITA, and Zimbabwe's African National Liberation Army were decisive in their struggles for independence. Algeria unwaveringly sustained, promoted and guarded the core of Chinese political interests. It strongly supported the One-China policy towards Taiwan and China's views on Tibet and Xinjiang. The independence of many nations in Africa, the Middle East, Asia and the Third World increased the number of seats at the United Nations. China had a great opportunity to cultivate co-operation and goodwill through forums such as the Non-Aligned Movement, and to secure the support of its membership in the organization. In addition, with the US's deep involvement in Vietnam, Laos and Cambodia, it was impossible not to involve China in international affairs; America wanted to secure tacit support for its disengagement and withdrawal from Vietnam. Thus, the US and China began their rapprochement process towards the end of 1968. Along with Albania, Algeria sought to take advantage of the international political developments conducive to the admission of China to the United Nations, and therefore introduced resolution GA-2758 which was passed on 25 October 1971 with 76 countries supporting it, 35 opposing it, 17 members abstaining and three non-voting members present.[7]

Between 1962 and 1976 Algeria developed a reputation for being a 'world-leading diplomat', taking initiatives in resolving some regional and international conflicts, and advancing the cause of friends and allies such as China. After China's admission to the UN, China and Algeria co-ordinated closely on issues on the UN's agenda such as the Arab–Israeli conflict, the Iran–Iraq border disputes, the apartheid regimes in South Africa and Angola, the Vietnam War, US–Soviet relations and their impact on Third World countries and national liberation movements in Africa, Latin America, the Middle East and the Far East. While China struggled to give major concessions to some countries so they would recognize and abide by the One-China policy, with Algeria it found itself on the same page. Algeria strongly advocated that African countries increase China's involvement in African and international affairs; it firmly committed to China's core issues and supported China's negotiations to unite Hong Kong and Macao with the homeland – a historical achievement realized in 1997 and 1999 respectively – and to its territorial integrity over Tibet and Xinjiang.

Algeria added another milestone accomplishment to its portfolio in assisting China to make inroads in Africa. Although Algeria was going through a civil war in the 1990s, which resulted in the deaths of over 200,000 people, its diplomacy managed to maintain a relatively active role on the world scene. When it chaired the African Union (AU) in 1999–2000, Algeria rallied African backing by establishing the Forum on China–Africa Co-operation (FOCAC), serving as a primary platform for comprehensive Sino–African engagement. The forum held its first meeting at ministerial level in October 2000 in Beijing. It was attended by eighty ministers of foreign affairs, international co-operation and international trade from 45 African countries, with a total attendance of over 500 officials. The conference resulted in the so called Beijing Declaration. The documents set forth an ambitious Sino-Africa plan for economic, cultural and political co-operation. So far, three more FOCAC meetings have been organized in Addis Ababa in 2003, in Beijing in 2006 and in Sharm el-Sheikh (Egypt) in 2009. The last meeting was attended by China and the representatives of forty-nine African countries and accomplished significant bilateral trade agreements. Chinese Premier Wen Jiabao summed up commitment towards Africa stating that China pledges to assist Africa in addressing climate change, in developments in science and technology, in finance and in opening its market to African agricultural products. He added that China would increase the number of its agricultural technology demonstration centres in Africa to 20, send 50 agricultural technology teams to Africa and train 2,000 agricultural technology personnel for Africa in order to help boost the continent's food security, the development of human resources and medical care and health and education. China will expand people-to-people and cultural exchanges.[8]

Trade relations

The fierce struggle between Algeria's national liberation movement and the French authorities caused millions of scientists, bureaucrats, entrepreneurs and health providers, the overwhelming majority of whom were French, to evacuate Algeria during the War of Independence (1954–62), leaving behind a vacuum in all sectors. The health sector in particular was paralysed, so that Algeria issued an international appeal in 1963 asking for world assistance to meet the population's health needs. China was one of the very first countries to respond by sending thousands of medical doctors, nurses and health personnel. 'Since then, China has sent a total of 21 batches of medical staff to Algeria, numbering more than 2,800 Chinese medical personnel.'[9] This appeal provided China with a new framework of co-operation with Africa, health care assistance. China sent significant numbers of health teams to the continent, to Latin America and to Asian neighbours. Other countries, such as Cuba, replicated this model in providing health assistance to needy countries, to the extent that Cuba became a pioneering country sending thousands of medical doctors around the world. Cuba and China also provided some students from Third World countries with scholarships to study medicine.

One of the vital fields of co-operation between China and Algeria has been the construction sector. Algeria sought Chinese expertise in building major infrastructure projects and, as China excelled in this sector, the China State Construction Engineering Corporation (CSCE) carried out Algeria's major construction projects such as highways, airports, ports, water canals, pipelines, bridges, telecommunication towers, hotels, etc. In addition to CSCE, there are over 50 other major Chinese companies operating in the construction sector, housing, mining, oil, natural gas and minerals. They are supported by a Chinese community of over 45,000 people. Some of their projects include Algiers Airport, Sheraton Hotel Algiers, Algeria's Grand Mosque and the East–West Highway. CSCE's latest massive project in Algeria is to build the Grand Mosque, a contract signed on 1 March 2012, to be completed in 42 months. Current President Bouteflika wants to leave a legacy for several centuries to come: 'The mega mosque will sit on 20 hectares (49 acres) of land in the Mohammadia area of the capital, with its minaret soaring 270 metres (almost 900 feet) into the sky. The one billion euro ($1.3 billion) house of worship will be able to accommodate 120,000 people, will also feature a library containing one million works and seating for 2,000 people, as well as a museum and a research centre. It will be the world's third largest mosque after those in Mecca and Medina in Saudi Arabia.'[10]

The East–West Highway is another mammoth project carried out by Chinese corporations. The highway project phase one, estimated at $6.2 thousand million, consists of 1,216 kilometres connecting east to west, strengthening Algeria's ties with neighbouring Maghreb countries.[11] The other two phases are still under way, and Chinese corporations are ahead of schedule, which highlights their efficiency in carrying out such a large-scale project. The overall cost of the East–West Highway's three phases is estimated at $12.00 thousand million. The China Civil Engineering and Construction Corporation was awarded a $2.1 thousand million contract to construct railways in the western region of Algeria similar to those under way in Saudi Arabia.

Commensurate with China's involvement in the Algerian economy, bilateral trade grew drastically. In 2000, it was $198.85 million, mostly in the construction sector; it increased to $292.34 million a year later, reaching a landmark point in 2007 of $3.8 thousand million, growing steadily to $5.17 thousand million in 2010, progressively increasing its goal of $20 thousand million by 2015. Table 9.2 illustrates bilateral trade value from 2000 to 2010. The trend is only expected to improve given that Algeria's Five Year Plan for 2010–14 is under way, and it includes major construction projects that are being carried out by Chinese corporations. Chinese oil companies have just begun their upstreaming and downstreaming joint ventures with Sonatrach, Algeria's national oil company. Chinese foreign direct investments (FDI) in Algeria up to 2010 amounted to $1,000 million, which is also expected to rise after signing new agreements.

Algeria's economic development

Over the past 10 years, Algeria has embarked on a process of economic development and national reconciliation after a devastating decade of civil war that led to the massacre of over 200,000 people by government security agencies and Islamist rebels. The election of Bouteflika in 1999 brought relative stability to the country and reduced tensions between the armed forces and

Table 9.2 Sino–Algerian bilateral trade in millions of dollars for the period from 2000 to 2010

Year	*Trade volume in $ million*
2010	5,177.32
2009	5,127.46
2008	4,601.13
2007	3,866.41
2006	2,090.64
2005	1,768.15
2004	1,239.60
2003	745.15
2002	433.81
2001	292.34
2000	198.85

Source: 2010 China Statistical Yearbook, p. 238.

the opposition. Algeria's economy grew modestly, averaging 3 percent, which is far below its potential growth rate. 2010 was critical because it marked the beginning of the Five Year Plan (2010–14) in which China was requested to implement major construction projects. The Five Year Plan continues the trend of co-operation begun in the 1950s, a decade before Algeria's independence.

Trade forums

China and Algeria's trade relations are served by a multitude of bilateral and multilateral entities, organizations and forums. Algeria's strategic geographical position in the MENA region and in Africa provides a wide range of opportunities to be included in Sino–Middle Eastern and Sino-African trade forums, protocols and agreements. The China–Africa Co-operation Forum and the China–Arab States Co-operation Forum are the two main umbrella organizations that boost multilateral trade relations, formal economic attaché offices, diplomatic missions, chambers of commerce and friendship associations. Their main goal is to maintain, nurture and promote the distinguished status of Sino–Algerian relations, and bring them to a higher level. The China–Algeria Joint Commission of Economics, Trade and Technology, established in 1982, made significant strides and has become a model for Algeria in its bilateral trade relations with other countries such as India, the US and Turkey. The commission promotes co-operation in major sectors such as oil and natural gas, consumer goods and services, construction and investment. It has also expanded its scope to include new energy sources, nuclear energy and scientific co-operation.

–Algerian Cultural Co-operation Agreement was signed on 11 53, followed by the Executive Plan for Sino–Algerian Cultural

Co-operation Agreement in 1964 and 1965.[12] A major street in the capital city of Algiers was named Beijing Street to commemorate historical relations between the two sides, China's recognition of Algeria [-] the first among non-Arab countries – and its valuable assistance during national liberation. In 2003, Algeria unveiled a stamp commemorating the forty-fifth anniversary of diplomatic relations between the two countries: 'it features the national flags of the two countries in the form of two doves of peace flying side by side, implying the friendly relations of the two countries and the sustained reciprocal effort for peace and development.'[13] From 1958 to 2002, their cultural relations were characterized by delegation visits and cultural weeks. Both sides validated their previous pacts in the 2002 implementation of the Plan for Cultural Agreement, and explored avenues for enhancing bilateral cultural relations in the areas of education, Sino–Algerian studies, festivals and exhibitions. The growth of their bilateral trade since 1979 has led to an increase in Chinese nationals residing in Algeria estimated at 50,000, the largest Chinese community in Africa.

In spite of generally peaceful co-existence, some repeated clashes have occurred between members of the Chinese community and Algerians, the worst of which were those in the summer of 2009. Such clashes are usually ignited by minor incidents such as disputes over a parking spot or opposition to some habits such as alcohol consumption, prevalent among the Chinese community; but the deeper reasons have to do with Algerian complaints over Chinese corporations' labour policies. Typically, Chinese construction companies bring their own labour force, but Algerian nationals want to see more employment opportunities for themselves at a time when the national economy is crippled by structural problems and high unemployment, currently estimated at 20 percent. Chinese corporations prefer Chinese nationals, and they accuse locals of being less disciplined, less productive and less committed to work than their Chinese counterparts. The construction corporations also offer low pay, under harsh work conditions, both of which are unacceptable to Algerian nationals. Usually, Chinese and Algerian officials downplay the significance of such clashes and highlight the historical and mutually beneficial relations. In reality, the clashes between the emerging Chinese community and Algerian locals can be detrimental to bilateral relations. Although these communities are considered a great asset to China in advancing its trade worldwide, they can also be a colossal liability.[14] They have raised some questions over China's responsibility and influence; therefore, senior officials advocate peace between the Chinese diaspora and hosting countries, and instruct their companies to act with greater accountability.

There are countless methods that both sides can pursue to maintain social peace and harmony. Chinese companies under direct instruction from the Chinese government have begun paying considerable attention to their social responsibility: 'Our company will attach greater importance to repaying society and building harmonious and friendly ties with local residents.'[15] The Chinese community's presence in Algeria is critical to China's and Algeria's economies and to their national prosperity; therefore, both sides should take the necessary steps to reach a peaceful settlement of disputes. Algerian locals should engage and interact with their guest community by exchanging visits, holding cultural events, organizing educational and awareness programmes and highlighting Arab Islamic values of hospitality and generosity towards foreigners. The Chinese community can develop sensitivity towards alcohol consumption, or at least refrain from public use as it is forbidden in Islam.

Although, currently, the Chinese community is seeking to establish a Chinatown, where Chinese nationals live in isolation from their surroundings, this approach is in contradiction of the aim and the spirit of Chinatowns worldwide. It is not the best approach in dealing with communal discord. In other countries, Chinatowns serve as cultural centers, whereas clashes in Algeria are promoting a 'Ghetto Chinatown' rather than being a symbol of cultural and commercial co-existence. Some intermarriage cases have been reported among the two communities, which, according to Arab tradition, are the best method for creating intercommunal and interfamily peace. Mutual understanding can be generated by enhancing cultural interaction and cultural activities, producing social peace. Teaching the Chinese language and Arabic and Algerian traditions is another step towards that goal. A senior Chinese official stated that 'the Chinese government will encourage Chinese enterprises to establish business and invest in Algeria, adopt open policy on technology transfer to Algeria and launch various training programs for Algerian personnel in an effort to contribute to Algeria's economic structure adjustment and employment enlargement.'[16]

Another step towards communal peace could be Confucius Institutes. In 2007 Algeria requested that branches be established in the country, but no institute has been built to date, which is out of character with Sino–Algerian relations. Algeria is keeping up with the global trend interested in learning about China's culture, language and history, while the Chinese response is way below the increasing demand and out of line with its notable bilateral relations. It is also below the efforts devoted by the Chinese to the US, Canada and European countries in terms of the number of Confucius Institutes in Europe and North America.

Another aspect of Sino-Algeria cultural co-operation is the recent announcement by the Chinese government of a donation of $40 million to build an opera house in Algeria. The project will be in the Ouled Fayet suburb of Algiers City and includes 14,000 seats. It is 'an important symbol of Chinese–Algerian friendship'[17] that serves as a cultural monument in Algeria. In the Shanghai International Expo, 2010, millions of visitors flocked to Algeria's national pavilion. The building is a unique piece of art symbolizing Algeria's historical houses with a theme of 'the house of my father', with reference to the *Casbah* 'as a historical, architectural and cultural patrimony'[18] well represented in Algeria's pavilion.

country to recognize in just five days the Algerian provisional government formed in December 1958. In the post-independence era, China supplied Algeria with much needed health professionals to offset the shortage caused by their departure to France. China and Algeria signed several agreements that cover culture, political co-ordination, trade, health, science, sports and tourism. Algeria, along with Albania, introduced a landmark resolution at the General Assembly in 1971 to admit China as a member of the UN. Algeria also paved the way for China to approach Africa's markets and has supported Chinese causes in international organizations. Their close ties have withstood local, regional and international challenges over the past six decades. In the post-Mao era, Sino–Algerian trade, investment and energy co-operation have accelerated. Algeria has entrusted Chinese construction corporations with the task of building major infrastructure projects such as airports, bridges, highways, oil and gas pipelines, ports, hotels, hospitals, housing projects and exploring for oil and natural gas across the country. Both countries aim to boost their bilateral trade to $20 thousand million by the year 2015.

Conclusion

The nine chapters in this book have highlighted the depth of Sino–Middle Eastern relations from the Silk Road to the current Arab Spring. China is increasingly viewing the region as strategic to its national interests defined in terms of territorial integrity, regime survival and economic prosperity. On these three fronts, the Middle East is exceptionally vital to China. In sovereignty and territorial integrity vis-à-vis the three core issues of Xinjiang, Tibet and Taiwan, Middle East support is of paramount importance to China. Xinjiang is spiritually and historically linked to the Middle East with ethnic and religious bonds. Middle Eastern people are also very concerned about religious freedom in China and its treatment of Muslims, especially in Xinjiang. They are horrified at the level of violence used against civilians during frequent conflicts in the province, most recently in the summer of 2009.

Middle Eastern support for China's sovereignty over Xinjiang is critical to China's territorial integrity. Xinjiang is the largest province in China, predominantly Muslim, ethnically tied to the forefathers of current Turkey and tightly linked with ethnic, familial and linguistic ties to Central Asia. Xinjiang's Muslims are followers of the Sunni sect; therefore, Saudi Arabia's support for China's territorial claims over Xinjiang is vital. In fact, during the civil war and the communists' Long March, several hundred Muslims from Xinjiang and other provinces fled the conflict and took up residence in the two holy cities of Mecca and Medina, while further thousands from Xinjiang in particular migrated to Turkey. In Mecca and Medina, Chinese Muslims established a prosperous community, albeit maintaining a strong emotional attachment to their homeland, China.

In order to secure Saudi and Turkish support for its policies in Xinjiang and to deny support for the East Turkistan Liberation Organization (ETLO) and its East Turkistan Islamic Movement (ETIM), China has pursued a diplomatic offensive on both the Turkish and the Saudi fronts. It bargained with Turkey by providing strategic missiles systems and other types of military technology. In exchange, it wanted Turkey to reduce and eliminate its support for East Turkistan's movements. China extracted clear commitments in writing on its claims of sovereignty over Xinjiang from the current Turkish president, the prime minister and the speaker of the Grand National Assembly of

Turkey. It also provided concessions in terms of bilateral trade by opening up its markets to Turkish corporations.

For Saudi Arabia, China provides arms, defence co-operation and strategic energy collaboration in upstreaming and downstreaming, while Chinese construction companies are carrying out major building projects throughout the kingdom. In this tradeoff, the Chinese goal is to continue to neutralize Saudi support for Muslims in Xinjiang. In fact, during the communal conflict between the Han and the Uyghur Muslims in the province in the summer of 2009, Saudi Arabia refrained from criticizing China's use of violence against Muslims. The Saudi government also prevented Saudi citizens of Chinese background from expressing their resentment or mobilizing support for their fellow Uyghur Muslims. This continued mistreatment of Muslims in Xinjiang reflects China's contradictory policy towards religion vis-à-vis its strong Middle Eastern ties and business interests in the region.

While Chinese corporations are building the Grand Mosque of Algeria – the third largest shrine after the two Holy Shrines in Mecca and Medina – China seems to have different standards and policies in dealing with the 'Muslim question' within its territory: it denies its 10 Chinese Muslim ethnic minorities full freedom of worship, a concern the Muslim world has had with China since the ninth century. To be fair, it has made some progress: of them all, Xinjiang Muslims are the most restricted, while the other nine minorities have a better margin of religious freedom. Lately, China has been channelling some of its development projects into its western regions. Xinjiang's major cities are changing, and economic change is noticeable.[1] If political authority, oppression and intolerance have failed to eradicate dissent in Xinjiang, China hopes that economic prosperity might. Other Muslim minorities and autonomous regions in China are greatly encouraged and supported by the state to take a lead in building business ties with the Middle East and the Muslim world. For example, from 12–16 September 2012, the Ningxia Hui Autonomous Region is organizing the Ningxia International Fair for Investment and Trade and hosting the China–Arab Economic and Trade Forum meetings. Negotiations between the Ningxia Hui Autonomous Region and the Abu Dhabi Chamber of Commerce took place in early March 2012. The goal was to establish a base for its Halal food distribution centre in Abu Dhabi to expand its industry to Middle Eastern markets.

The process of economic prosperity is effective and productive even among Muslim communities, but China has no room for dissent when it comes to the legitimate rights of Muslims, especially in the political sphere. It has declared war against the so called 'three ills', extremism, separatism and terrorism, all of which seem to apply to Muslims, especially in Xinjiang. Tibetan or even Hong Kong (anti-unification) opposition was never termed extremist or terrorist but, curiously, Muslims are diagnosed with these 'diseases', and the state intervenes with massive force whenever it feels any of these three ills is present. Historically, Tibet has always been an ally of Muslims. The Tibetan National Liberation movement is concentrated in India and Nepal, and spreads across Europe, Canada and the United States but, oddly, it is inactive in the Middle East. In fact, Middle Eastern countries officially conceded to Chinese territorial claims but, at the non-governmental level, civil society organizations are sympathetic to the Tibetan cause and the cause of Xinjiang. Finally, the Middle East as a whole has either cut off its relations with the Republic of China (ROC) or reduced its ties with Taiwan to a minimum. Middle Eastern countries abide by the One-China policy, although some Middle Eastern countries such as Saudi Arabia, the United Arab Emirates (UAE), Israel, Jordan, Oman and Turkey maintain trade offices in Taipei, and Taiwan still maintains some trade and cultural offices in the region.

The Arab Spring is viewed as threatening to China's territorial integrity, sovereignty and economic interests in the Middle East as it serves as a liberation framework not only for Arabs and Muslims, but also for East Turkistanis and Tibetans. For the first time since the golden age of Islam (eighth to ninth centuries), the Middle East has become a source of inspiration for people around the world who are desperate for freedom and justice and weary of state tyranny and abuses from multinational corporations. The depth of resentment towards the status quo and the vibrant role of young people, women, children and the elderly have revived the global spirit for resistance to injustice across the Middle East, Europe, North America and elsewhere.

China views unsettling Arab regime changes as Western supported rather than a genuine effort by the people in the Middle East to obtain justice. It feels that the Arab Spring can be used by its competitors, namely the United States and 'old' enemies Japan, South Korea and Taiwan to mobilize unrest similar to the massive student demonstrations in 1989. It realizes the vulnerability of large segments of its population to the revolutionary fever coming from the Middle East. It fears an alliance of uprooted labourers, urban democratic forces and separatist movements in Tibet and Xinjiang. If such scenarios should occur, then China would be vulnerable to external intervention through existing United Nations mechanisms. Subsequently, to prevent them from happening again and to avoid repercussions domestically, China (naively) believes that it needs to oppose the changes. This explains its fierce opposition to the role of the Security Council and the threat of using force against governments such as Syria.

China's energy interests in Syria, Iraq, Kuwait, Algeria, Iran, Saudi Arabia, Libya, the Sudan, Yemen and elsewhere put it at odds with the revolutions. Stability, not change, best serves its interests in the Middle East. Therefore, it prefers to keep the status quo and reverse the three decades of promoting revolutionary change that it has followed in the Middle East between 1950 and 1980. Here are the perplexing reasons: Middle Eastern democratic governments would be more likely to support freedom, democracy and human rights in China. They would also be more supportive of the rights of Tibet, Taiwan and Xinjiang in terms of their right to self-determination. Democratic governments in the region would be less likely to engage in inequitable oil deals with China. The equity share system that China follows to secure oil in the region might not be acceptable to democratic governments that are seeking to maximize their monetary gains from oil trade; unlike authoritarian regimes, they will favour development, protect and promote domestic producers and double domestic manufacture that would eventually put a strain on China's exports to the Middle East. These reasons explain why China opposes the Arab Spring and strives hard to break its momentum, particularly in Syria, a country that shares structural similarities with China.

In addressing China's views on revolutionary changes in the region, Chapter 4 concludes that its policy towards the Arab Spring is imprudent in the sense that it validates those who advocate that China's foreign policy is immoral and pure Realpolitik. While China's aim is stability to ensure its interests, it has put itself in a predicament and a situation characterized by inconsistency. On the one hand, Chinese officials continue to highlight that China supports the Arab people and respects their choices, while on the other, they provide massive amounts of weaponry to oppressive regimes such as Syria and the Sudan, and previously, the Libyan regime. In particular, China and Russia provided the political shield and the diplomatic support for Syria to continue to oppress its people. In doing so, China is precluding any collaboration with a post-Assad government.

The people of the region are accustomed to political violence and foreign intervention, but they always emerge triumphant, and the Syrian case will prove that China is unsound in its decision to support Assad. Recent events in Libya have already shown China that Gaddafi's regime (and Chinese, Cuban, Venezuelan, Russian and Algerian support) was not a match for the determination of the Libyan people to end his dictatorship. Currently, Chinese businesses are finding it difficult to return to Libyan markets because of the negative impression free Libya has of China's support for the *ancien régime;* 8,000 more people lost their lives after the infamous Chinese and Russian veto. Now, after more than a year of ongoing killing in Syria, China's diplomats continue to rehash the same statements repeated at the foreign ministry, at UN meetings, etc. that China 'supports the Syrian people.' Frankly, the Syrian people do not feel the sympathy, compassion, support or affection that China claims to have towards them. What they see is deliberate support for their oppressors, the Syrian government, its security agencies and its paramilitary *Shabeha* forces.

This book has also examined China's interests in the Middle East in what I call the five pillars: energy, arms sales, trade, culture and political ties. On all of these indicators, Sino–Middle Eastern relations have made remarkable progress. Currently, the Middle East provides nearly half of China's oil imports. China is the second oil importer from the Middle East after the United States, but it is expected to surpass it by 2020. It has strategic energy ties with Saudi Arabia, Iran, Algeria, Kuwait and the United Arab Emirates that include co-operation in oil upstreaming and downstreaming, natural gas, building oil storage, pipelines and clean and nuclear energy. China is the first and second trading partner with several Middle Eastern countries, but strives to be the leading one with them all. Towards the realization of this goal, it has made strategic alliances. Arms sales to the region peaked between 1980 and 1987 as a result of the Iran–Iraq war and declined after the conflict. Arms sales have always served as a vehicle towards trade partnerships, such as with Israel, Turkey, Iran and Saudi Arabia. Among the existing powerhouses in the region, the Sino–Israeli military partnership is exceptionally vital as Israel exports to China high-tech defence products such as drones, radar systems and jetfighter designs such as the Israeli Lvi (China's J-10) in exchange for political support, trade partnerships and markets for Israeli products.

Both China and Middle Eastern countries are taking the necessary steps to enhance their cultural relations. Iran and China set a precedent over 2,000 years ago when Persian cultural traditions, folklore and musical instruments found their way to China. Recently, China has established the Confucius Institutes, cultural entities worldwide with the goal of disseminating Chinese language, culture, tradition and customs. Among the 358 institutes around the world, 12 are in the Middle East. Algeria and several other countries in the region have requested that more be established. Chinese studies are becoming popular in Egypt, Israel and Turkey. Middle Eastern languages, Arabic, Persian, Turkish and Hebrew, are being taught at major Chinese universities and colleges, and these are becoming a destination for Arab students seeking higher education in China. There are 10,000 Arab students studying in China, and 1,500 of them come from Saudi Arabia. Similarly, the Chinese language is becoming popular in the Middle East among students and the business community interested in learning about China. By the same token, the Middle East has become a major destination for Chinese tourists coming to Egypt, Israel, the UAE and Turkey.

In terms of political co-operation, China's main interest in the region from 1949 to 1978 was diplomatic recognition and anti-colonialist co-ordination. However, the new China's political interests are broader and oriented towards peace and stability. China is involved in the Middle East peace process through its Middle East Envoy. The office seeks to provide support for the Palestinian National Authority, encourage bilateral relations with Israel and promote a peaceful settlement of the Arab–Israeli conflict, but declines an invitation to become part of the Quartet (US, Russia, EU and the UN). China's goal is to be associated with the success of the settlement, not to be part of its failure; fragmentation of the Palestinians and botched peace negotiations can be attributed to the current Israeli government, to Tony Blair and to the Bush Administration. In truth, China wants to be free from the entanglements of the peace process in order to maintain its manoeuvrability and relations with all sides, without exception. China is also active in providing peacekeeping forces in the Middle East, especially in Lebanon, and is heavily involved in resolving the Iranian–Western standoff over Iran's nuclear programme.

This study has also developed a tridimensional approach to Sino–Middle Eastern relations by analysing the interaction between three nations at a time. For example, Chinese diplomacy has been successful in maintaining a balance between foes such as Iran and Saudi Arabia; another dimension is China's partnership with Israel and the Palestinians, and the delicate balance between the US and the Middle East. China's ultimate goal is to secure energy and trade interests, and to stake out a space of manoeuvrability between the powerhouses in the region. In most of these partnerships, China is not only succeeding, but has mastered the art of balancing in the midst of a turbulent Middle East.

In the section on bilateral and case studies, the book highlights Sino–Israeli, Sino–Iranian, Sino–Saudi, Sino–Emirati and Sino–Algerian relations. Each of these countries has a comparative advantage that is vital to China's prosperity. Israel provides China with advanced technology in both the military and the civilian spheres, while Saudi Arabia and Iran provide the oil necessary for the continuity of its industrial growth. China is currently involved in major development projects in Algeria as it seeks to displace France and the EU as Algeria's top business partners. Celebrated political ties have enabled China to access North Africa and Africa at large and take a leading role in the current Algerian Five Year Plan, in addition to securing markets for its products and services. Its oil corporations are infiltrating the Algerian market as a result of fierce competition with Western oil corporations, but are already well positioned. China is entrusted to build major Algerian highways such as the East–West Highway, airports, housing projects and hotels.

China's success has spilled over to other forms of co-operation after being involved with each of these five countries on at least one core issue. China–Israeli collaboration is not confined to defence, but extends to agriculture, clean energy, high-tech products and, most recently, to the oil and natural gas sector. China and Iran's partnership extends to non-oil sectors such as the construction of major highways, dams and bridges. It is also involved in Iran's nuclear programme and managing the current standoff with the world. The Chinese–Saudi Arabian alliance is impressive in the sense that, in the span of three decades, their bilateral ties have shifted from animosity to strategic partnership in the areas of defence, energy and trade. China is involved in the Saudis' most ambitious railway network that connects north to south at a cost of over $4 thousand million. Finally, the United Arab Emirates provides China with a hub for its corporations and access to Middle East markets. Sino–Emirati ties include building oil storage, pipelines and defence strategies. Highlighting Chinese relations with these five countries does not diminish the importance of its relations with other countries in the Middle East. China's ties with Turkey, Egypt, Syria, Morocco, Kuwait, Qatar and Oman merit a study beyond the scope of this research, but to truly grasp the depth of Sino–Middle Eastern relations, I must underline the need for more research and publications on this topic.

Energy

The Energy Information Administration (EIA) lists Algeria as the fourth largest African oil- and gas-producing country after Nigeria, Angola and Libya. It is also an active member of OPEC. Its hydrocarbons sector accounts for 60 percent of its annual revenue, 36 percent of its GDP and 97 percent of its total export earnings. Algeria's oil and natural gas partners are mainly Western corporations such as Total, BP, Conoco-Phillips, Eni, Shell and Statoil. 'Algeria produced an estimated average of 1.27 million barrels per day of crude oil in 2011, about the same as it produced in 2010. Together with 270,000 bd of condensate and 340,000 bd of natural gas liquids not included in its OPEC quota, Algeria averaged 1.88 mbd of total oil liquids production during 2011.'[19] The country produces high-quality crude oil with very low sulphur and mineral content that makes it easy to refine; it is in huge demand and, in spite of being far below its production potential, net exports exceed domestic needs (Figure 9.1).

Chinese operations in Algeria are expected to increase oil and gas production, but CNPC will definitely face stiff resistance from Western oil companies resentful of Chinese involvement in the country. CNPC enjoys the support of the Algerian government and has huge assets it can easily utilize to maximize its opportunities. The same applies to the natural gas sector, which is ample enough to accommodate a Chinese presence. Modest national needs enable Algeria to export most of its production to external markets, including the European, Chinese and Asian markets (Figure 9.2).

In 2002, Sinopec signed a $525 million contract with Sonatrach, Algeria's national oil company, to develop the Zarzaitine oil field, located in Algeria's south-eastern Illizi Basin. Sinopec funds the project at a rate of 75 percent to

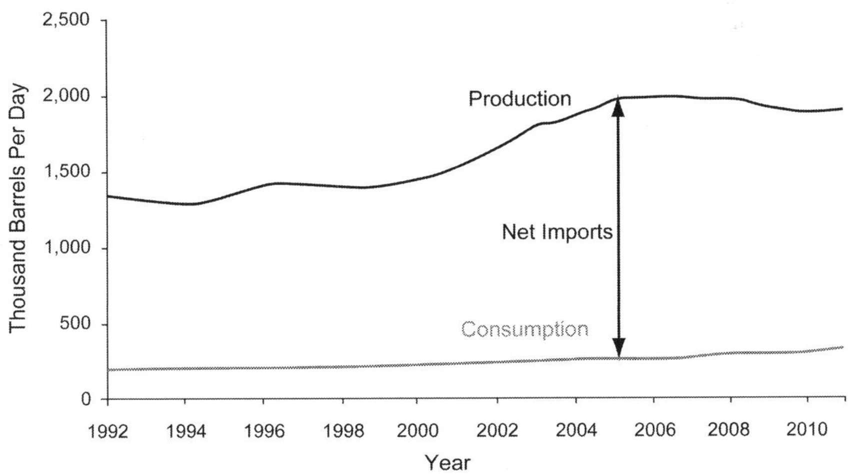

Figure 9.1 Algeria's total oil production and consumption from 1992 to 2011

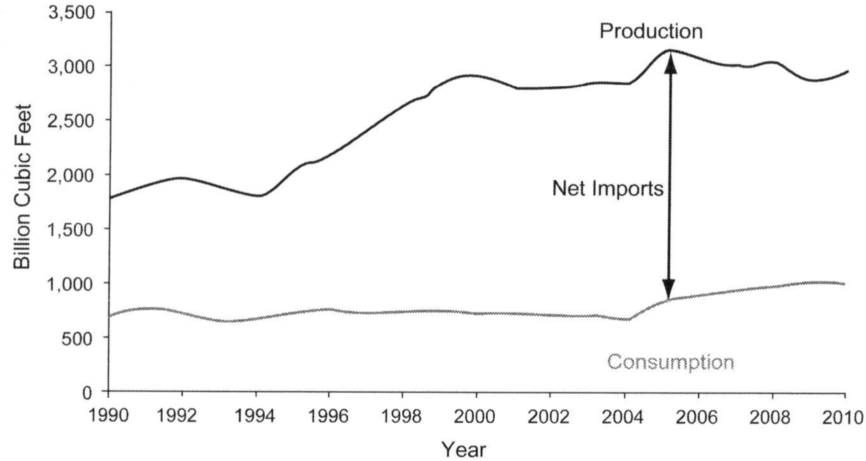

Figure 9.2 Production and consumption of natural gas in Algeria

25 percent with Sonatrach. It is estimated that the Zarzaitine produces two million tons of crude oil annually.[20] 'In 2003 CNPC purchased a number of Algerian refineries for US$350 million and signed a deal to explore for oil in two blocks, while PetroChina signed a contract with Algeria's Hydrogen Carbide to jointly develop oil fields and construct a refinery.'[21] Building refineries is one of the most challenging aspects of oil investment in Africa, which explains why Western corporations are reluctant to embark on such construction projects. Shell, Total, ExxonMobil, Chevron and other Western corporations' goals are to ensure African consumers' continued dependence on Western refined oil. China took on the challenge and built the Adrar refinery in northern Algeria, similar to several other refineries across Africa: 'On May 12, 2003, CNPC won the tender for the Adrar upstream and downstream integrated project with a contract term of 23 years. The project is composed of three parts: oil field appraisal and development, construction of a refinery, and marketing of refined products.'[22] Two months later, CNPC and Algeria's Sonatrach signed the Shareholders Agreement: 70 percent to Sonatrach and 30 percent to CNPC. In 2006, exploration and production of the Adrar oil field was completed, and in April 2007 the refinery became fully operational, with an annual capacity of 600,000 tons of refined oil. It is estimated that China imported 1,612,828 tons, equivalent to 1.02 percent of its overall imports in 2007.[23] In May 2005 CNPC won an engineering contract to build Sonatrach's $5 million ton/year condensate oil refinery in Algeria's Skikda Province, with a total investment of US$385 million.[24] By 28 July 2009 the refinery had a processing capacity of 10,000 bd. The consortiums CNOOC and PTTEP won the bid 50/50 to develop the Hassi Bir Rekaiz in south-eastern Algeria. It covers an area of 5,670 square kilometres. Algeria continues to increase its refinery capacities. Sonatrach received bids from

leading international corporations, and Sinopec made it to the short list, but granting of the contract was postponed four times. The last postponement was reported on 27 March 2011, although Sonatrach gave no justification.[25]

China and Algeria have also extended their co-operation to nuclear energy. Algeria's capacity to produce electricity is very limited, although Algeria is endowed with oil and natural gas. Therefore, Algeria is pursuing nuclear energy as a source to boost its electricity production capacity. China has built two out of three confirmed nuclear installations in Algeria. Algeria also co-ordinates closely with the International Atomic Energy Agency (IAEA), and its installations are under the direct supervision of the agency. Algeria also has nuclear co-operation agreements with the US, Germany and Argentina, signed the non-proliferation treaty, and its nuclear co-operation with China, the US, Argentina, South Africa, France and Germany is well known to the relevant agencies.[26] American and French support is crucial to eliminate suspicion and opposition to Sino–Algerian co-operation, unlike US opposition to Sino–Iranian nuclear co-operation. Algeria hopes that by 2017 it will have a fully functional nuclear reactor.

Arms sales and security co-operation

China prides itself on being Algeria's consistent friend, assisting it during critical times in its modern history. The earliest military co-operation occurred in the Algerian War of Independence in the 1950s, during which China provided the FLN with arms. Since then, a strategic partnership has grown and security co-operation has become essential. Based on the SIPRI's method of calculation of arms exports, Taylor reports that, between 1990 and 2006, the 'foremost importers of Chinese arms are Egypt, Algeria, Sudan, Tanzania, Nigeria and Zimbabwe.'[27] SIPRI confirms that, in 2010, the estimated total military expenditures in Africa were $30.1 thousand million, of which $10.6 thousand million were in North Africa (Morocco, Algeria, Tunisia and Libya). Military spending in Africa was 5.2 percent higher than in the previous year, and North Africa accounted for 5.6 percent of that increase, while sub-Saharan Africa accounted for 4.9 percent. Africa's military spending in 2010 was 64 percent higher than in 2001.[28] Algeria's, Angola's and Nigeria's military spending is associated with the increase in their respective oil production and accumulation of large foreign reserves. Algeria's arms purchases are closely related to the increase in oil prices. Table 9.3 illustrates Algeria's military expenditures in million of US dollars for the period 2001–10.

SIPRI estimates that Algeria imported arms from China worth $250 million between 1987 and 2011, a modest figure in comparison with Algeria's arms purchase of $8.7 thousand million for the period between 2003 and 2010. Algeria's main sources of weapons remain the US, France, Britain and Russia. Since 2001, US–Algerian security co-operation has increased dramatically, providing Algeria with military capabilities, advanced weapons systems, drones and reconnaissance to combat Al-Qaeda and the growing terrorist threat in North and Western Africa. Algerian–Chinese co-operation has

Table 9.3 Algeria's military expenditure in constant US millions of dollars for 2001–10

Year	*Expenditure*
2001	2,914
2002	2,978
2003	2,914
2004	3,314
2005	3,470
2006	3,557
2007	4,173
2008	4,862
2009	5,281
2010	5,586

Source: SIPRI Yearbook, 2011, p. 205.

touched on domestic and regional security threats. In the summer of 2009, China faced a wave of collective violence between the Han and the Uyghur Muslims in Xinjiang where hundreds of people were killed. It coincided with violence in Algeria between some Chinese shopkeepers and local Algerian merchants. The level of violence in Xinjiang was widely covered by major Middle Eastern TV stations. The coverage and the level of violence used by the state and the Hans against the Muslims in Xinjiang mobilized resentment towards China. Muslim clergy called for a boycott of Chinese products, demonstrations in front of Chinese diplomatic missions and demanded that Arab and Muslim governments exercise pressure on China to treat Muslims fairly. On its part, Al-Qaeda in the Islamic Maghreb threatened to target the Chinese community in Algeria if the violence against Muslims in Xinjiang did not end. Given the formidability of Al-Qaeda in North Africa, its threat was taken seriously.

Al-Qaeda in Afghanistan has always been accused of training East Turkistan units to fight for independence from China. This has prompted closer Sino–American, Sino–Russian, Sino-Central Asian, Sino-Turkish and Sino–Algerian co-ordination to combat the threat. The clashes between the Chinese and Algerian communities received national security exposure and direct attention from both governments. The Chinese ambassador to Algeria swiftly visited the neighbourhood and instructed the Chinese community to pursue 'good neighborly relations' with Algerian society and to respect local traditions and customs. Algeria's senior government officials also reminded the Algerian people of the long-standing friendship and co-operation between China and Algeria, condemned Al-Qaeda threats against the Chinese community in Algeria and boosted security around the country.

Conclusion

The Sino–Algerian partnership is deeply rooted in Algeria's War of Independence and China's support for the FLN. China provided Algeria with military, political and diplomatic support, and prides itself on being the first non-Arab

Promoting Middle East and Chinese studies

This book stresses the urgent need for an intellectual foundation and infrastructure to support bilateral relations similar to those in the business sector. This entails organizing and shaping an intellectual community of students, scholars, entrepreneurs, diplomats and any individuals or entities interested in Sino–Middle Eastern connections, with the common goal of piecing together the needed components of Chinese–Middle Eastern studies at universities and colleges in the Middle East. An important component would be to add to the curriculum a degree course in Chinese studies, and to promote Middle Eastern studies, Arab studies, Iranian studies and Israeli studies in China. Israeli institutions are more advanced in this aspect than other Middle Eastern countries. The Israel–China Institute has established the *Journal of Asian and Middle Eastern Studies* (JAMES). Israeli universities also teach courses on China, Chinese language and politics. Hebrew, Arabic Turkish and Persian languages are being taught at major Chinese universities as well.

Another component would be to establish the Middle East Association for Chinese Studies. Currently, Sino–Middle Eastern relations are incorporated in international and some national professional associations such as the International Studies Association, the Middle East Studies Association of North America, the American Political Science Association, the French Political Science Association, the Association of Chinese Political Studies (ACPS), the German Political Science Association, the Arab Association of Political Science, the Russian Political Science Association, the Association of Chinese Political Studies, the Chinese Social and Political Studies Association and the Canadian Political Science Association. However, there is no broad Middle Eastern professional association with the sole mission of promoting Chinese studies in the region, while on the Chinese side, there are several entities that deal with Middle Eastern affairs, among which are the Chinese Association for Middle East Studies, the Institute of West-Asian and African Studies, the Chinese Academy of Social Sciences and other related strategic studies centres. This is added to the fact that Asian scholars maintain the Asian Federation of Middle East Studies Association composed of several members, including the Japanese Association of Middle East Studies, the Korean Association of Middle East Studies and the Mongolian Association of Middle East Studies. This lack of an institutional framework and the absence of a Middle Eastern Association for Chinese Studies is a major deficiency on the part of the Middle East, although all the necessary resources are abundantly available in the region. Associations are essential components that organize and mobilize interested individuals and entities in the area of Chinese studies. An organization would also be in a better position to secure funding for research and to direct students towards critical research enquires. An association is also essential in organizing conferences and producing manuscripts and journals. While the general support is present and there are tremendous resources that can be built to articulate an association, the organizational aspect is missing.

Establishing Confucius Institutes is also important to promote bilateral relations. China is concentrating its efforts on the US, Canada and Europe and ignoring its allies and friends in the Middle East. There are 72 established Confucius Institutes in the US alone, but only 12 in the entire Middle East and North Africa. The 12 institutes are totally disproportionate to China's growing interests in the region. There is significant interest and need to learn Chinese history and traditions, but China does not seem ready to respond to the growing need in the Middle East.

Data availability

One of the challenges of doing research on China and the Middle East is the lack of data and accurate historical accounts of Sino–Middle Eastern relations. I was struck by the unavailability of major statistics and yearbooks on China at some Chinese diplomatic missions. The early Islamic period, in particular, is characterized by conflicting Chinese and Arab accounts of major issues such as the Talas Battle, the exchange of diplomatic missions and episodes of violence and massacres that occurred in China against the Hui communities. On current issues, data are available on oil, natural gas and the volume of trade, although scattered in several online sources and manuscripts. Obtaining copies of China's statistics and yearbooks was challenging. It is my hope that references on trade, energy and arms sales, in particular, will be made available to future researchers. One of the purposes of the office of a cultural attaché is to assist researchers in their endeavours and to make all needed research material available. However, it would be wonderful if there was a centralized library on China somewhere in the Middle East where researchers could find the references and the resources they need because, while Chinese diplomats are accessible, it is difficult to get answers or conduct interviews on basic issues related to China's foreign policy in the Middle East. It is unproductive to view research with suspicion based on the nationality or birthplace of the researchers. Chinese diplomats should be willing and able to meet researchers, exchange intellectual debates and assist researchers in their search for facts. Chinese diplomatic missions should refrain from viewing students of Chinese and Middle East studies as agents for certain governments; instead, they should assist and open up to intellectuals and academics who seek information and knowledge from and about China.

There is also a need for governments in the region to assist departments of social sciences and humanities at their universities and colleges to establish Chinese studies and Middle East studies programmes on their respective campuses, given the fact that well-funded universities in the Middle East are those that are state owned, not those owned by the private sector. It is only through educational exchanges that mutual understanding and continued friendships can be built on solid ground.

Future research on Sino–Middle Eastern relations

This study has highlighted China's increasing involvement in the Middle East through the five pillars approach developed in the previous chapters. However, there are endless research questions and issues of a bilateral and multilateral nature to be investigated. Although the general approach embodied in Chinese studies is still applicable, there is a need to study China's relations with each and every Middle Eastern country, given that they are comprehensive in scope and substance and multifaceted in nature. Within this bilateral approach, there are endless research questions that deal with energy security, trade policy, labour, tourism, culture and political ties. At a multilateral level, China's politics in the region encompass a wide range of questions that still need to be investigated. Some of these enquiries pertain to the status of the Middle East with respect to American–Chinese rivalry, the genuine Chinese motives behind its policies towards the Arab Spring, the Iranian nuclear programme and the Arab–Israeli conflict. These questions are not only of regional importance, but also of an international nature. Why is China reluctant to get involved wholeheartedly in resolving the Arab–Israeli conflict, although it enjoys the admiration of both sides? Why is China's role destructive when it comes to the Arab Spring? Why can China not put the interests of the Syrian people ahead of its self-centred interests? Why is its rivalry with the West manifesting itself in such a destructive way for the Syrian people? For many decades to come, the future of the Middle East hinges on each of these questions.

China's stance vis-à-vis the Iranian nuclear programme is also problematic. On the one hand, it provided Iran with some nuclear technology in the 1990s but, on the other, it is playing a vital role in resolving the current international confrontation. In this aspect, there are also endless questions about China's nuclear policy in the Middle East and the prospect of jeopardizing Arab national security. Is China, along with the US, Europe and Russia, willing to compromise with Iran on its nuclear programme, thus driving the region towards a new nuclear arms race? Is China seeking to exploit the standoff to advance its energy interests with Iran? How would China react to a nuclear programme in Saudi Arabia, Egypt, the United Arab Emirates or Algeria? Would China support the nuclearization of the Middle East? Furthermore, in terms of trade, is China's model of development applicable to the Middle East? How can China assist the Middle East in building its own developmental and industrial infrastructure? Is China's dumping policy assisting or hurting local Middle Eastern producers? Are Chinese corporations genuine about their corporate responsibility towards hosting countries?

China has always expressed its admiration for Middle Eastern cultures and heritage, value systems, creeds and faiths. However, endless questions can be raised about China's commitment to these principles. Is China willing to allow its Muslim communities to practise their faith free from the harassment of Chinese security agencies? Is China willing to allow its Muslim population to perform Hajj freely, free from state intervention, supervision and regulations? Is China willing to incorporate Muslim provinces and autonomous regions in its developmental project? Is China willing to negotiate a peaceful resolution to its conflict with Xinjiang's liberation movements? Would China invite Saudi or Turkish mediation to resolve the conflict? There are also endless questions open to future enquiry. Students and scholars in the field should investigate whether the calls for China's involvement in the affairs of the region are genuine or mere expressions of frustration against the United States and Europe. What are the goals and motives of Middle Eastern governments' relations with China? Are these governments genuine about the implementation of the Chinese model of development in the Middle East? Is the Middle East ready for massive Chinese involvement in the region? Would the governments in the region open up their countries to Chinese influence in the same way as the US and Europe enjoy now across the region?

I want to conclude with one last open question: China's support of the Syrian Government will certainly mobilize Arab sentiments against it. If it continues in this direction, China's influence in the Middle East may not endure as long as the US presence has. Before the Arab Spring, the people of the Middle East were very enthusiastic about Chinese involvement in the affairs of the region, but the same scenario was displayed at the beginning of the twentieth century when the Arab masses, movements and governments solicited US involvement and the US became an integral part of the region. Are the people of the Middle East ready for another massive cultural, political and economic invasion?

Notes

1 Sino-Middle East relations: an overview

1 Reichelt, Karl Ludvig, 1951. *Religion in Chinese Garments*, James Clarke & Co., Cambridge, p. 155.
2 Reichelt, Karl Ludvig, 1951. *Religion in Chinese Garments*, James Clarke & Co., Cambridge, England, p. 155.
3 Reichelt, Karl Ludvig, 1951. *Religion in Chinese Garments*, James Clarke & Co., Cambridge, p. 155.
4 Reichelt, Karl Ludvig, 1951. *Religion in Chinese Garments*, James Clarke & Co., Cambridge, p. 155.
5 Ibn Al Athir (1160–1233), [n.d.]. *Al Kamil: The Complete History*, International Ideas Home, Amman, Jordan, p. 664.
6 Ibn Al Athir (1160–1233), [n.d.]. *Al Kamil: The Complete History*, International Ideas Home, Amman, Jordan, p. 787.
7 Keay, John, 2009. *A History of China*, Basic Books, New York, p. 265.
8 Reichelt, Karl Ludvig, 1951. *Religion in Chinese Garments*, James Clarke & Co., Cambridge, p. 240.
9 Reichelt, Karl Ludvig, 1951. *Religion in Chinese Garments*, James Clarke & Co., Cambridge, p. 157.
10 Hassan, Ahmad Sanusi, 2010. Islam came to South East Asia from China: Evidence from Chinese Roof Design in Kampung Laut's Old Mosque in Malaysia, *Canadian Social Science*, Vol. 6, No. 5, p. 2 (2–15).
11 Reichelt, Karl Ludvig, 1951. *Religion in Chinese Garments*, James Clarke & Co., Cambridge, p. 157.
12 Reichelt, Karl Ludvig, 1951. *Religion in Chinese Garments*, James Clarke & Co., Cambridge, p. 157.
13 Ebrey, Patricia Buckley, 2010. *China*, Cambridge University Press, London, p. 36.
14 Ebrey, Patricia Buckley, 2010. *China*, Cambridge University Press, London, p. 169.
15 Ebrey, Patricia Buckley, 2010. *China*, Cambridge University Press, London, p. 173.
16 Ebrey, Patricia Buckley, 2010. *China*, Cambridge University Press, London, p. 77.
17 Gillette, Maris Boyd, 2000. *Between Mecca and Beijing*, Stanford University Press, Stanford, CA, p. 11.
18 Ebrey, Patricia Buckley, 2010. *China*, Cambridge University Press, London, p. 209.
19 Jacques, Martin, 2009. *When China Rules the World*, The Penguin Press, New York, p. 78.
20 Jacques, Martin, 2009. *When China Rules the World*, The Penguin Press, New York, p. 239.
21 Jacques, Martin, 2009. *When China Rules the World*, The Penguin Press, New York, p. 239.

22 Jacques, Martin, 2009. *When China Rules the World*, The Penguin Press, New York, p. 239.
23 Ebrey, Patricia Buckley, 2010. *China*, Cambridge University Press, London, p. 243.
24 Jacques, Martin, 2009. *When China Rules the World*, The Penguin Press, New York, p. 89.
25 Jacques, Martin, 2009. *When China Rules the World*, The Penguin Press, New York, p. 90.
26 Jacques, Martin, 2009. *When China Rules the World*, The Penguin Press, New York, p. 90.
27 Gillette, Maris Boyd, 2002. *Between Mecca and Beijing: Modernization and Consumption Among Urban Chinese Muslims*, Stanford University Press, Stanford, CA, p. 14.
28 Gillette, Maris Boyd, 2000. *Between Mecca and Beijing*, Stanford University Press, Stanford, CA, p. 18.
29 Shichor, Yitzhak, 1979. *The Middle East in China's Foreign Policy 1949–1977*, Cambridge University Press, Cambridge and London, p. 2.
30 Shichor, Yitzhak, 1979. *The Middle East in China's Foreign Policy 1949–1977*, Cambridge University Press, Cambridge and London, p. 2.
31 Shichor, Yitzhak, 1979. *The Middle East in China's Foreign Policy 1949–1977*, Cambridge University Press, Cambridge and London, p. 2.
32 Shichor, Yitzhak, 1979. *The Middle East in China's Foreign Policy 1949–1977*, Cambridge University Press, Cambridge and London, p. 22–27.
33 Shichor, Yitzhak, 1979. *The Middle East in China's Foreign Policy 1949–1977*, Cambridge University Press, Cambridge and London, p. 12.
34 Shichor, Yitzhak, 1979. *The Middle East in China's Foreign Policy 1949–1977*, Cambridge University Press, Cambridge and London, p. 12.
35 Shichor, Yitzhak, 1979. *The Middle East in China's Foreign Policy 1949–1977*, Cambridge University Press, Cambridge and London, p. 13.
36 Shichor, Yitzhak, 1979. *The Middle East in China's Foreign Policy 1949–1977*, Cambridge University Press, Cambridge and London, p. 13.
37 Shichor, Yitzhak, 1979. *The Middle East in China's Foreign Policy 1949–1977*, Cambridge University Press, Cambridge and London, p. 32.
38 Shichor, Yitzhak, 1979. *The Middle East in China's Foreign Policy 1949–1977*, Cambridge University Press, Cambridge and London, p. 33.
39 Shichor, Yitzhak, 1979. *The Middle East in China's Foreign Policy 1949–1977*, Cambridge University Press, Cambridge and London, p. 35.
40 See Shichor, Yitzhak, 1979. *The Middle East in China's Foreign Policy 1949–1977*; and Behbehani, Hashim S. H., 1981. *China's Foreign Policy in the Arab World: 1955–1975*.
41 Behbehani, Hashim S. H., 1981. *China's Foreign Policy in the Arab World: 1955–1975*, KPI, London, p. 98.
42 Shichor, Yitzhak, 1979. *The Middle East in China's Foreign Policy 1949–1977*, Cambridge University Press, Cambridge and London, p. 35.
43 Behbehani, Hashim S. H., 1981. *China's Foreign Policy in the Arab World*, KPI, London, p. 89.
44 Behbehani, Hashim S. H., 1981. *China's Foreign Policy in the Arab World*, KPI, London, p. 193.
45 *China Brief*, Vol. VII, Issue 14, 11 July 2007, p. 13.
46 Mawdsley, Emma, 2007. China and Africa: Emerging Challenges to the Geographies of Power, *Geography Compass*, Vol. 1, No. 3, pp. 410, 405–21.
47 UN Security Council Resolution 1368, accessed at http://daccess-dds.
48 Resolution 11373/2001, accessed at http://daccess-dds-ny.un.org/doc/UNDOC/GEN/N01/557/43/PDF/N0155743.pdf?OpenElement [n.d.].

49 Gifford, Rob, 2007. *China Road: A Journey into the Future of a Rising Power*, Random House, New York, p. 262.
50 Gifford, Rob, 2007. *China Road: A Journey into the Future of a Rising Power*, Random House, New York, p. 262.
51 Gifford, Rob, 2007. *China Road: A Journey into the Future of a Rising Power*, Random House, New York, p. 262.
52 Gifford, Rob, 2007. *China Road: A Journey into the Future of a Rising Power*, Random House, New York, p. 118.
53 Document 19, p. 1 accessed at www.purdue.edu/crcs/itemResources/PRCDoc/pdf/Document_no._19_1982.pdf [n.d.].
54 Document 19, p. 1 accessed at www.purdue.edu/crcs/itemResources/PRCDoc/pdf/Document_no._19_1982.pdf [n.d.].
55 Document 19, p. 2 accessed at www.purdue.edu/crcs/itemResources/PRCDoc/pdf/Document_no._19_1982.pdf [n.d.].
56 Document 19, p. 3 accessed at www.purdue.edu/crcs/itemResources/PRCDoc/pdf/Document_no._19_1982.pdf [n.d.].
57 Document 19, pp. 1–15 accessed at www.purdue.edu/crcs/itemResources/PRCDoc/pdf/Document_no._19_1982.pdf [n.d.].
58 Veselic, Maja, 2011. Managing Religion in Contemporary China: the Case of Islam, *Journal of Ethics Studies*, No. 65, September 2011, pp. 114–37.
59 Veselic, Maja, 2011. Managing Religion in Contemporary China: the Case of Islam, *Journal of Ethics Studies*, No. 65, September 2011, p. 120.
60 Veselic, Maja, 2011. Managing Religion in Contemporary China: the Case of Islam, *Journal of Ethics Studies*, No. 65, September 2011, p. 121.
61 Veselic, Maja, 2011. Managing Religion in Contemporary China: the Case of Islam, *Journal of Ethics Studies*, No. 65, September 2011, p. 126.
62 Veselic, Maja, 2011. Managing Religion in Contemporary China: the Case of Islam, *Journal of Ethics Studies*, No. 65, September 2011, p. 126.
63 Kal Shi Chuan et al. in Wai-Yip Ho, 2010. Islam, China and the Internet: Negotiating Residual Cyberspace between Hegemonic Patriotism and Connectivity to the Ummah, *Journal of Muslim Minority Affairs*, Vol. 30, No. 1, March 2010, p. 63 (63–78).

2 A five-dimensional paradigm: energy, trade, arms sales, cultural relations and political co-operation

1 See CNN's reporting and analysis of the event at www.cnn.com/2012/06/11/world/asia/china-female-astronaut/index.html?hpt=wo_c1 [n.d.].
2 Grumbine, R. Edward, 2007. China's Emergence and the Prospects for Global Sustainability, *Bioscience*, Vol. 57, No. 3, p. 249.
3 Gökay, Bülent, 2009. Tectonic Shifts and Systemic Fault-lines: A Global Perspective to understand the 2008–9 World Economic Crisis, *Alternatives: Turkish Journal of International Relations*, Vol. 8, No. 1, p. 33.
4 Douglas, John Keefer, Nelson, Matthew B. and Schwartz, Kevin 2006. Fueling the Dragon's Flame: How China's Energy Demands affect its Relationships in the Middle East, *US–China Economic and Security Review Commission*, p. 1.
5 Yetiv, Steve A. and Chunlong Li, 2007. China, Global Energy, and the Middle East, *The Middle East Journal*, Vol. 61, No. 2, pp. 199–218.
6 Beng, Phar Kim and Li, Vic Y.W. 2007. China's Energy Dependence on the Middle East: Boon or Bane for Asian security? *The China and Eurasia Forum Quarterly*, Vol. 3, No. 3, p. 19.
7 Zha, Daojiong, 2005. China's Energy Security and its International Relations, *The China and Eurasia Forum Quarterly*, Vol. 3, No. 3, pp. 39–54.

8 Taylor, Ian, 2006. China's Oil Diplomacy in Africa, *International Affairs*, Vol. 82, No. 5, p. 937.
9 Mawdsley, Emma, 2007. China and Africa: Emerging Challenges to the Geographies of Power, *Geography Compass*, Vol. 1, No. 3, p. 407.
10 Chen, Shaofeng, 2008. Motivations behind China's Foreign Oil Quest: A Perspective from the Chinese Government and the Oil Companies, *Journal of Chinese Political Science*, Vol. 13, No. 1, p. 80.
11 Chen, Shaofeng, 2008. Motivations behind China's Foreign Oil Quest: A Perspective from the Chinese Government and the Oil Companies, *Journal of Chinese Political Science*, Vol. 13, No. 1, p. 80.
12 Wu, Kang and Fereidun Fesharaki, 2002. Managing Asia Pacific's Energy Dependence on the Middle East: Is there a role for Central Asia? *AsiaPacific Issues*, Vol. 60, p. 1.
13 Wu, Kang and Fereidun Fesharaki, 2002. Managing Asia Pacific's Energy Dependence on the Middle East: Is there a role for Central Asia? *AsiaPacific Issues*, Vol. 60, p. 6.
14 Bubalo, Anthony and Thirlwell, Mark P. 2004. Energy Insecurity: China, India and the Middle East Oil, *Issues Brief*, No. 7, December, p. 7.
15 Bubalo, Anthony and Thirlwell, Mark P. 2004. Energy Insecurity: China, India and the Middle East Oil, *Issues Brief*, No. 7, December, p. 7 and 12.
16 Bubalo, Anthony and Thirlwell, Mark P. 2004. Energy Insecurity: China, India and the Middle East Oil, *Issues Brief*, No. 7, December, p. 8.
17 Russell, Richard L., 2005. China's WMD Foot in the Greater Middle East's Door, *Middle East Review of International Affairs*, Vol. 9, No. 3, pp. 108–24.
18 Grumbine, R. Edward, 2007. China's Emergence and the Prospects for Global Sustainability, *Bioscience*, Vol. 57, No. 3, p. 249.
19 Grumbine, R. Edward, 2007. China's Emergence and the Prospects for Global Sustainability, *Bioscience*, Vol. 57, No. 3, p. 250.
20 Douglas, John Keefer, Nelson, Matthew B. and Schwartz, Kevin 2006. Fueling the Dragon's Flame: How China's Energy Demands affect its Relationships in the Middle East, *US–China Economic and Security Review Commission*, p. 1.
21 Figures for production and consumption from the BP database at www.bp.com [n.d.].
22 Beng, Phar Kim and Li, Vic Y.W. 2007. China's Energy Dependence on the Middle East: Boon or Bane for Asian Security? *The China and Eurasia Forum Quarterly*, Vol. 3, No. 3, p. 19.
23 Kynge, James, 2006. *China Shakes the World*, Houghton Mifflin Co., Boston, MA, p. 133.
24 Zha, Daojiong, 2005. China's Energy Security and its International Relations, *The China and Eurasia Forum Quarterly*, Vol. 3, No. 3, pp. 39–54.
25 Navarro, Peter, 2008. *The Coming China Wars: Where They will Be Fought and How They Can Be Won*, Pearson Education, Upper Saddle River, NJ, p. 45.
26 BP Statistical Review of World Energy, 2011, at www.bp.com/statisticalreview.
27 Taylor, Ian, 2006. China's Oil Diplomacy in Africa, *International Affairs*, Vol. 82, No. 5, pp. 937–59.
28 Mawdsley, Emma, 2007. China and Africa: Emerging Challenges to the Geographies of Power, *Geography Compass*, Vol. 1, No. 3, p. 407.
29 www.chinadaily.com.cn/china/2010–09/10/content_11288046.htm [n.d.].
30 www.china.org.cn/english/BAT/108359.htm [n.d.].
31 Klare, Michael T., 2009. *Rising Powers, Shrinking Planet*, Metropolitan Books, New York, p. 135.
32 http://news.xinhuanet.com/english2010/china/2011–02/03/c_13717889.htm (accessed 2 March 2011).
33 Lee, Henry and Shalmon, Dan A. 2007. Searching for Oil: China's Oil Initiatives in the Middle East, Harvard University, Faculty Working Research Papers Series RWP07–017, p. 9. The paper can be accessed at http://ssrn.com/abstract=976536.

34 Wu, Kang and Fereidun Fesharaki, 2002. Managing Asia Pacific's Energy Dependence on the Middle East: Is there a role for Central Asia? *AsiaPacific Issues*, Vol. 60, p. 1.
35 Navarro, Peter, 2008. *The Coming China Wars*, Pearson Education, Upper Saddle River, NJ, p. 47.
36 Russell, Richard L., 2005. China's WMD Foot in the Greater Middle East's Door, *Middle East Review of International Affairs*, Vol. 9, No. 3, p. 180.
37 Russell, Richard L., 2005. China's WMD Foot in the Greater Middle East's Door, *Middle East Review of International Affairs*, Vol. 9, No. 3, pp. 108–24.
38 Ikenberry, G. John, 2008. The Rise of China and the Future of the West: Can the Liberal System Survive? *Foreign Affairs*, Vol. 87, No. 1, p. 23.
39 Ikenberry, G. John, 2008. The Rise of China and the Future of the West: Can the Liberal System Survive? *Foreign Affairs*, Vol. 87, No. 1, p. 23.
40 Alterman, Jon B. and Garver, John W. 2008. *The Vital Triangle: China, the United States, and the Middle East*, Center for Strategic and International Studies, Washington, DC, p. 100.
41 Ikenberry, G. John, 2008. The Rise of China and the Future of the West: Can the Liberal System Survive? *Foreign Affairs*, Vol. 87, No. 1, p. 23.
42 Alterman, Jon B. and Garver, John W. 2008. *The Vital Triangle: China, the United States, and the Middle East*, Center for Strategic and International Studies, Washington, DC, p. 100.
43 Baker, Peter and Kessler, Glenn 2006. US Campaign is aimed at Iran's Leaders, *Washington Post*, 13, A01.
44 World Bank, 2008. Strengthening MENA's Trade and Investments Links with China and India, World Bank Documents at http://siteresources.worldbank.org/INTMENA/Resources/MENA_China_India_Sept08.pdf [n.d.].
45 The International Monetary Fund, World Economic Outlook Update, January 2012, Washington, DC, at www.imf.org/external/pubs/ft/weo/2012/update/01/pdf/0112.pdf [n.d.].
46 For more information on the chamber, see www.arabcci.org/ [n.d.].
47 www.arabbusinessclub.cn/index.php (accessed 24 April 2012).
48 http://laoag.china-consulate.org/eng/lgxw/t466439.htm [n.d.].
49 www.ameinfo.com/218228.html [n.d.].
50 www.kuwaitchina.com [n.d.].
51 Turkey–China Co-operation Forum, 14 March 2012, at http://blog.tcp.gov.tr/?p=5634.
52 www.focac.org/eng/ltda/dyjbzjhy/DOC12009/t606796.htm [n.d.].
53 Wu Xia, 1 January 2012, Xinhua, China Readier to Share its Diverse Culture with the World, at http://news.xinhuanet.com/english/indepth/2012–01/24/c_131374941.htm.
54 Wu Xia, 1 January 2012, Xinhua, China Readier to Share its Diverse Culture with the World, at http://news.xinhuanet.com/english/indepth/2012–01/24/c_131374941.htm.
55 Motti Golani, at www.jstor.org/discover/10.2307/4283762?uid=3737432&uid=2129&uid=2&uid=70&uid=4&sid=47698760706477 [n.d.].
56 Shichor, Yitzhak in Dittmer, Lowell and George T, Yu, 2010. *China, the Developing World and the New Global Dynamic*, Lynne Rienner Publishers, Boulder, CO, p. 162.
57 Shichor, Yitzhak, in Dittmer, Lowell and Yu, George T. 2010. *China, the Developing World and the New Global Dynamic*, Lynne Rienner Publishers. Boulder, CO, p. 163.
58 Shichor, Yitzhak, in Dittmer, Lowell and Yu, George T. 2010. *China, the Developing World and the New Global Dynamic*, Lynne Rienner Publishers, Boulder, CO, p. 170.

59 www.sipri.org/research/armaments/production/Top100 [n.d.].
60 Shichor, Yitzhak in Dittmer, Lowell and Yu, George T. 2010. *China, the Developing World and the New Global Dynamic*, Lynne Rienner Publishers. Boulder, CO, p. 162.
61 Shichor, Yitzhak in Dittmer, Lowell and Yu, George T. 2010. *China, the Developing World and the New Global Dynamic*, Lynne Rienner Publishers, Boulder, CO, p. 162.
62 Sutter, Robert G., 2010. *Chinese Foreign Relations*, Rowman and Littlefield Publishers, Boulder, CO, p. 123.

3 Walking on thin ropes: a tridimensional perspective

1 Dittmer, Lowell, 2005. The Sino–Japanese–Russian Triangle, *Journal of Chinese Political Science*, Vol. 10, No. 1, p. 1.
2 Alterman, Jon B. and Garver, John W. 2006. *China & Iran*, University of Washington Press, Seattle, WA, p. 5.
3 For more information on Sino–Israeli relations, see Shichor, Yitzhak in Dittmer, Lowell and George T. Yu, 2010. *China, the Developing World and the New Global Dynamic*, Lynne Rienner Publisher, Boulder, CO, pp. 152–76. Also, Shichor, Yitzhak, 1979. *The Middle East in China's Foreign Policy 1949–1977*, Cambridge University Press, London.
4 Hashim S.H. Behbehani provides a detailed account of China's support for the Palestinians in his book *China's Foreign Policy in the Arab World, 1955–75: Three Case Studies*, 1981, KPI, London.
5 Yetiv, Steve A. and Chunlong Lu, 2007. China, Global Energy and the Middle East, *Middle East Journal*, Vol. 61, No. 2, p. 213.
6 Yetiv, Steve A. and Chunlong Lu, 2007. China, Global Energy and the Middle East, *Middle East Journal*, Vol. 61, No. 2, p. 110.
7 *China Brief* Vol. 7, No. 21 (November 2007), p. 5.
8 Alterman, Jon B. and Garver, John W. 2006. *China & Iran*, University of Washington Press, Seattle, WA, p. 178.
9 Douglas, John Keefer, Nelson, Matthew B. and Schwartz, Kevin 2006. Fueling the Dragon's Flame: How China's Energy Demands Affect its Relationships in the Middle East, *US–China Economic and Security Review Commission*, p. 2.
10 Leverett, Flynt and Bader, Jeffrey 2005–6. Managing China– US Energy Competition in the Middle East, *The Washington Quarterly*, Winter 2005–6, p. 191.
11 For more information on Iran's gas sector, see http://aljazeera.net/NR/exeres/D85C46BD-5760-42B9-B5F2-BDD18128307D.htm [n.d.].
12 Boutwell, Jeffrey, 2003. Middle East Security and Iran, CIAO Center (September 2003), at www.ciaonet.org/wps/jeb03/index.html, p. 3.
13 President Obama's message at www.whitehouse.gov/Nowruz/ [n.d.].
14 For more detailed information on the Saudi–Chinese deal, see Alterman, Jon B. and Garver, John W. 2008. *The Vital Triangle: China, the United States, and the Middle East*, Center for Strategic & International Studies, Washington, DC, p. 32.
15 Russell, Richard L. 2005. China's WMD Foot in the Greater Middle East's Door, *Middle East Review of International Affairs*, Vol. 9, No. 3 (September 2005), p. 114.
16 Yetiv, Steve A. and Chunlong Lu, 2007. China, Global Energy and the Middle East, *Middle East Journal*, Vol. 61, No. 2, p. 205.
17 Telhami, Shibley 2004. *The Stakes: America in the Middle East*, Westview Press, Boulder, CO, p. 132.
18 Bubalo, Anthony and Thirlwell, Mark P. 2004. Energy Insecurity: China, India and the Middle East Oil, *Issues Brief*, December, p. 11.
19 http://uk.reuters.com/article/2008/06/18/sabic-sinopec-idUKPEK4672020080618.
20 For a unique perspective on the depth of American–Middle Eastern relations since the seventeenth century, please see Oren, Michael B., 2007. *Power, Faith and*

Fantasy: America in the Middle East, 1776 to the Present, W. W. Norton & Co., New York.
21 Alterman, Jon B. and John W. Garver, John W. 2006. *China & Iran*, University of Washington Press, Seattle, WA, p. 93–122.
22 Alterman, Jon B. and Garver, John W. 2006. *China & Iran*, University of Washington Press, Seattle, WA, p. 95.
23 Alterman, Jon B. and Garver, John W. 2006. *China & Iran*, University of Washington Press, Seattle, WA, p. 100.
24 Alterman, Jon B. and Garver, John W. 2006. *China & Iran*, University of Washington Press, Seattle, WA, p. 100.
25 Alterman, Jon B. and Garver, John W. 2006. *China & Iran*, University of Washington Press, Seattle, WA, p. 100; also Ikenberry, G. John 2008. The Rise of China and the Future of the West: Can the Liberal System Survive? *Foreign Affairs*, Vol. 87, No. 1, p. 23.
26 www.bloomberg.com/news/2011-03-16/china-approves-9-billion-sinopec-kuwait-guangdong-refinery-1-.html.
27 BP Statistical Review of World Energy, June 2011, p. 7 at www.bp.com/statisticalreview.

4 China's reaction to the Arab Spring

1 Fisher, Marc, 27 March 2011. In Tunisia, the act of one fruit vendor unleashes wave of revolution through Arab world, *Washington Post* at www.washingtonpost.com/world/in-tunisia-act-of-one-fruit-vendor-sparks-wave-of-revolution-through-arab-world/2011/03/16/AFjfsueB_story.html [n.d.].
2 Fisher, Marc, 27 March 2011. In Tunisia, act of one fruit vendor unleashes wave of revolution through Arab world, *Washington Post* at www.washingtonpost.com/world/in-tunisia-act-of-one-fruit-vendor-sparks-wave-of-revolution-through-arab-world/2011/03/16/AFjfsueB_story.html [n.d.].
3 Anderson, Roy R., Robert F. Seibert and John G. Wagner, 2012. *Politics and Change in the Middle East*, Longman, Boston, MA, p. 194.
4 Lam, Willy. 2011. Beijing Wary of 'Color Revolutions' Sweeping Middle East/North Africa, *China Brief*, Vol. 11, Issue 3, 10 February 2011, p. 2.
5 www.koreatimes.co.kr/www/news/include/print.asp?newsIdx=105186.
6 United Nations, at http://daccess-dds-ny.un.org/doc/UNDOC/GEN/N12/223/75/PDF/N1222375.pdf?OpenElement (accessed 4 February 2012).
7 United Nations, at http://daccess-dds-ny.un.org/doc/UNDOC/GEN/N12/223/75/PDF/N1222375.pdf?OpenElement (accessed 4 February 2012).
8 http://daccess-dds-ny.un.org/doc/UNDOC/GEN/N12/223/75/PDF/N1222375.pdf?OpenElement [n.d.].
9 http://daccess-dds-ny.un.org/doc/UNDOC/GEN/N12/223/75/PDF/N1222375.pdf?OpenElement [n.d.].
10 Gifford, Rob, 2007. *China Road: A Journey into the Future of a Rising Power*, Random House, New York, p. 241.
11 McDonald, Mark, 5 February 2012. The Arab Spring is Coming to China, *International Herald Tribune*, the Global Edition of *New York Times*, at http://rendezvous.blogs.nytimes.com/2012/02/05/the-arab-spring-is-coming-to-china/.
12 For the Sino–Russian alliance, especially in Central Asia, see Klare, Michael T., 2008. *Rising Powers, Shrinking Planet: the New Geopolitics of Energy*, Henry Holt and Co., LLC, New York, pp. 132–3.
13 Xinhua Press Agency, at http://news.xinhuanet.com/english/world/2012–02/17/c_122713543.htm (accessed 17 February 2012).
14 United Nations at www.un.org/News/Press/docs/2012/ga11207.doc.htm [n.d.].
15 United Nations at www.un.org/News/Press/docs/2012/ga11207.doc.htm [n.d.].

16 United Nations at www.un.org/News/Press/docs/2012/ga11207.doc.htm [n.d.].
17 http://english.alarabiya.net/articles/2012/02/22/196356.html.
18 United Nations at www.un.org/News/Press/docs/2012/ga11207.doc.htm.
19 United Nations at www.un.org/News/Press/docs/2012/ga11207.doc.htm.
20 United Nations at www.un.org/News/Press/docs/2012/ga11207.doc.htm.
21 United Nations at www.un.org/News/Press/docs/2012/ga11207.doc.htm.
22 www.fmprc.gov.cn/eng/xwfw/s2510/t904275.htm [n.d].
23 www.fmprc.gov.cn/eng/xwfw/s2510/t904275.htm [n.d.].
24 www.fmprc.gov.cn/eng/xwfw/s2510/t904275.htm [n.d.].
25 www.fmprc.gov.cn/eng/xwfw/s2510/t904275.htm [n.d.]. Foreign Ministry spokesperson Liu Weimin's regular press conference on 10 February 2012.
26 www.fmprc.gov.cn/eng/xwfw/s2510/t904275.htm [n.d].
27 www.chinadaily.com.cn/kindle/2012–02/10/content_14575866.htm [n.d.].
28 www.chinadaily.com.cn/kindle/2012–02/10/content_14575866.htm [n.d.].
29 www.chinadaily.com.cn/kindle/2012–02/10/content_14575866.htm [n.d.].
30 www.chinadaily.com.cn/kindle/2012–02/10/content_14575866.htm [n.d.].
31 http://online.wsj.com/article/SB10001424052970204062704577222891820566360.html?mod=googlenews_wsj [n.d.].
32 Sonmez, Felicia, 15 February 2012. China's Xi Jinping visits Capitol Hill, *Washington Post*, at www.washingtonpost.com/blogs/2chambers/post/chinas-xi-jinping-visits-capitol-hill/2012/02/15/gIQA2qUkFR_blog.html.
33 http://english.people.com.cn/90883/7730434.html [n.d.].
34 Meng, Liu, Chinese VP Xi holds talks with US Congress, at http://english.peopledaily.com.cn/90883/7730440.html.
35 http://news.xinhuanet.com/english/china/2012–02/22/c_131423550.htm [n.d.].
36 *People's Daily*, at http://english.people.com.cn/102774/7732458.html (accessed 17 February 2012).
37 *People's Daily*, at http://english.people.com.cn/102774/7732458.html (accessed 17 February 2012).
38 *People's Daily*, at http://english.people.com.cn/102774/7732458.html (accessed: 17 February 2012).
39 *People's Daily*, at http://english.people.com.cn/102774/7732458.html (accessed 17 February 2012).
40 *People's Daily*, at http://english.people.com.cn/102774/7732458.html (accessed 17 February 2012).
41 *People's Daily*, at http://english.people.com.cn/102774/7732458.html (accessed 17 February 2012).
42 A statement given by Ambassador Zhai Jun before his first trip to Syria as envoy, at http://fj.chineseembassy.org/eng/zgdt/t905622.htm.
43 http://english.peopledaily.com.cn/90883/7732455.html [n.d.].
44 http://english.peopledaily.com.cn/90883/7732455.html [n.d.].
45 The United Nations Information Center, at www.un.org/apps/news/story.asp?NewsID=42140&Cr=Syria&Cr1= [n.d.].

5 China and Israel

1 Ebrey-Buckley, Patricia 2010. *China*, 2nd edn, Cambridge University Press, New York, p. 118.
2 Ebrey-Buckley, Patricia 2010. *China*, 2nd edn, Cambridge University Press, New York, p. 88.
3 Bo, Jin, 31 October 2003. An unforgettable history, *China Daily*, at www2.kenyon.edu/Depts/Religion/Fac/Adler/Reln270/Judaism/Harbin-Jews.htm (accessed 24 April 2012).

4 Ebrey-Buckley, Patricia 2010. *China*, 2nd edn, Cambridge University Press, New York, p. 21.

5 Stockholm International Peace Research Institute. *SIPRI Year Book 2011, Armament and International Security*, Oxford University Press, New York, p. 237.

6 Stockholm International Peace Research Institute. *SIPRI Year Book 2011, Armament and International Security*, Oxford University Press, New York, p. 238.

7 Stockholm International Peace Research Institute. *SIPRI Year Book 2011, Armament and International Security*, Oxford University Press, New York, p. 238.

8 Stockholm International Peace Research Institute. *SIPRI Year Book 2011, Armament and International Security*, Oxford University Press, New York, p. 238.

9 Stockholm International Peace Research Institute. *SIPRI Year Book 2011, Armament and International Security*, Oxford University Press, New York, p. 251.

10 Alterman, Jon B. and Graver, John W. 2008. *The Vital Triangle: China, the United States and the Middle East*, The CSIS Press, Center for Strategic and International Studies, Washington, DC, p. 71.

11 *Defense Industry Daily*, 9 November 2011, Indian AWACS Moving Forward on 2 Fronts, at www.defenseindustrydaily.com/Indian-AWACS-Moving-Forward-on-2-Fronts-04855/ [n.d.].

12 *Defense Industry Daily*, 24 June 2012, Indian AWACS Moving Forward on 2 Fronts, at www.defenseindustrydaily.com/Indian-AWACS-Moving-Forward-on-2-Fronts-04855/.

13 Arms Control Association, November 1999, Mixed U.S. Signals on Israel–China Deal, at www.armscontrol.org/node/3129.

14 Abramson, Jeff and Warren, Meghan October 2010. US Arms Deals Decline in Shrinking Market, *Arms Control Today* at www.armscontrol.org/act/2010_10/USArmsDeals.

15 Abramson, Jeff and Warren, Meghan October 2010. US Arms Deals Decline in Shrinking Market, *Arms Control Today* at www.armscontrol.org/act/2010_10/USArmsDeals.

16 For more information on the drones, see Shichor, Yitzhak, 15 September 2008. The US Factor in Israel's Military Relations with China, *China Brief*, Vol. 5, No. 12, at www.jamestown.org/single/?no_cache=1&tx_ttnews%5Btt_news%5D = 3864.

17 Israel Ministry of Foreign Affairs, 24 January 2007. Israel and China Mark 15 Years of Diplomatic Relations, at www.mfa.gov.il/MFA/MFA+events/Around+the+world/Israel+and+China+mark+15+years+of+diplomatic+relations+24-Jan-2007.htm.

18 For more information on the Trade Representative Office, see www.israeltrade.org.cn/english/doing_business_with_china/bilateral_trade/000052/ [n.d.].

19 Bresnahan, Timothy F. and Gambardella, Alfonso 2004. *Building High-Tech Clusters: Silicon Valley and Beyond*, Cambridge University Press, p. 42.

20 Israel–China Institute, 2010. China's Mating Call to Israeli Knowhow and Hi Tech, at www.israelchinainstitute.com/index.php/News/info/t/104/id/63 [n.d.].

21 Israel–China Institute, at www.israelchinainstitute.com/index.php/News/info/t/69/id/86 [n.d].

22 Israel–China Institute, at www.israelchinainstitute.com/index.php/News/info/t/69/id/86 [n.d.].

23 Israel–China Institute, at www.israelchinainstitute.com/index.php/News/info/t/85/id/129 (accessed 28 April 2012).

24 Israel–China Institute, at www.israelchinainstitute.com/index.php/News/info/t/86/id/130.

25 www.israeltrade.org.cn/english/ [n.d.].

26 For more information, see IsCham, at http://beijing.ischam.org/ (accessed 28 April 2012).

27 http://ischamshanghai.org/index.php?option=com_content&view=article&id=1&Itemid=2 (accessed 28 April 2012).
28 www.chinaisrael.com/en/index.asp [n.d.].
29 www.usgs.gov/newsroom/article.asp?ID=2435#.T5BuaKtDyFg [n.d.].
30 2009 estimates as reported at www.indexmundi.com/israel/oil_consumption.html [n.d.].
31 2009 estimates as reported at www.indexmundi.com/israel/natural_gas_consumption.html [n.d.].
32 Peter Lee, US Peace Institute, China Flirts with Israel amid Gulf Crisis, at www.upi.com/Business_News/Energy-Resources/2012/02/01/China-flirts-with-Israel-amid-gulf-crisis/UPI-21281328121090/ [n.d].
33 For detailed discussion on early Israeli–Chinese relations, see Shichor, Yitzhak, 1979. *The Middle East in China's Foreign Policy 1949–1977*, Cambridge University Press, Cambridge and London.
34 Shichor, Yitzhak, 1979. *The Middle East in China's Foreign Policy 1949–1977*, Cambridge University Press, Cambridge and London, p. 21.
35 Shichor, Yitzhak, 1979. *The Middle East in China's Foreign Policy 1949–1977*, Cambridge University Press, Cambridge and London, p. 23.
36 Sutter, G. Robert, 2010. *Chinese Foreign Relations: Power and Policy Since the Cold War*, Roman & Littlefield Publishers, London, p. 303.
37 Shanghai 2010 Expo, at http://en.expo2010.cn/c/en_gj_tpl_32.htm [n.d.].

6 China and Saudi Arabia

1 Shichor, Yitzhak, 1979. *The Middle East in China's Foreign Policy: 1949–1977*, Cambridge University Press, London, p. 44.
2 Shichor, Yitzhak, 1979. *The Middle East in China's Foreign Policy: 1949–1977*, Cambridge University Press, London, p. 44.
3 Kissinger, Henry, 2011. *On China*, The Penguin Press, New York, p. 351.
4 Behbehani, Hashim S.H., 1981. *China's Foreign Policy in the Arab World*, KPI, London, p. 231.
5 For an interesting perspective, see Henry Kissinger's book, *On China*, 2011, The Penguin Press, New York.
6 Behbehani, Hashim S.H., 1981. *China's Foreign Policy in the Arab World*, KPI, London, p. 231.
7 For more information on US assistance in building the Jihadi infrastructure and mobilization in the 1980s, see Telhami, Shibley, 2004. *The Stakes: America in the Middle East*, Westview Press, Boulder, CO, pp. 1–37.
8 For a comprehensive work on Xiaoping, see Vogel, Ezra F., 2011. *Deng Xiaoping and the Transformation of China*, The Belknap Press of Harvard University Press, Cambridge, MA.
9 Sutter, Robert G., 2010. *Chinese Foreign Relations: Power and Policy since the Cold War*, Roman & Littlefield Publishers, UK, p. 70.
10 For more information on the terrorist attacks, see Telhami, Shibley, 2004. *The Stakes: America in the Middle East*, Westview Press, Boulder, CO.
11 Xinhua, 12 May 2010. China, Arab states eye new 'Silk Road' seek elevated ties, at http://news.xinhuanet.com/english2010/china/2010–05/12/c_13290704.htm.
12 Mouwad, Jad, 2010. *New York Times*, at www.nytimes.com/2010/03/20/business/energy-environment/20saudi.html?pagewanted=all.
13 Xinhua, 21 February 2012. Iran oil ban triggers Chinese oil reserve concerns, at http://news.xinhuanet.com/english/indepth/2012–02/21/c_131423403.htm.
14 Xiaocong, Wang, *Caixin*, 16 January 2012. Sinopec, Aramco to Build Oil Refinery in Saudi Arabia, at http://english.caixin.com/2012–01-16/100349089.html.
15 *People's Daily*, 2010. China, Saudi Arabia to boost trade, at http://english.peopledaily.com.cn/90001/90778/90861/6865894.html [n.d.].

16 *People's Daily Online*, 12 January 2010. China, Saudi Arabia to boost trade, at http://english.peopledaily.com.cn/90001/90778/90861/6865894.html.
17 This figure is provided in an interview with a senior official at the Saudi Ministry of Higher Education.
18 The Shanghai Expo, at http://en.expo2010.cn/documents/indexf.htm [n.d.].
19 This figure is provided by the CIA's *World Facts Books*, at www.cia.gov/library/publications/the-world-factbook/geos/sa.html [n.d.].
20 Alterman, Jon B. and Garver, John W. 2008. *The Vital Triangle: China, the United States and the Middle East*, CSIS: Center for Strategic & International Studies, Washington, DC, p. 66.
21 Alterman, Jon B. and Garver, John W. 2008. *The Vital Triangle: China, the United States and the Middle East*, CSIS: Center for Strategic & International Studies, Washington, DC, p. 66.
22 www.sinodefence.com/army/artillery/plz45.asp [n.d.].
23 Shichor, Yitzhak in Lowell, Dittmer and Yu, George T. 2010. *China, the Developing World, and the New Global Dynamic*. Lynne Rienner, Boulder, CO, p. 164.
24 Grimmett, Richard. Congressional Research Service, Annual Report on Conventional Arms Transfers to Developing Nations, 2003–10, p. 13.

7 China and Iran

1 For more information on the PFLOAG, see Behbehani, Hashim S.H., 1981. *China's Foreign Policy in the Arab World*, KPI, London, pp. 144–48.
2 For more information on Sino–Iranian relations, please see *Encyclopedia Iranica, Chinese–Iranian Relations*, Section v on Diplomatic and Commercial Relations, 1949–90, at www.iranicaonline.org/articles/chinese-iranian-v [n.d.].
3 Dittmer, Lowell and Yu, George T. 2010. *The Developing World, and the New Global Dynamic*, Lynne Rienner Publishers, Boulder, CO, p. 164.
4 Alterman, Jon B. and Garver, John W. 2008. *The Vital Triangle: China, the United States, and the Middle East*, Center for Strategic & International Studies, Washington, DC, p. 69.
5 Alterman, Jon B. and Garver, John W. 2008. *The Vital Triangle: China, the United States, and the Middle East*, Center for Strategic & International Studies, Washington, DC, p. 66.
6 Dittmer, Lowell and Yu, George T. 2010. *China, the Developing World and the New Global Dynamic*, Lynn Rienner Publishers, Boulder, CO, p. 164.
7 Alterman, Jon B and Garver, John W. 2008. *The Vital Triangle: China, the United States, and the Middle East*, Center for Strategic & International Studies, Washington, DC, p. 65.
8 Kemp, Geoffrey, 2010. *The East Moves West: India, China, and the Asia's Growing Presence in the Middle East*, Brookings Institute, Washington, DC, p. 77.
9 Dittmer, Lowell and Yu, George T. 2010. *The Developing World, and the New Global Dynamic*, Lynne Rienner Publishers, Boulder, CO, p. 164.
10 Grimmett, Richard F. 2011. *Conventional Arms Transfers to Developing Nations, 2003–2010*, Specialist in International Security, Congressional Research Service, Washington, DC, p. 10.
11 Remarks by the US Secretary of State Hillary Clinton, US State Department, at www.state.gov/secretary/rm/2012/03/187245.htm [n.d].
12 Remarks by the US Secretary of State Hillary Clinton, US State Department, at www.state.gov/secretary/rm/2012/03/187245.htm [n.d].
13 Hameed, Rashad, 2010. Sino–Iranian Relations Current Developments and Future Scenario, *Policy Perspective*, Vol. 7, No. 2, January–June 2010, p. 10.
14 *People's Daily*, 11 January 2001. Sinopec Taps Oil Block in Iran, at http://english.people.com.cn/english/200101/11/eng20010111_60163.html [n.d].

15 Xinhua, 29 January 2002. China's Iran-Ordered Giant Oil Tanker to Be Delivered in April, at http://news.xinhuanet.com/english/2002–01/29/content_259354.htm.
16 Alterman, Jon B. and Garver, John W. 2008. *The Vital Triangle: China, the United States, and the Middle East*, Center for Strategic & International Studies, Washington, DC, p. 66.
17 http://iranprimer.usip.org/resource/iran-and-china [n.d.].
18 Kemp, Geoffrey 2010. *The East Moves West: India, China, and the Asia's Growing Presence in the Middle East*, Brookings Institute, Washington, DC, p. 77.
19 Xinhua, 10 December 2007. China's Sinopec, Iran sign oilfield development contract, at http://news.xinhuanet.com/english/2007–12/10/content_7221433.htm [n.d].
20 FARS News Agency, 29 June 2012. Iran Starts Early Production in Yadavaran Oil Field, at http://english.farsnews.com/newstext.php?nn=9102111085.
21 Kemp, Geoffrey, 2010. *The East Moves West: India, China, and the Asia's Growing Presence in the Middle East*, Brookings Institute, Washington, DC, p. 77.
22 Tran, Mandy Zuo and Liu, Irene Jay Friday 6 April 2012. *South China Morning Post*, Sanctions against Iran drive up China trade tenfold in decade, at http://topics.scmp.com/news/iranshellgame/article/Sanctions-against-Iran-drive-up-China-trade-tenfold-in-decade1 [n.d.].
23 Xinhua, 15 February 2010. Saudi Arabia, Angola, Iran remain Top 3 Oil Suppliers to China, at http://news.xinhuanet.com/english2010/china/2010–02/10/c_13171039.htm.
24 Xinhua, 15 February 2010. Saudi Arabia, Angola, Iran remain Top 3 Oil Suppliers to China, at http://news.xinhuanet.com/english2010/china/2010–02/10/c_13171039.htm.
25 *International Business Time*, 8 March 2010. Iran inks Pact with China for Oil Rig, at www.ibtimes.com/articles/9978/20100308/iran-inks-pact-with-china-oil-rig.htm [n.d.].
26 Wan, Xiao, 16 January 2009. *China Daily*. CNPC to develop Azadegan oilfield, at www.chinadaily.com.cn/business/2009–01/16/content_7403699.htm.
27 Sahana Network, 7 June 2009. To Be Realized by the End of the Year: $18 bn Investment in South Pars, at www.shana.ir/142654-en.html.
28 Shana Network, 8 June 2009. Petronas Stays in Iran Gas, to Review Role with CNPC, at www.shana.ir/142687-en.html.
29 Shana Network, 4 April 2012. $30 Billion to Be Invested In Oil Industry This Year, at www.shana.ir/186896-en.html.
30 Kemp, Geoffrey, 2010. *The East Moves West: India, China, and the Asia's Growing Presence in the Middle East*, Brookings Institute, Washington, DC, p. 75.
31 Mandy Zuo and Liu, Irene Jay Friday 6 April 2012. *South China Morning Post*, Sanctions against Iran drive up China Trade Tenfold in Decade, at http://topics.scmp.com/news/iranshellgame/article/Sanctions-against-Iran-drive-up-China-trade-tenfold-in-decade1 [n.d.].
32 Kemp, Geoffrey 2010. *The East Moves West: India, China, and the Asia's Growing Presence in the Middle East*, Brookings Institute, Washington, DC, p. 74.
33 Confucius Institutes, at http://college.chinese.cn/en/article/2009–08/29/content_22308.htm.
34 Shanghai International Expo's homepage, at http://en.expo2010.cn/c/en_gj_tpl_72.htm [n.d.].
35 Xinhua, 16 February 2012. China, Iran set up Committee to enhance Cultural Exchanges, at http://news.xinhuanet.com/english/china/2012–02/16/c_131414684.htm.

8 China and the United Arab Emirates

1 Behbehani, Hashim S.H., 1981. *China's Foreign Policy in the Arab World*, KPI, London, p. 215.
2 www.chinaconstruction.ae/about%20us.htm [n.d.].

3 The China State Construction Engineering Corp. Ltd homepage, at www.chinaconstruction.ae/about%20us.htm (accessed 30 April 2012).
4 For more information on Nakheel's projects, see Nakheel's website, at www.nakheel.com/en/developments [n.d.].
5 DubaiCity, at www.dubaicity.com/what_to_do_in_dubai/dubai_dragon_mart.htm [n.d.].
6 www.arabianbusiness.com/china-uae-sign-5-54bn-currency-swap-deal-441097.html. (accessed 2 May 2012).
7 Sambidge, Andy. Mashreq Inks Deal to Boost UAE–China Opportunities, at www.arabianbusiness.com/mashreq-inks-deal-boost-uae-china-opportunities-399655.html (accessed 2 May 2012).
8 The Industrial and Commercial Bank of China Limited, ICBC, at www.icbc-ltd.com/icbcltd/about%20us/news/icbc%20opens%20its%20subsidiary%20in%20the%20middle%20east.htm [n.d.].
9 The Oil and Gas Year, at http://theoilandgasyear.com/week/2012/03/20/togy-talks-to-gao-yusheng/ [n.d.].
10 Arabian Business.com, 21 March 2011. PetroChina in Talks for Fujairah Oil Storage Deal, at www.arabianbusiness.com/petrochina-in-talks-for-fujairah-oil-storage-deal-389115.html (accessed 2 May 2012).
11 Xinhua, 30 December 2009. CNPC Allies Win $9.7 billion Gas Contract, at http://news.xinhuanet.com/english2010/business/2009–12/30/c_13139130.htm [n.d.].
12 www.csc.edu.cn/Laihua/universitydetailen.aspx?collegeId=79 [n.d.].
13 China University of Petroleum-Beijing's website, at www.cup.edu.cn/internationaloffice/en/about/ (accessed 3 May 2012).
14 For more information on Plan Abu Dhabi 2030, please see http://gsec.abudhabi.ae/Sites/GSEC/Navigation/EN/publications,did=90378.html [n.d.].
15 For more information, see Stockholm International Peace Research Institute database, at www.sipri.org/databases/armstransfers/background [n.d.].
16 Grimmett, Richard F., 2011. *Conventional Arms Transfers to Developing Nations*, Congressional Research Service, Washington, DC, p. 12.
17 Wolf, Jim, *Reuters*, 31 December 2011, at www.reuters.com/article/2011/12/31/us-usa-uae-iran-idUSTRE7BU0BF20111231 [n.d.].
18 Stockholm International Peace Research Institute, 2011. *SIPRI Yearbook* 2011, Oxford University Press, London, p. 211.
19 Xinhua, 17 January 2012, at http://news.xinhuanet.com/english/china/2012–01/18/c_122598763.htm (accessed 3 May 2012).
20 Xinhua, 17 January 2012. China, UAE issue Joint Statement on establishing Strategic Partnership, at http://news.xinhuanet.com/english/china/2012–01/18/c_122598763.htm (accessed 3 May 2012).
21 Broomhall, Elizabeth, 22 April 2012. What the Great Economy of China means for MENA, in Arabianbusiness.com, at www.arabianbusiness.com/what-great-economy-of-china-means-for-mena-454570.html?page=2.
22 Chinese tourists flock to UAE, 29 December 2011, CNN, Dubai, United Arab Emirates, at http://business.blogs.cnn.com/2011/12/29/chinese-tourists-flock-to-uae/.
23 Bundhun, Rebecca, 8 January 2011. Chinese Tourism takes off across the Emirates, at www.thenational.ae/featured-content/channel-page/business/travel-tourism/chinese-tourism-takes-off-across-the-emirates [n.d.].
24 Shanghai Expo 2010 at www.e-architect.co.uk/shanghai/uae_expo_pavilion.htm [n.d.].

9 China–Algeria Relations

1 CIA Fact Book, Algeria: Country Profile, at www.cia.gov/library/publications/the-world-factbook/geos/ag.html [n.d.].

2 For more information, see Fanon, Frantz, 1964, *The Wretched of the Earth, Black Skin, White Masks*; 2008, *A Dying Colonialism*, 1994; *Toward African Revolution*, 1994.
3 Shichor, Yitzhak, 1979. *The Middle East in China's Foreign Policy 1949–1977*, Cambridge University Press, Cambridge, p. 71.
4 Behbehani, Hashim S.H., 1981. *China's Foreign Policy in the Arab World*, KPI, London, p. 5.
5 For a list of Sino–Algerian agreements, see Behbehani, Hashim S.H., 1981. *China's Foreign Policy in the Arab World*, KPI, London, pp. 351–52.
6 For more information on the exchange of delegations and co-ordination in this period, see Behbehani, Hashim S.H., 1981. *China's Foreign Policy in the Arab World*, KPI, London, pp. 329–58.
7 The United Nations Bibliographic Information System, Resolution 2758, at http://unbisnet.un.org (accessed 16 May 2012).
8 For more information on the FOCAC's eight principles, please check FOCAC's website, at www.focac.org/eng/dsjbzjhy/t625619.htm [n.d.].
9 Long-standing China–Algeria ties show strong momentum for growth, at http://lr.china-embassy.org/eng/gyzg/a123/t417111.htm [n.d.].
10 Foreign Policy Blog, at http://blog.foreignpolicy.com/ (accessed 16 May 2012).
11 Xinhua, at http://news.xinhuanet.com/english/2006–12/21/content_5516158.htm [n.d.].
12 For a list of Sino-Algeria cultural agreements, see Behbehani, Hashim S.H., 1981. *China's Foreign Policy in the Arab World*, KPI, London, p. 351.
13 Weizhong, Xu, 2011. *A Review of Sino–Algerian Relations in Retrospect*, at www.sinoalgerie.com (accessed 21 May 2012).
14 For more discussion on Chinese diaspora communities, see Liu Hong, 2010. *Chinese Overseers and a Rising China*, in *China and International Relations*, edited by Zheng Yongnian, Routledge, London, pp. 177–199.
15 Xinhua, 7 August 2009, Statement issued by Zhuo Lei, General Manager of a Joint Highway Project undertaken by China CITIC Group and China Railway Construction Corporation Limited, at www.chinadaily.com.cn/china/2009–08/07/content_8543666.htm [n.d.].
16 Wu Bangguo, Chairman of the Standing Committee of China's National People's Congress, at www.npc.gov.cn/englishnpc/Special4/2008–11/06/content_1456975.htm [n.d.].
17 Chikhi, Lamine, 22 April 2012. China donates $40 million Opera House to Algeria, in Reuters, at www.reuters.com/article/2010/04/22/us-algeria-china-opera-idUSTRE63L4HF20100422.
18 Official website of the 2010 Shanghai Expo, at http://en.expo2010.cn/c/en_gj_tpl_52.htm [n.d.].
19 US Energy Information Administration, Country Profile: Algeria, at www.eia.gov/countries/cab.cfm?fips=AG (accessed 14 May 2012).
20 Albawaba.com, at www.albawaba.com/business/china%E2%80%99s-sinopec-develop-algeria%E2%80%99s-zarzaitine-oil-field [n.d.].
21 Taylor, Ian, 2009. *China's New Role in Africa*, Lynne Rienner Publishers, Boulder, CO, p. 45.
22 Adrar Upstream and Downstream Integrated Project, at www.cnpc.com.cn/en/cnpcworldwide/algeria/ [n.d.].
23 Dittmer, Lowell and Yu, George T. 2010. *China, the Developing World, and the New Global Dynamic*, Lynne Rienner Publishers, Boulder, CO, p. 46.
24 www.sudantribune.com/China-reinforces-oil-investment-in,18931 [n.d.].
25 Abdelghani, Henni, 27 March 2011. Sonatrach indefinitely halts Tiaret Refinery Work, at www.arabianoilandgas.com/article-8670-sonatrach-indefinitely-halts-tiaret-refinery-work/ [n.d.].

26 Meftah, Brahim, 2009. Outlook of Nuclear Energy in Algeria, International Atomic Energy Agency, IAEA-CN-164-1S02, at www-pub.iaea.org/MTCD/publications/PDF/P1500_CD_Web/htm/pdf/topic1/1S02_B.%20Meftah.pdf.

27 Taylor, Ian, 2009. *China's New Role in Africa*, Lynne Rienner Publishers, Boulder, CO, p. 120.

28 Stockholm International Peace Research Institute, *SIPRI Yearbook 2011*, Oxford University Press, London, p. 184.

Conclusion

1 For more information on Muslims in China, see Gifford, Rob, 2007. China Road: A Journey into the Future of a Rising Power, Random House, New York; Boyd Gillette, Maris, 2000. Between Mecca and Beijing, Stanford University Press, Stanford, CA; Jacques, Martin, 2009. When China Rules the World, The Penguin Press, New York.

Index

Note: page numbers in *italic* type refer to Figures; those in **bold** type refer to Tables.

21275890R00134

Printed in Great Britain
by Amazon